Prosperity Amidst Crisis

WILHELM HANKEL

Translated by Jean Steinberg

Prosperity Amidst Crisis

Austria's Economic Policy and the Energy Crunch

Westview Press / Boulder, Colorado

Copyright © 1981 by Westview Press, Inc.

Published in 1981 in the United States of America by
   Westview Press, Inc.
   5500 Central Avenue
   Boulder, Colorado 80301
   Frederick A. Praeger, Publisher

Library of Congress Cataloging in Publication Data
Hankel, Wilhelm, 1929–
   Prosperity amidst crisis.
   Translation of Prosperität in der Krise.
   Includes bibliographical references.
   1. Austria—Economic policy—1945– I. Title. II. Series.
HC265.H3213   330.9436'053   80-22133
ISBN 0-86531-101-3

Printed and bound in the United States of America

CONTENTS

TABLES

FIGURES

FOREWORD

At the beginning of the seventies it seemed as though the industrial nations stood on the threshold of an era of strong economic growth and almost unlimited possibilities. Their optimistic view of the future was grounded in the experience of twenty-five years of impressive postwar reconstruction and accomplishments. But the seventies did not live up to their expectations. The very bases of their hopes were undergoing profound changes.

The protest movements of the students brought the awareness that established values were being questioned. Belief in progress gave way to vague uneasiness.

In the economic area, the dismantling of the monetary system underscored the weakening economic position of the United States. And the political ascendancy of the Third World brought worldwide economic and political realignments in its wake.

The oil shock put an end to the age of cheap energy and raised serious questions about the nature of industrial society. The recession of the mid-seventies was not followed by the expected strong recovery but by a period of limited growth and continued high unemployment.

Global interdependence and sophisticated methods of mass communication spread moods and attitudes throughout the world with lightning speed.

In an interdependent world of interrelated world markets no country—and that of course includes Austria—can remain detached. Measured by the yardsticks of growth and full employment as well as social stability, Austria has more than held its own among the industrial nations of the world.

The international economic order is undergoing profound changes, and traditional beliefs in "preordained" rises in production and the level of prosperity are being shaken. A solution to the conflict between the Northern world and the developing countries—both oil producers and those without their own sources of crude oil—does not seem imminent.

In the industrial nations the number of citizens who will have to be integrated into the labor market continues to rise. A sense of responsibility toward our youth dictates that in the provision of jobs we plan for qualitative as well as quantitative factors— that means that we also have to deal with the problem of "psychological unemployment."

Given this array of problems, economic policy now more than ever before cannot afford to limit itself to short-term measures geared to ephemeral political considerations, to issues that already have entered into the public consciousness, or to only those issues that are forced upon us. Such an approach would reduce our sphere of action so severely that even the most essential steps could no longer be taken.

If it takes a generating plant ten to fifteen years before it can become fully productive, or if industrial structural improvements do not become effective immediately, a responsible leadership cannot afford policies geared solely to the next election campaign.

The design of our future is a political task. But the more complex the decisions that have to be made and the more they depart from those of the past, the greater the need for expert knowledge and understanding of contemporary problems and the greater the need for enlightened political policies and an expanded range of action.

This book grew out of a study I commissioned in the fall of 1978. It was meant to offer a comprehensive survey of the development, condition, and possibilities of the Austrian economy, to assist in policymaking and decisionmaking. The international theoretical and practical experience of Wilhelm Hankel and his personal interest in the development of our country made him the ideal choice for presenting Austria's development within the broader international framework.

The publication and discussion of this book are a contribution to "public marketing" and a step toward the process of consciousness raising, which in a democracy is the precondition for action.

Vice-Chancellor Dr. Hannes Androsch

PREFACE

Small National Economy—
Big Economic Policy

*The separate economic blocs and all the friction and
loss of friendship they must bring with them are ex-
pedients to which one may be driven in a hostile
world, where trade has ceased over wide areas to be
co-operative and peaceful and where are forgotten the
healthy rules of mutual advantage and equal treatment. But it is surely crazy to prefer that. Above all,
this determination to make trade truly international
and to avoid the establishment of economic blocs
which limit and restrict commercial intercourse outside them, is plainly an essential condition of world's
best hope.*

> —From Lord John Maynard
> Keynes's last address before
> the House of Lords, De-
> cember 18, 1945 (in Parlia-
> mentary Debates, *Hansard*,
> House of Lords, vol. 138,
> no. 41).

In large economic areas policymaking may be easier than in small ones. But is policy therefore also better, as those who sing the theoretical and political praises of what they call "optimal" economic areas (be it Europe or elsewhere) maintain? Alas, recent events support the view that the world economy would most likely be in better shape today if some of the fatal decisions that still haunt us had not been made in the early seventies in the large areas on either side of the Atlantic—in the United States and in that part of Western Europe under the economic leadership of the German Federal Republic. The decisions of 1973 culminated in the dismantling of the world monetary system developed at Bretton Woods, flawed though it may have been, and in the failure to respond to the sudden OPEC reach for more favorable terms of trade with a well-thought-out policy of internal readjustments. Instead, the decision makers fell back on traditional export and balance-of-payments surpluses.

In small economic areas economic policy is incomparably more difficult. Almost all the plans made by a government and a central bank to protect the people against the twin scourge of inflation and unemployment can easily and off-handedly be destroyed by outside economic forces that put their own interests ahead of their neighbors'.

In the thirties, small economies were compelled to import the depressions that their big neighbors were unable to contain within their own borders. Since the sixties, the small areas have been the victims of the suicidal battles of their big brothers, who accuse one another of exporting their inflations. Regardless of who is right—the "German school," which seeks to lay all responsibility at the door of the U.S. balance-of-payments deficit that floods the world economy with U.S. dollars, or the "American school," which sees German unwillingness to reduce its balance-of-payments surplus as the source of all inflationary evil since every new deutsche mark (DM) appreciation sets in motion a new decline in the dollar price—the "forced" importers of this worldwide inflation are always the small economies dependent on the world market.

And since the big areas seem to be able to trigger both depressions and inflation, and are always trying to export both— depression via a (neomercantile) export-surplus policy and inflation via either a currency depreciation that sends domestic prices soaring or currency appreciation that inflates export prices—the small areas seem to live in the worst of all possible world economies. They are forced to import both unemployment as well as the deterioration of money values, which their big friends with domestic problems deposit at their doorsteps.

What are those small, dependent entities to do? Economic common sense would seem to dictate that the best course is to join forces with one of the big areas, the strongest if possible, and try to adopt its employment, price, and inflation levels. How? The easiest way is by tying their currency to that of the big area, letting their own currency continue (formally) to circulate but handing its (material) purchasing power over to the big neighbor. The small entities thus become co-occupants of a neighboring economic and monetary unit and co-users of the economic and monetary policy of an outside power whose risks they share but in the policy formulation of which they play no part. They thereby relinquish an autonomous policy, which according to prevalent economic wisdom they cannot pursue at home in any case. Therefore they actually give up "nothing."

In terms of individual entrepreneurial magnitudes, small may be beautiful; but in terms of economic magnitudes, this unfortunately is not so. The only "beautiful" aspect of the above widely espoused course of action is that it is obviously only half true, as the example of Austria's small economy amidst the economic world crisis of the seventies demonstrated. Even though Austria, in line with the described scenario, voluntarily surrendered its monetary sovereignty early on and tied the schilling to the strong DM and saw the schilling skyrocket along with the deutsche mark, it did not relinquish one iota of a highly active independent domestic economic policy. Even more astonishing, this small country fared better with its homemade economic policy than its big neighbor, and far better also than most Western industrial nations, big and small. The sum of Austria's achievement, measured against even the most complex and ambitious set of goals, is compelling: domestic economic growth, full employment, no inflation (neither imported nor self-made), continued real income growth, unprecedented technological progress, industrial growth, and expansion of export capacities—and all this combined with the country's growing economic integration in a world apparently eager to invest its capital in Austria, rather than the other way around.

Austria's accomplishments demonstrate something that is no longer self-evident in any of the leading industrial nations of the West—something Austria achieved by a semi-autonomous economic policy that despite the most serious and profound economic crisis since the thirties has not curtailed its economic independence. This miracle—protecting the domestic economy against the shock waves of inflation and depression emanating from the economic crisis that engulfs the world—happened not in the homeland of the social market economy, the German Federal Republic, but in Austria. It accords with the as yet unfulfilled hope, voiced by John Maynard Keynes in his famous 1943 farewell address before the House of Lords, that all countries, big and small, may one day be free to break the chains binding them to the walls of old prisons, and not be compelled to import the depressions or inflations that other, more powerful countries cannot contain at home.

What makes Austria's example so interesting is that here a small, not particularly advantageously situated, landlocked country at the fringes of the world economy was able to swim against almost every fashionable current of the seventies and against a far more powerful neighbor—and that it succeeded so admirably.

Austria has not participated in the popular pastime of floating, nor is it officially knocking on the door of a regional monetary club. It simply acts as though the Bretton Woods system did not collapse, and ties the stable schilling exchange rate not to the continually softening U.S. dollar but to the increasingly hardening DM, while at the same time avoiding an exchange appreciation that would damage its own economy.

Yet Austria also does not play the monetarist game of substituting monetary for fiscal policy. It refrains from proclaiming monetary goals in more or less mystical types of money from M_1 to M_7, which are not adhered to and which in the end hardly anyone can tell apart since the various countries that agree on this policy delimit it differently—the German Federal Republic differently than the United States.

Austria by contrast follows an old-fashioned growth and full-employment policy à la Keynes built around the almost archaic idea of budget deficit, which, conventional wisdom has it, only stimulates inflation and stirs up discord among the social partners about the distribution of the social product and the distribution of real income and real profits.[1] And all this, oddly enough, is happening in Austria, a country whose leading economic theorists, dead and living, turned their backs on Keynesian economics. Despite years of living fiscally beyond its means, Austria has a stable price structure and the social partners have preserved the peace, as though reality had the right to supersede the most revered theories of the most venerable economists of one's own country. True, domestic and foreign indebtedness continues to rise, but contrary to expectations the creditors are not unduly concerned, unlike those critics who fear the debt will put an intolerable burden on future generations. The fact of the matter is that later generations tend to castigate their elders for not having left them with more infrastructure and more productive capacity— a complaint sounded by some of the most passionate anticolonialists in the developing countries about their unloved former rulers.

The following analysis is an attempt to explore these contradictions. It was tempting for a German economist to investigate why Austria should have been so successful with a policy that ran counter to Germany's policy—to continue its foreign-trade deficit instead of turning it around and to compensate for the slack by concentrating on the domestic market instead of engaging in ruinous competition for world markets with other nations, regardless of the economic and political consequences.

This book has two concerns. First, the aim is to dispose of theories and doctrines that, however appropriate in their time, today tend to make a bad situation worse—regardless of whether they are the brainchildren of Austrian "monetarists," of Anglo-Saxon "fiscalists," or of the recently revived European "optimal zone" school (which has yet to prove that its claim to "stability" is justified).

Second, this book deals with the far more important and exciting question of whether the world economic crisis can in fact be stopped only by a fight among all against all by forcing others to make painful adjustments in their demand, price, and employment levels—a game in which the German Federal Republic has achieved unparalleled mastery over the years. To put it more bluntly: Is the oil war preventable?

The Austrian model demonstrates that a sensible economic policy can overcome a worldwide recession brought on by oil prices without making life difficult for others. It can therefore be assumed that the world economy would be in better shape if it were less concerned with optimal areas and more with optimal national policies.

Austria's policy is a case in point, but since it has been practiced in a small country, it has gone unnoticed. Yet such a policy deserves serious consideration, its minor and major flaws (which will be discussed in some detail in the course of this study) notwithstanding. The list of missed opportunities of Austrian economic policy is admittedly long—from the excessive financing incentives for business (a sort of "domestic capital transfer tax" that, by building internal protective fences around factory gates, works to block that most effective of all development laws, the "law of profit-rate equilibrium" [an Austrian invention at that]) to the negative investment bonuses and the failure to stimulate the growth of an atrophied capital market (the most effective defense against lopsided concentrations of property, capital, and capacity, with all the economic and social evils such concentrations entail).

Once we have come to see where Austria has erred, what its sins of commission and omission are, we will be able to arrive at a fairly objective appraisal of the overall effectiveness of Austrian policy and to explore whether it lends itself to the different conditions of other countries. This answer can be given only after we determine whether the Austrian model can be sustained over longer periods; whether the benefits are greater than the costs; and whether the sizable internal (budget) and external (foreign-exchange) indebtedness, in addition to curtailing Austria's financial breathing space, will not be seen (and justifiably so) as the anticipation, not to say prefinancing, of expected "unavoidable" foreign-exchange and revenue surpluses.

We therefore must direct our full attention to this "money" question: How long can an economic and financial policy of "prosperity on credit" be sustained? This is the leitmotiv of our analysis.

In launching our inquiry we are not concerned with meaningless financial calculations the assumptions of which anticipate the outcome; nor are we concerned with speculations about the future behavior of markets, central banks, and officialdom. What we are concerned with is the existing or anticipated growth of the production capacity of the Austrian economy—the expected "free portions" of its real social product. Should it turn out that Austria will in the future absorb inherently smaller, not larger, portions of its current production for domestic private and public consumption and domestic private and public investment, no limits will be set to a future reduction of the borrowed (part consumed, part invested) means. On the contrary, debt liquidation then becomes the same sort of compelling by-product of development as the previous indebtedness, assuming that no one comes up with the insane idea to stop the development process itself—a piece of advice that despite its "insane logic" and misplaced "heroic assumptions" (to quote Thomas Balogh) was widely disseminated in 1929, and not only by Austrian economists.

Perhaps the most important lesson to be drawn from our examination of Austrian economic policy in the seventies is that if the Austrian economy is to continue on its successful course it must guard against letting the almost inevitable transition from current account and budget deficits to surpluses turn into a neomercantile policy of budget-induced export growth along the questionable lines of its West German neighbor or the equally questionable theories of Nicholas Kaldor's New Cambridge

xx   PREFACE

school. Were this to happen, Austria would lose the key to its
economic success: the almost total absence of troublesome conflicting goals. In that event, Austria, like any other normal
industrial nation (whether a soft-currency country like the
United States or a strong balance-of-payments country like West
Germany), would have to worry that most measures designed to
safeguard price stability (such as exchange appreciation or
domestic restrictions) would endanger its full-employment and
balance-of-payments equilibrium, while almost everything designed to safeguard its balance of payments (currency depreciation, deflation, or reflation) would adversely affect employment
or price stability or both. But Austria did not experiment with
any "new" doctrine; rather, it drew the only correct conclusion
from a changed international economic situation: If out there in
the world economy there is less (real) investment and more
(nominal) saving, then it is quite all right to make more (real)
investments at home than can be saved (nominally). And by
following a fairly straightforward course one comes back to the
old, eternally new truism of Adam Smith: that the wealth of a
nation (of all nations, not just one) is best served by stimulating
domestic growth and, via a balance-of-trade deficit, that of all
others as well.

If our findings should prove that Austria's economic policy
of the seventies can rightly claim to have found a way out of
the deadlock of Western economic policy—beyond the old economic nationalism, which inevitably runs up against the problem
that in the long run a *single* world economy must agree on a
policy that protects the interests of all, and also beyond the new
economic nationalism on that higher European plane that could
escalate the problems to a still more dangerous confrontation
of the blocs, including a fight over increasingly scarce resources—
then it will become clear that this is not simply a play performed
on a local stage but one that, having survived the try-outs in the
provinces, could play on all the major stages of the world, particularly if international stars would also agree to act in it.

We will begin our analysis with a look at the interrelation-
ships and connections of a range of economic policy decisions.
The failure of the market to perform in accordance with expectations is a policy matter—whether the issue is business or oil

prices—though not necessarily in the sense that those economic
models do not add up when "something" changes in the predicted reaction of people to economic conditions, whether
these people are cast in the role of entrepreneur or not. The
lesson we still have to learn is that the "old" textbooks are not
wrong, but that we have merely forgotten how to read them
correctly. The great crisis theoreticians of the thirties, from
the then rather conservative head of the Chicago school, Frank
Knight, to the "revolutionary" John Maynard Keynes of the old
Cambridge school, postulated something that could not be more
up to date: the predictions and calculations about the behavior
of the economy will accord with the model only when the reactions of the participants constitute a sort of constant, regardless
of time or milieu. Keynes spent the greater part of his life working on the book that proves how little reliance can be placed on
such constants, particularly in times of crisis. He began working
on his *Tract on Probability* in 1906 and published it in 1921.
Keynes's battle with the econometricians of whatever school or
direction that still rages on is based on a working hypothesis
reiterated in Chapter 15 of his *General Theory:* As long as
economic theory creates or fails to resolve doubt among the participants, he said, it cannot be certain of its effects—a process
that in turn underscores and intensifies the uncertainty of
those involved.

This factor—and not the "errant" textbooks—lies at the heart
of the inadequacy of the economic policy of almost every
Western industrial nation since the collapse of the international
monetary system of Bretton Woods and the onset of the oil
crisis of 1973. If today nothing "adds up," no prognosis and no
projection—if wise men become fools and economic policy
makers commit the most egregious blunders jeopardizing not
only their own credibility but, far worse because of the potentially far graver consequences, that of the whole system, they
do so because they continue to nurse illusions about the efficacy
of their proposals, whether these be designed to fight inflation,
stimulate business, or balance the budget. These policy makers
would do far better if, instead of hurling accusations at all and
sundry—at "indolent" businessmen, "undisciplined, irresponsible" trade unions, "speculative" Euro- and other banks—

they examined the underlying assumptions of their policies to see whether they are still "correct" and "timely" (in the sense of Walter Eucken's postulate) and asked themselves self-critically whether perhaps they contributed to the insecurity and attitudes of those under their aegis.

Austria is living proof that appropriate economic measures can alleviate the painful effects of currency and oil crises. That is why the Austrian policy mix of the seventies is at the center of this study. It proves that a policy based on the "correct" diagnosis of the international economic situation and the expected reactions of the participants can be successful even if it operates with such old-fashioned concepts as a Keynesian full-employment and an old (rather than neo-) classical exchange policy. As mentioned earlier, the fact that Austria's policy is so compelling is no reason to gloss over its obvious mistakes and shortcomings. On the contrary, if our presentation is perhaps painted in too bright colors, it is more likely to err on the side of the shortcomings rather than the positive features, if for no other reason than that an examination of defects helps one see the possibilities for improvement for Austria as well as for other countries.

I could never have taken the risk of dissecting the economic policy of a foreign country had it not been for the friendly assistance given me in the gathering and evaluation of the voluminous material. I am extremely grateful for the help given me by Dr. H. Cordt, Mr. Sellner, Mr. Ziehengraser, Dr. A. Stanzel, and Dr. A. Rainer of the Finance Ministry in Vienna. As in almost all my previous work, the statistical work in this volume was supervised and executed by my colleague H. Kupky. However, any errors and omissions are solely my responsibility.

Wilhelm Hankel
Bologna Center of the Johns Hopkins University

PART 1

AUSTRIA'S ACHIEVEMENTS, UNREALIZED CHANCES, AND FUTURE POSSIBILITIES

Optimality is here defined in terms of the ability to stabilize national employment and price levels.
—Robert Mundell, 1961

1

MAXIMAL CAPITAL FORMATION AND PLANNING DATA CONSTANCY

For the past decade Austria has maintained one of the highest investment ratios of all Western industrial countries. While in almost every other Western industrial nation the share of investment spending on the social or national product has been stagnant or declining since the end of the sixties—a process that has sharply accelerated since the intensification of the international economic crisis following the Organization of Petroleum Exporting Countries (OPEC) price offensive of 1973–1974—the trend in Austria has been in the opposite direction. Austria's investment quota increased both in nominal and real terms, even though the mood in the German Federal Republic, a considerable factor in Austria's business sector, has grown increasingly gloomy (see Figures 1 and 2). The age of uncertainty foreseen by J. K. Galbraith[1] has not come to Austria. The question is: Will it still come?

A comparison with Austria's German neighbor is particularly revealing in this context. After all, German and Austrian investors share the same monetary fate, so why not the same business fate?

Since the beginning of the seventies the DM and the schilling have risen at approximately the same rate—by more than 50 percent compared to the soft currencies. Yet even though the percentage increase in the investment position and consequently the lure of foreign investment were approximately the same for both countries, only the German investors chose to look for opportunities outside their own country. German foreign investment between 1971 and 1977 rose more rapidly than at

3

Figure 1. Growth Through Investment

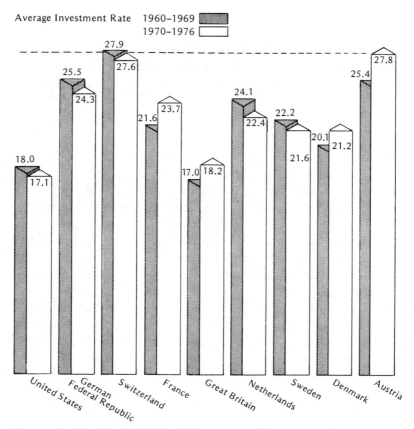

Average Investment Rate   1960–1969
                           1970–1976

Source: Austrian Finance Ministry, Vienna.

any time since the end of World War II, to the tune of some 80 percent. Nothing like this took place in Austria. On the contrary, because of its hard-currency policy, Austria remained a net-capital import country, not only in nominal terms (in credits), but also in real terms (in direct investments). Why?

*   *   *

Figure 2. Business Profits and Their Utilization in the German Federal Republic, 1960–1975

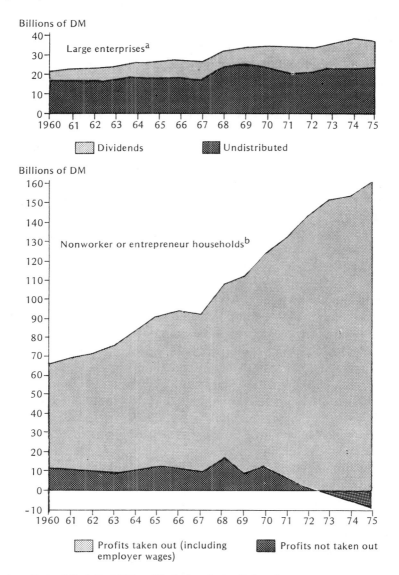

Source: Federal Statistical Office, Wiesbaden, Series N, Part 1.

  a. Corporate enterprises.
  b. Noncorporate enterprises (mostly small and medium-sized businesses, including professions).

Investment behavior is always governed by expectations. Keynes devotes three (rarely read) chapters of his *General Theory* (Chapters 5, 13, and 15) to this simple, basic phenomenon. Yet critics are still not convinced that Keynesianism is anything more than merely a bleak "total-quantity mechanism" (according to Wilhelm Röpke). What it is, in fact, is a doctrine of explainable and provable psychological reactions of investors, savers, moneylenders, currency traders, and other economic factors to expected or feared changes in the "planning data" (of Walter Eucken)—the most important of these being the reaction of investors. If they fear a new wave of instability or riskiness, they make adjustments in their investment time schedule; and in the event of a more sustained period of instability or riskiness, they make adjustments in the type of investments as well. F. Lutz described the operation of this mechanism in the crisis of the thirties;[2] the present author showed a very similar pattern for the German Federal Republic of the seventies. The small and middle-sized German entrepreneurs not protected by mammoth (outside) capital and who "risk" their own capital have behaved in almost exemplary Keynesian fashion since the beginning of the sixties.[3]

At first, at the beginning of the crisis, only net investments are reduced, which in turn shortens the remaining terms of the not-yet-written-off capitalization. As the crisis continues or intensifies, business reinvestment declines and investment capital becomes savings capital. Why? Because this is a way of turning excessive investment risks into a sure thing. In both instances, the change in the investment time schedule and the transformation of investments into savings, the entrepreneur is adjusting to the increasingly problem-ridden situation of his markets. He anticipates threatened income and capital losses by changing his role from one who ventures to one who does not, or more properly, by becoming a "rentier" who invests his holdings safely.

If, moreover, as happened in West Germany, the road is cleared for him by a monetary policy of extraordinarily high real interest rates, or a finance policy granting tax advantages for investments outside one's own enterprise—measures allegedly designed to counteract an inflationary mentality but that in fact reward a rentier mentality—the process accelerates. The private sector saves, instead of investing, thereby forcing fiscal policy into a deficit, for if the state wants to prevent a further downward slide of internal investment demand, it must, despite the loss of revenue, try at least to maintain its level of spending. The result is that the deficit, which can be financed only through indebtedness, provides the "secure" and "high-interest" money capital instruments grabbed up by investors turned savers.

The rates and relations in Figure 2 show this to be the reality of the German Federal Republic. While the anonymously controlled capital corporations (which without misrepresentation may be equated with big business), in line with the market-control thesis of the Galbraith-Baumol-Harris school, reduce only their net investments and reinvest the earned write-offs in their own enterprises, the growing tendency of small and medium-sized businesses since 1972 has been to maximize their take-out. Ultimately they even took out more than they were earning: They transformed increasingly large portions of their freed investment capital into savings.

How do we know that these were really savings and not an increase in consumer spending? We can figure it out from the way the crisis developed since 1972. If in that period the marginal investment quotas in the German Federal Republic had been higher than the marginal savings quotas, neither consumption nor profit nor employment could have declined. The expectations of all investors, corporate as well as noncorporate, would then have been fulfilled by the total demand for consumer and investment goods and the investors would not, in the absence of any serious (crisis) dislocations, have had to shop around for readjustment strategies. The big firms would not have had to withdraw into the debt-neutral fortress of cash-flow financing of current investment programs through just barely earned write-offs, and the small firms would not have been forced to become public financiers and pensioners out of fear of unavoidable losses.

Table 1 also shows that marginal savings rates overtook marginal investment, with an average marginal savings rate of +11 percent in 1974–1977 as opposed to a marginal net (dis)-investment rate of –6 percent, while the Austrian savings and

Table 1. Marginal Investment and Savings Rates

Year	National Income (NI) (in billions of schillings)	Annual Changes in Investments				Savings[a]	
		Gross (in billions of schillings)	Gross (dNI = 100)	Net (in billions of schillings)	Net (dNI = 100)	(in billions of schillings)	(dNI = 100)
AUSTRIA							
1974	+ 58.3	+23.0	+39.5	+11.4	+19.6	+ 4.1	+ 7.1
1975	+ 30.2	−15.4	−51.0	−23.4	−77.5	+19.4	+64.2
1976	+ 54.1	+37.2	+68.8	+31.6	+58.4	+16.3	+30.2
1977	+ 48.6	+26.9	+55.3	+19.2	+39.5	−32.8	−67.5
1974–1977	+191.1	+71.7	+37.5	+38.8	+20.3	+ 7.1	+ 3.7
	(in billions of DM)	(in billions of DM)	(dNI = 100)	(in billions of DM)	(dNI = 100)	(in billions of DM)	(dNI = 100)
GERMAN FEDERAL REPUBLIC							
1974	+ 51.4	−10.7	−20.8	−22.3	−43.4	+12.9	+25.1
1975	+ 30.2	− 9.7	−32.1	−19.4	−64.2	+18.6	+61.6
1976	+ 69.2	+29.4	+42.5	+20.9	+30.2	− 5.9	+ 8.5
1977	+ 54.5	+16.6	+30.5	+ 7.7	+14.1	− 2.2	− 4.0
1974–1977	+205.3	+25.6	+12.5	−13.1	− 6.4	+23.4	+11.4

Sources: Statistisches Handbuch für die Republik Österreich 1978 (Vienna, 1978); Annual Report, 1978, of the Austrian National Bank; Monthly reports of the German Federal Bank, Frankfurt/Main.

[a]For Austria, development of the most important forms of savings; for German Federal Republic, private households.

investment figures for that same period stood at +4 and +20 percent, respectively. Because the investment risks in Austria were assumed to be smaller, investments were higher and savings assured there than in neighboring Germany.

Before going into an explanation of the interesting difference in the savings and investment behaviors between German and Austrian business, we ought to point out two conclusions of this analysis. First, Keynes's model of the endogenously intensifying employment crisis is as relevant today as it was forty-five years ago. Today's galloping inflation and excessive liquidity, accompanied by worldwide deflationary pressure on demand, international trade, production, and employment, certainly fits into Keynes's scheme. The model he offered in his *General Theory* is absolutely timely. Then as now, the crisis grew out of the self-legitimating fear reaction of insecure entrepreneurs.

This demand deficit in the investment sector is not merely a short-term phenomenon. The process, which turns entrepreneurial investors into savers, and which Keynes still considered largely cyclically reversible, changes the structure of the entire economy and creates a milieu in which policy making becomes more rather than less difficult.

If the adjustment to crisis is confined predominantly to the small and medium-sized private business sector, three long-range factors of any market economy change immediately: employment, competition (and its counterpart, monopoly), and the basis for estimating entrepreneurial efficiency. Because the last of these will be discussed in some detail in connection with the income policy of the economic partners—employees and labor (Chapter 4)—this discussion will be confined to the consequences of the first and second points.

* * *

Not all of the investment/savings adjustments were equally successful. In West Germany, some fifty thousand enterprises have closed down since 1972, almost every one a business with fewer than five hundred employees. This translates into a job loss of about 250,000, which would explain more than half the rise in West Germany's unemployment since 1972. This may not be a particularly satisfactory explanation, but this may work quality presents a more serious problem, for the empss in in this sector were primarily the kind of specialized, higs skilled workers who cannot be trained overnight and are har to replace.

A still graver problem from the social perspective relates to the fact that this shrinking small and medium-sized business sector is not part of the oligopolistic group that can dominate markets and set prices. Rather, they are the businesses that must adjust costs to prices. If they fail, it is because the price-adjustment route is closed to them, partly because of their disproportionately high credit financing and indebtedness rate compared to big business. In West Germany, the share of business-financing debts has risen from 56 percent in 1954 to 71 percent in 1974.[4] According to German banking groups and major banks, over the last twenty years small and medium-sized businesses showed a greater decline in the proportion of self-owned capital investment compared to outside financing than big business. It would thus seem obvious that if the little guys were big, they, like the monopolistic price setters, could have improved their self-financing position at the expense of their customers and balanced even long-lasting declines in demand with their (self-created) cash flow.

The freedom of movement that monopolistic self-financing affords will be discussed further in Chapter 5. The interest here is in a structural aspect: the cyclical temporary decline in expected demand, profits, and jobs that becomes irreversible if the total number of active businesses in the economy decreases. The shrinkage of private business permanently removes jobs from the marketplace and profoundly changes the nature of economic competition and monopoly. The survivors of the crisis wind up with a more favorable market, free of competition, but not even their professional defenders claim that this sort of purge improves the quality of the market economy. The dominance of the anonymous, manager- rather than owner-controlled national and multinational capital enterprises, and the death of small, privately owned business are obviously connected with the defects of the financial structure, not with problems of allocation.

The cost of this dual petrifaction of the economic process— the gigantism of business and the cementing of its monopoly— is invariably borne by a public that is allowed to live with fewer available jobs and lower income, higher social costs, greater social tensions, and a precarious overconcentration of reduced real growth combined with still higher monopolistic prices. Almost all the manifestations of unease of this socially far too costly policy of stability are due to the failure to read or understand the texts about crisis management. The monism that persists in the belief that fighting inflation is all that need be done has given us negative structures that will continue to cast their shadow for a long time to come.[5]

*   *   *

The vitality and crisis resistance of Austria's medium-sized entrepreneurial structures testify to the effectiveness of its market policy. If, of all European OECD countries, Austria continues to have one of the highest added-value and employment ratios in enterprises employing fewer than one hundred workers, this is not a regressive feature but rather the opposite. Austrian economic policy of the seventies has managed what Germany's has failed to do: to keep monopoly and concentration levels low despite a crisis that favors the survival of big enterprise. Recently a spokesman of Austria's Federal Business Chamber complained that the "concentrations [on big enterprises with more than five hundred employees] have resulted in only marginal changes since the beginning of the seventies."[6] The department would do well to read something Wilhelm Röpke wrote twenty-five years ago in a report on German economic policy commissioned by Konrad Adenauer (*Is German Economic Policy Right?*). Röpke's findings could apply verbatim to Austria's policy today, as analysis as well as a guide:

> An economic system of free prices, competition, private property, and independent entrepreneurs does not seem possible in the long

run if at the same time no effort is made to change the social base (individualization and deproletarization). . . . The measures that are to be considered in this context concern above all the promotion of economic and social decentralization in line with the dictates of economy, by encouraging the spread of small and medium-sized enterprises, population dispersion between city and country and between industry and agriculture, by breaking up big industry and by promoting small property holdings of the people, and other measures that would help today's urban and industrial nomads put down roots. . . . It would serve the cause of harmony if one were to start out from the premise that the modern big enterprise poses one of the most difficult human and social problems of our time . . . [and] that the opacity of modern economic life, whose vast ramifications and real functions the ordinary person can no longer understand, not only makes real competition more difficult, but seems to be one of the deepest sources of today's social discomfort, for nothing makes people more bitter than the feeling that they are the easily exploitable pawns of obscure processes.[7]

*   *   *

What is surprising is not that Austria actively pursues a market economy and market order but rather that this policy born out of concern for the middle class is being pursued by a "socialist" regime and is tolerated by the trade unions, while the spokesmen for industry have obvious analytical (and ideological) difficulty in comprehending the tendered opportunities. If any Western industrial nation in these times of permanent business crisis can be said to have succeeded in saving small private enterprise and preserving the jobs created by it—so vital a part of every market economy—it is the Austria of the seventies. If the spokesmen of industry are heard to complain that in those crisis years neither the share of aggregate industrial added value of the gross domestic product (27 percent) nor the share of aggregate industrial employment (approximately 1.225 million, or 44 percent of total employment) has gone up significantly, it proves not only how well their sector has kept pace with the growing productivity of the total economy, but also that it managed to avoid excessive substitution of labor by capital, a danger inherent in every highly industrialized society.

(This point will be discussed in greater detail in Chapter 4.)

Table 2 shows the divergent trends of bankruptcy rates (largely among the middle class) in West Germany and Austria. In West Germany the rate more than doubled since 1970; in Austria it declined by more than 20 percent compared with the 1970–1972 averages.

What factors were to feed this pro-business bias in Austria? The answer must be sought in Austria's external hard-currency and domestic demand and full-employment policy mix. This Archimedean principle of the Austrian model, combining external dependency with internal autonomy, which exerts leverage down to the very last enterprise, is so important a factor that it will be discussed on separate theoretical planes: comprehensively (descriptively) in Parts 2 and 3 and in mathematical terms in Part 4.

The following analysis of the impact of Austria's hard-currency policy on the investment decisions of Austrian businessmen speaks for itself.

In the countries with free, or rather (since the halfhearted monetary agreement reached in Kingston, Jamaica, in January 1976) semi-tied exchange rates, the balance of payments has

Table 2. Bankruptcies Prior and Subsequent to 1973

Year	Austria		German Federal Republic	
	Number	1970–1972 = 100	Number	1970–1972 = 100
Average:				
1970–1972	1226	100	4404	100
1973	1049	85.6	5515	125.2
1974	1276	104.1	7722	175.3
1975	1105	90.1	9195	208.8
1976	1016	82.9	9362	212.6
1977	1020	83.2	9562	217.1

Sources: For Austria—*Statistisches Handbuch für die Republik Österreich 1978*, Vienna, 1978; for German Federal Republic—*Statistisches Jahrbuch 1978*, Stuttgart and Mainz, 1978.

been left to the activities of privately determined and financed money and credit movements, a system investigated more closely in Chapter 9. The crucial aspect of this policy mix is that fixed (nonvariable) exchange rates free monetary policy from having to serve the balance-of-payments goals and allow it to concentrate on the regulation of internal demand flows. Yet wherever this monetary reorientation of economic policy has been seriously attempted it has led to the following dual destabilization of the base underlying entrepreneurial invest-ment calculations.

1. This policy allows an unforeseeable restriction of domestic demand and credit, particularly since the new orthodoxy de-nounces all countersteering of an anticyclical fiscal policy as being basically wrong whereas in fact the contrary is the case: Given this policy, the fiscal instruments regulating demand are weakened still more by excessive tax reductions (especially in the United States and West Germany) because in times of over-saving, such restrictive deficit spending does not stimulate an already weak investment trend but rather an already all too powerful savings trend.

2. On the world markets, on the other hand, demand and credit facilities expand, thanks to the favorable price and interest-rate relations brought about by domestic restrictions. Foreign prices expressed in dollars rise above domestic levels, and foreign interest rates, also expressed in dollars, fall below those of domestic markets; as a result dollar expectations are becoming negative and consequent excessive efforts to stabilize one's own exchange rates (which weaken the dollar still further) vitiate the efforts to balance the disparities via a floating exchange rate.

*   *   *

Given this climate of inflation abroad and deflation at home, the nonmultinational (small and medium-sized) enterprises are faced with the loss not only of the formerly assured domestic demand but also of credit refinancing at reasonable terms. Thus they lose sure profits and sustain substantial capital-value losses on their investments because of the higher domestic interest rates.

If these excessive and inevitable exchange-rate swings are

downward (tending to devaluations), they intensify pressure on foreign competition, but if they are upward (tending to revaluations), they add to the uncertainty of these businesses. If small business were to attempt to gain the advantageous monetary foreign positions of the multinationals, it would have to have the assurance that the gains won by shifting positions would at least survive the amortization of their investments—an assurance they neither have nor can expect. The leading responsible policy makers in the appreciation areas (the DM and Swiss franc) never tire of assuring their "clients" that overvaluation is about to slow down or come to a complete stop—one more method designed to rob domestic business and investors of the last shred of planning certainty and to spread justified doubt about the reliability of that sort of economic policy.

The victory of monetarist policy, which has its merits at best in times of assured full employment (when, except for price stability, nothing is threatened), and the rediscovery of the early Keynes of "competing depreciations" (which predates his Bretton Woods proposals)—at a time of declining aggregate demand—made everything more difficult. The appreciation (or monetarist hard-currency) nations like the German Federal Republic, or at times the United States, repeated the orthodox but self-destructive error of the post-1929 era in trying, through domestic deflation, to win back world market positions that had been lost because of domestically uncontrollable, exogenous events. Thus after 1929 Germany and Austria destroyed the basis of their internal stability when (inspired largely by the economists of the Austrian school) they sought to stop the outflow of foreign credits by curbing instead of expanding domestic demand, production, and employment, only because falling quotations on the New York Stock Exchange from time to time caused U.S. interest levels to soar above those of the debtor nations. The depreciation (or Keynesian soft-currency) nations like Great Britain, Italy, and occasionally France repeated the self-destructive error of the post-1933 years by seeking to regain in world market positions through external depreciation what had been lost through internationally uncontrollable, endogenous events. After 1933 France, Great Britain, and the United States destroyed the productivity of a world economy based on the division of labor in which specialization, not monetary differentiation, would have determined surplus and deficit positions.

The price move of the OPEC nations in October 1973 played a catastrophic role similar to the New York stock market crash of October 1929. The monetarist appreciation nations responded to the heavily increased price of the most important of all energy raw materials by increasing the prices of their currencies, and in this way managed to cushion the deterioration of their terms of trade. The Keynesian depreciation nations responded by decreasing the prices of their currencies, and used their deteriorated terms of trade to avoid reserve losses by depreciation floats and to gain trade and export advantages by lowering their export prices.

Although both these unquestionably cleverly plotted defensive maneuvers took the OPEC leaders and their advisers by surprise, neither one was successful. The appreciation nations may have won the battle against balance-of-payment deficits and inflation at home but they lost the war against unemployment. The depreciation nations lost everything: balance-of-payment equilibrium, price stability, and full employment.

Even though the monetary appreciation policy clearly was the better one, in the short run—though not necessarily from the point of view of long-range national interests—it too failed in its most important objective: domestic full employment.

What caused this failure? Both these "clever" reactions saw the OPEC move only as an inflationary attack on prices and costs and not as an act of real (world) income distribution; yet even in the absence of any theoretical understanding, the ecstatic reaction of Third World countries, even though they too were affected by the OPEC thrust, should have been a warning. Their theoretically less well versed but politically more astute economists were quick to recognize that the OPEC nations had succeeded in making deep inroads into the structure of world income distribution erected at the end of World War I (not, as is generally believed, World War II). Raw material suppliers no longer had to suffer under poor terms of trade, and raw material processors were no longer able to buy at any price they pleased. Price brought about a worldwide income policy, and price was the instrument that replaced aid by trade.

Because the Western industrial nations, despite their different concepts and different motives—in a rare display of unanimity—saw the primary danger of the oil price hike in the inflationary push instead of in the deflationary real-income and real-demand transfer from oil-consuming to oil-producing countries, they made wrong economic policy decisions. And because all oil-consuming Western nations sought to minimize the OPEC grab for their currency reserves, both camps failed to develop a long-term strategy, substituting cheaper energy sources for the now too expensive oil, and other internal revenues for the losses on domestic income and demand for the tribute extracted by OPEC. That is why both groups of countries, to differing degrees (depending on the success of their export offensives against other markets), slid into the same crisis.[8] That is, all except one: the small country of Austria. All the others, ignoring danger signals, continued either their monetarist policy of price-level stabilization with a deflationary bias, or an early Keynesian reserve-losses-avoiding policy through competing depreciations, when what was indicated was a late Keynesian combination of internal anticyclical measures and external control of the international money and capital flows. The combined outcome of both failures was not only the conservation of the international monetary crisis, but a long and continuing confusion about vital internal planning and policy data bases.

The real reason for Austria's divergence from the worldwide trend toward higher inflation and unemployment rates lies in the different response to the oil embargo. Austria's economic policy, by not falling victim to the illusion that price-level stability is always endangered but unemployment never is or to the illusion that exchange rates can be left to the tender mercies of sensible(!) speculators as though speculation is directed toward "social" rather than "private" benefits and no overblown expectations existed, exhibited a high degree of realism and social responsibility. It neither relied on untested theories nor burdened its businessmen and investors with costs they could neither anticipate nor afford. Austria's post-1973 economic policy protected its businessmen and investors against the danger to investment planning posed by completely incalculable monetary exchange- and interest-rate risks.[9]

What, if anything, would have changed in the world had other roads been taken? The renewed tying of exchange rates plus a reorientation of interest rates from price level to balance of payments (a high-interest-rate policy for deficit nations, a low-interest-rate policy for surplus nations) after the oil shock would have changed the Petrodollars in search of investment into "real" U.S. dollars instead of interim Eurodollars, and thus stabilized rather than destabilized the U.S. dollar. The assumption that floating helped in the recovery from the oil shock is, as should be obvious, devoid of even a kernel of truth.

What would the process of real-demand and real-income transfers have looked like at the time of the oil embargo or immediately thereafter had exchange rates been firm? First, the real-income transfer from the deficit-incurring, oil-consuming to the surplus-achieving, oil-exporting nations would have brought an immediate price-level split in the industrial nations—price increases in the energy sector, deflationary price pressure in the "ultimately" affected other (income-elastic) sectors, as well as (because of the balance-of-payment deficits and reserve losses) a rise in interest rates. In the case of so much transparency no government could have been persuaded to ignore the "inevitable" improvements in the terms of trade of the OPEC nations, and—as did happen—absorb them either through competing depreciations (the error of the soft-currency nations) or through appreciation without the simultaneous replacement of the drop in foreign demand by domestic demand (the error of West Germany—the result of illusions about money, exchange rates, and expectations, which will be treated in some detail in Chapter 7).

Second, had the U.S. dollar been stabilized with the help of an interest-rate policy that conformed to the real balance-of-payments deficit, the exchange-rate fluctuations of the Euro-markets and hence the worldwide inflationary impact would have been substantially less severe because a substantially smaller amount of balance-of-payment deficits would have had to be financed and the industrial deficit nations would have had to fall back either on existing reserves or on controllable refinancing facilities of official monetary agencies (International Monetary Fund [IMF], European Economic Community [EEC],

Inter-Central bank lines). Thus credit multipliers of the Euro-markets would have had less breathing space and scope, and many of the (speculative) covering operations to finance the exchange-rate split might have been avoided (see Chapter 9).

Third, and most decisive as far as domestic business is concerned: In the case of a stable, possibly even rising (but certainly not depreciated) U.S. dollar, all Western businesses and investors would have been able to plan and allocate with far more certainty and over a longer range. Why? Because two risk factors that make the investment plans of the (small) domestic business a gamble would have been eliminated: In the absence of unpredictable foreign-exchange fluctuations, foreign prices as well as the financing costs for the individual businessman over normal amortization periods on domestic and foreign markets would have been sure and calculable. If an investor cannot, with any degree of certainty, estimate current investment yields that depend on competitive prices or effective financing costs of new plants and equipment at different places at home or abroad because they are influenced by floating but not predictable exchange rates, why should he invest? Particularly if he can instead invest (or save) his money risk-free and in titles at fixed rates of interest! More important still: so long as monetary policy is "used" at the exchange-rate front, interest-rate formation will follow predictable market developments rather than unpredictable central bank interventions. Nor should market surprises be ruled out. The effect of comparatively stable exchange rates on domestic and foreign competitors and domestic and foreign positions is more or less equal. In the case of integrated worldwide money and credit markets (which since the end of the fifties have become a permanent fixture of the "real existing world economy") the difference between domestic and foreign interest rates is due not so much to differing national refinancing costs as to differing national (and that ultimately means subjective) risk estimates. The development of an expanding twilight zone of risk premiums believed to be essential for covering feared losses, the result of the practically unchecked growth of currency (exchange) riskiness, thus became a "sure" way of widening the spread between domestic and foreign interest rates. The role of floating as a regulator of monetary fears will be discussed in the analysis of the so-called Eurodollar money and credit markets in Chapter 9. Here the concern is for the effect of floating on domestic investment. The policy of high domestic interest rates (compared to foreign money and credit markets) behind the domestic protective wall of overblown foreign-exchange risks brought about by appreciation floats, and perhaps even necessary in the case of depreciation floats, always hits domestic investors harder than their foreign counterparts, and it is thus no accident that floating has been accompanied by a proliferation of multinational corporations.

Furthermore, the increased financing costs brought on by monetary policy affect investment calculations, an intrusion that is all the more troublesome the more figuring an investor has to do. As a rule this involves the undercapitalized small and medium-sized enterprises dependent on credit rather than the well-capitalized big businesses with plenty of cash flow and not dependent on credit. The first victim of any sustained restrictive high-interest policy is the smaller entrepreneur whose business collapses not because he overextended himself in the flush of previous inflationary excesses, but because, lacking market and monopoly power, he is unable to load unexpected additional financing costs onto his prices (which he cannot "set" but must accept). It is therefore axiomatic that monetary restrictions always affect already-decided-upon or about-to-be-decided-upon investment plans, and that they measure with two different yardsticks—one for the credit-dependent small business, and one for the big business with disposable cash flow.

And what about the restrictions imposed by fiscal policy? Budget factors (surpluses as well as deficits) do not influence the investment plans of business either directly or with regard to size or capital equipment. All they do is change the data on which the entrepreneur bases his investment calculation. A budget surplus alerts investors to an imminent cooling off of demand and prices, and a budget deficit tells them that they may count on a continued benign economic climate, and perhaps even on some heating up. Every investor is free to, and should, draw his own conclusions from these indicators. They do not directly interfere with his plans.

Yet it is part of the mistaken perception of almost all investment groups that the restrictions imposed by central banks are "good," whereas the fiscal policies of the government constitute interference in entrepreneurial decision making. In fact, however, the exact opposite is true. Even a restrictive fiscal policy (big budget surplus) is neutral with respect to business size and financing—it affects small business dependent on credit the same as big business not dependent on credit; it puts no heavier a burden on externally financed long-term investments than on self-financed short-term investments.

Not only do prejudices have a long life, but like sleeping dogs they are easily aroused. Perhaps the gravest sin of omission of modern fiscal policy is its failure to acknowledge the pro-business cameralist tradition it rediscovered in the thirties because of its sweeping rejection of all aspects of mercantilism. However, when mercantilism was in full flower it did not limit its efforts to favorable trade balances and export-based growth. Again it was Keynes who in Chapter 23 of his *General Theory* showed the historic importance and the political effectiveness of governmental activity aimed at utilizing the nation's potential for development as well as showing concern for the independent entrepreneur. No modern industrial nation owes its development to free enterprise unencumbered by governmental support. The premises on which the entrepreneur can base his "private" calculation—laws, calculability, infrastructure, and protection against unpredictability—had to be created by a concerned state.

*   *   *

Austria's economic policy decisions of the seventies to keep the exchange value of the schilling stable and monetary policy out of the regulation of domestic demand via changes of investment profitability have created an eminently pro–middle-class investment climate. Since 1971 Austria's investors have been protected against the undercutting of the exchange rate by their most dangerous competitor, West Germany (before 1971, in the days of acute DM undervaluation, this caused a great many headaches), yet they did not have to forgo the stabilizing effects of a hard-currency policy. Vis-à-vis the soft-currency countries, whence comes the threat of imported inflation, the appreciated schilling (in tandem with the DM and other hard currencies) "discounts" their inflated prices for the domestic consumer entirely (or almost entirely) to conform with the real purchasing parities. Thanks to its hard schilling Austria is able to buy in the inflationary countries (almost) as cheaply as at home.

The decision about how much and for how long to invest ultimately depends on two calculations: an actual and objective estimate based on the relation of the purchase prices of production facilities and materials (costs) to the selling price (returns), and an inevitably subjective estimate about which cost/proceeds assumptions (expectations) will or will not be fulfilled over time. The investor consequently must constantly compare his planning data with actual developments. If he decides that the fluctuations of economic policy make for an unpredictable degree of instability, the lack of confidence will act as a restraint—he will invest only what is absolutely necessary and every available free penny will go into savings.

Walter Eucken, the father of the German market economy, therefore saw the "constancy of planning data" as a double necessity. Planning data were needed first of all to safeguard the competitive position and deconcentration of society. "The insecurity brought on by the rapid changes in economic policy gives the push for participation in, or in the acquisition of, the firms of other branches of production," he noted in his *Grundsätze*,[10] as though foreseeing the future. The only thing he would have had to add today is "or make one give up the business altogether to become the pensioner of his own capital."

In fact, aside from the barter economy reserves of some of the developing countries, there hardly exists a monetary policy as stable as Austria's since the seventies. Its monetary authorities did not simply sit back and relax, even though the schilling did not demand their full attention. How little "happened" between 1973 and 1978 can be seen from the policy measures of the National Bank. In that period the official discount rates changed six times, and the minimum reserve rates fourteen. A comparison with the amount of space devoted to economic policy measures in the annual reports of the German Federal

Bank up to 1978—enough to make a ten-page pamphlet—is instructive. The German entrepreneurs, so it would appear, were rather put upon, and it is a near miracle that so many of them nonetheless stayed where they were instead of taking refuge in that oasis of monetary calm, Austria.

Looking at the expenditure of energy and the actual results of the respective monetary policies, we find that the German Federal Bank, in a frenzy of activity in 1978, managed to give the DM a stability edge of 0.5 percent over the practically "inactive" Austrian schilling. However, Austria's fiscal policy was able to stave off the German level of unemployment. (The Federal Republic's unemployment rate escalated from 1.1 percent of the total population in 1971 to 4.4 percent in 1978, a figure that would be higher still by at least 2 percent if the reduction or "export" of the foreign work force were included.)

The quiet on the employment front gave Austrian business yet another planning-data constant, and a rather significant one at that: the observed and hence predictable development of the income policy of the autonomous economic partners. Because of its importance this aspect will be discussed at greater length at a later point. Was Austria's growth in the seventies the result of its "active," "disciplined" trade unions, or did this explosive growth keep inevitable social conflicts from surfacing? This issue will be addressed in Chapter 4.

At a comparable level of stability of the Austrian and German systems, the Austrian investors had greater assurance than their German counterparts that the market rather than regulations would continue to determine their relative costs and profits. There was neither room nor a reason for monetary policy intervention in the investment process. The Austrian investors knew their markets and market developments, and there was little room for surprises to intrude between the planning and the actual data.

Austria's classical policy mix—the importation of the highest possible degree of international stability (namely Germany's) in return for protection of the internal price and cost structure against incisive changes in the financing climate—proved to be a boon for steady and long-range domestic investment. Moreover, because of the calm on the data front there was no reason for capital to flee to other countries, or from one's own enterprise, and certainly not into other (more reversible) types of investments like "revocable capital formations" in capital money titles. This of course also had its drawbacks. The excessive business and self-financing bias of Austrian fiscal policy (with its much too generous and undifferentiated approach to investment promotion via tax incentives) had already resulted in a far too one-sided capital agglomeration (not to say endogamy) in existing enterprises, branches, and sectors, an overconcentration whose effects on productivity and on innovative and capital markets will be discussed in the following chapter and also in Chapter 5.

2
DOMESTIC FISCAL POLICY: GLOBAL DEMAND AND SELECTIVE STRUCTURING

The effects of some adjustments are felt for a long time. As we have seen, the overwhelming majority of Western economic policy makers and theoreticians considered the oil-price "blackmail" in the wake of the Yom Kippur War of 1973 not as a forced real improvement in the terms of trade of the oil-exporting countries but as a nominal higher-cost effect comparable to across-the-board wage demands by unions. And they reacted accordingly, both verbally and politically. Nothing shows the influence of the monetarist, distorting view more clearly than the concerted and completely injudicious defensive reaction of the Western industrial complex, with the German Federal Republic and the United States in the lead. Instead of recognizing the inevitability of the real-income transfer aspect of the oil-price hike and the consequent inevitable reduction of domestic demand of the oil-importing industrial nations by the margin of difference between the old and the new oil bills (amounting initially to between 50 and 70 billion U.S. dollars of purchasing power), which opened up a demand gap for domestic products that somehow had to be closed, they saw only the effects on prices and payments balances. If one had to pay three to five times as much for the same quantity of imported oil, domestic thrift was the only way out: curbing domestic consumption and domestic investments to limit the demand for the now too expensive energy raw material, and thus prevent an imported cost push from turning into a domestic inflationary spiral. This, incidentally, is the policy for which Chancellor Schmidt solicited the support of the Carter Administration even after the economic summits of London (1977) and Bonn (1978), with complete "success," as we have since seen.

The crucial point now is this: the rolling-over of the higher oil prices to the domestic cost and price levels feared by the authors of this policy could not have come about in view of the flow of the amounts of former domestic demand to the OPEC nations. The OPEC measure was no union wage demand that could be answered, or rather punished, by "efficiency," but a "tax increase" whose proceeds its foreign collector had to hoard in the absence of domestic spending possibilities. And so, for the time being these moneys did not translate into purchasing power. Consequently, the oil buyers had the opportunity (and flexibility) to replace the missing domestic demand of their full-employment economy without fear of inflationary overheating and escalating balance-of-payment deficits. The high oil prices, which anyway could not be changed, would (in line with the law of the interdependence of prices) have led to a rearrangement in the "relative" prices, but not to an increase in the "absolute" cost and price levels of the Western industrial countries. To block this drop in prices and employment would have required building up of domestic demand, maybe not in the same amount as the loss suffered, for that would indeed have led to an inflation-financed roll-over of the oil-price increase to all domestic costs and prices.

The economic balance sheet that should have been drawn up looks like this: What was missing was domestic demand (dD), the amount of which was known because of the difference between the old and new oil bills.

What amount of budget-financed investment and consumer spending (dS) do the fiscal agencies have to plan on to avoid a drop in prices and employment or an inflationary overfinancing of the oil-price boom? Every surplus in domestic demand, whether of investment or consumption, falls into three parts or categories of use: (*a*) the part that is spent additionally and with (multiplicative) effects; (*b*) the part that becomes additional savings (putting a drain on demand); and (*c*) the part that turns into additional imports (foreign demand). The three are obviously determined by

$$1 - a = b + c$$

i.e., the sum of marginal-savings plus marginal-import quotas, the domestic-effect "multiplier" of dS. Since

$$dS = dD \div \frac{1}{1 - a}$$

$$= dD \div \frac{1}{b + c}$$

dS is always smaller than dD, if $b + c$ has a positive total value, i.e., when, with higher domestic spending and income, savings as well as imports increase, which seems to be the rule.[1]

A domestic spending and fiscal surplus policy must thus be concerned (and if possible quantifiably so) not only with the domestic-effect multiplier $(1 - a)$, but above all with the external-effect multiplier (c) involving the spending of foreign exchange.

It is not known whether the Austrian government drew up such a balance sheet after the oil shock of 1973, i.e., whether it anticipated the domestic effect of the multiplier and its conformation out of the relevant marginal spending (a) and "drainage" quotas $(b + c)$, nor whether their values (if they were established) had any significance. What is known is that the Austrian fiscal policy behaved as though it had always known and considered these effective connections. In calculating the budget deficits for the post-1974 period, the policy aim has been (1) to increase domestic demand (dD), (2) from the very beginning to set up the calculations so as to avoid an equally large increase of deficit-financed spending surplus (dS), because (3) an increase of the (marginal) savings and import rates $(b + c)$ was to be expected, and therefore (4) the additional currency and reserves (dR) inevitably required for the unavoidable increase in imports had to be incorporated into the budget's financing calculation: the amount of financing of foreign credits (or capital imports) required by the domestic program.

Assuming that the Austrian fiscal policy makers in 1973–1974 were convinced that one-third of the additional domestic spending (dS) provided for in the budget was domestic savings (thus not spent) and another third would result in the domestic production rather than import of goods and services, the effective domestic spending multiplier would be $1 \div 2/3 = 1.5$. Provided that a third of the amount could have been financed in foreign exchange (333 million schillings' worth of foreign credits), a 100 billion schilling program would have brought in a 150 billion schilling spending effect in the first year. If only half that amount, 75 billion schillings, were needed, a 50 billion schilling spending program and 167 million schillings' worth of foreign credits would have sufficed.

In Part 4 we will return to the connection between the fiscal domestic multiplier

$$\frac{1}{1-a} = \frac{1}{a+b}$$

and its outside financing through foreign credit that safeguards the gross currency reserve. At this point let us merely say that Austrian fiscal policy was planned conceptually and in full awareness of the domestic consequences. It is not the result of ad hoc improvisation or of experimentation without a concept, neither from the model nor the basic premises (substitution for the loss of foreign demand) nor in its economic and financial implementation: closing and financing of the domestic demand gap. If the government, for example, had failed to see the (negative) import multiplier, the entire program would have foundered simply because of the existing currency gap.

The same cannot be said of Germany's related policy. From beginning to end it lacked an underlying concept. Even at the time, the German declaration that more money was no substitute for a shortage of oil was wrong on three counts. First, there was no oil shortage; on the contrary, there was all the oil one might want, only it was more expensive. Second, no amount of "internal saving" would bring down the price of oil, except if one thought along the startling and revealing lines of international struggles of redistribution. And third, there was only one way to deal with the deterioration in the terms of trade forced by the OPEC states—and that was not taken, either by the German Federal Republic or by most of the big Western industrial nations—namely, to "compensate" for the losses on internal demand and expenditures, in line with Austria's fiscal model, which, if the calculation of the savings and import multipliers was only moderately accurate, would not have heated up inflation but ameliorated the depression of 1974–1975.

The increase in the budget deficit since 1973—between 1970 and 1972 Austria's credit share of the gross national product had fallen to 0.5 percent annually while from 1973 and 1975 it rose to 4.6 percent—perfected the division of labor between monetary and fiscal policy. The dual strategy balanced the dual effect of the crisislike developments in the wake of the OPEC decision—i.e., that the rising world market prices would necessarily import inflation and the falling demand brought on by rising oil-transfer payments would result in depression. Monetary policy prevented the importation of inflation, and in a bold gambit it even changed it into the importation of stability by letting the schilling appreciate in tandem with the DM vis-à-vis the U.S. dollar (and to that extent also vis-à-vis the dollar-denominated oil price). The deficit-based fiscal policy, on the other hand, warded off the importation of depression, which—despite permanent schilling appreciation—was the price paid for the higher real value of the oil imports and for the participation in the monetary and economic union with the big, strong, but deflationary neighbor.

How does this anticyclical fiscal policy, immune to the intrusion of depression, work? It "technically" combines three objectives:

1. The full financing of the recession-caused loss of income of the public sector to avoid a (cumulative) intensification of the decline in private domestic demand through a further decline in domestic public demand. To prevent a procyclical public spending adjustment to the receding level of state revenues, the treasury was given the role of credit adjuster. That meant it had to go into debt.

2. For reasons of effectiveness (the defense against negative import-multiplier impacts) the inevitable public indebtedness (with its effect on full employment) in turn should, as far as possible, conform to the balance of payments. The already weak reserve position of the central bank brought on by the deficit in the balance on current accounts must not be further weakened by the supplementary program; moreover, the reserve loss must not be allowed to set off any additional defla-

tionary movements. Therefore, without a foreign trade back-stop, such a program is bound to fail either because of the depletion of the foreign-exchange drawer (the depletion of the reserve position of the central bank) or the disproportionate balance on current accounts deficit (the transformation of domestic into foreign demand). If stable exchange rates and a basic aversion to import planning rule out any possibility of a closed border, there remains only one method of obtaining the indispensable fiscal freedom of movement and effectiveness: shifting most of deficit spending over to foreign credits.

At the same time, this method of external deficit financing (which at times approaches the 100 percent mark) allows a tangible easing of the domestic credit (interest rate) situation. The unencumbered domestic credit market thus remains open to the private domestic investor, without any of those crowding-out effects that in neighboring West Germany—despite substantially higher savings and liquidity supply (out of the official money-amount goal of the German Federal Bank and its re-nunciation of foreign-exchange-market interventions)—accompany the covering of the government's credit and influence the interest-rate trend pro- rather than anticyclically, both with regard to balancing external payments and domestic employment. This point will be discussed in Chapter 5.

3. The investment promotion via the incentives provided by the Austrian progressive income tax is intensified. To compensate for the brakes on self-financing imported along with the hard-currency policy, more and more fiscal sources of substitute financing are being made available to the private business sector at the expense of the general tax collection. Thus in addition to the greater possibilities of premature write-offs (which in 1978 climbed to 50 percent for movable investment goods, 30 percent for ordinary investments, and 60 percent for investments in environmental protection, energy conservation, and research), there are fresh incentives like free investment funds, investment reserves, as well as the possibilities of double tax write-offs through increases in the book value of already written-off investment capital and the tax neutrality of reserve transfers. According to calculations, the build-up in 1978 made possible an effective business profit after taxes of about 6 percent;

before the crisis it probably came to about one-third of this amount.[2]

But that is not all. There is also the annually increasing support of selective (or projected) investment financed by para-treasuries and governmental guarantees. (Because of the special financing framework this aspect need not be discussed here.) The relationship between general and selective public investment supports is explored in Chapter 5.

Some figures and relationships of the anticyclical fiscal mechanism of the deficit years since 1973 are discussed next. Table 3 shows the demand-stabilizing effect of public investment. The higher growth rates of public investment offset the weakness of private investment during the critical years of 1973, 1975, and 1978. Were it not for this offsetting factor, those years would without a doubt have registered zero or negative growth rates. However, it also demonstrates that the reasons for the slide into the recession trough of 1975 went beyond the previously described exogenous causes. Because a great many of the effects of public investment on spending and demand sparked in 1973 were obviously not felt until the next year, private and public investment spending accumulated in 1974. The timing of the 1973 program was thus not exactly optimal; it came too late to affect the weak investment of that year and too early for the deeper recession of 1975. Even if the boom diagnosticians, most of whom slept through the crisis of 1975—not only in Austria—would have alerted us to the impending recession in good time (something only a few outsiders did), the situation could probably not have been saved because of the time lags between diagnosis, program preparation, and execution. What happened in 1975 apparently was inevitable, not only because of the exogenous circumstances, but also because of the dispositive (endogenous) time lags. What matters, however, is the clearly visible firming of private investment activity since that time, and the growing realization in the wake of the 1975 recession that there existed a highly "visible hand" of governmental protection against the turbulence of the economic climate and, moreover, that this protection was effective. Summing up, we find that the post-1975 recession years show an unusually stable growth rate of

Table 3. Gross Investments, 1970–1979

	Total		Public Sector[a]		Private Sector		Industry Share	
	(in billions of schillings)	Increase (in percent)	(in billions of schillings)	Increase (in percent)	(in billions of schillings)	Increase (in percent)	(in billions of schillings)	Increase (in percent)
1970	97.2	15.8	17.5	12.9	79.7	19.0	16.4	34.2
1971	116.8	20.2	21.0	20.0	95.8	20.2	21.2	31.7
1972	144.7	23.9	25.1	19.5	119.6	24.8	24.2	14.2
1973	146.6	1.3	27.0	7.6	119.6	0.0	22.4	- 7.4
1974	172.3	17.5	32.2	19.3	140.1	17.1	25.0	11.6
1975	175.4	1.8	35.0	8.7	140.4	0.2	21.5	-14.0
1976[b]	190.4	8.6	36.9	5.4	153.5	9.3	22.8	6.1
1977[b]	215.6	13.2	38.8	5.2	176.8	15.2	28.0	22.8
1978[c]	227.9	5.7	44.9	15.7	183.0	3.5	30.0	7.1
1979[c]	247.1	8.4	49.0	9.1	198.1	8.3	33.0	10.0
1960–1969		8.4		9.4		7.9		3.7
1970–1979		10.9		12.1		10.6		8.3

Source: Austrian Institute for Economic Research.

[a]Share of aggregate.
[b]Estimated.
[c]Projected.

private gross plant investments in the range of 9 percent annually.

Tables 4 and 5 show the use, distribution, and extent of government financing of, and assistance to, private investment. In almost every year after 1975 the totals exceeded public investment. Thus in every year since 1975, Austria's fiscal policy sported a dual aspect: in addition to investing in the public sector it introduced a publicly financed investment quota into the private sector, and moreover one showing a rising and stabilizing tendency.

If the two components of the real and financial public share

Table 4. Public Investments and Investment Support, 1970–1979 (in billions of schillings)

Year	Government Investment and Maintenance Costs[a]	Investment Supports in the Economic Sector		Totals	Financing of Investments Authorized by the Federal Finance Law
		Housing Construction and Water Supply[b]	Other Sectors[c]		
1970	11.5	3.9	2.6	18.0	0.35
1971	13.2	4.5	2.4	20.1	0.40
1972	15.7	5.2	4.6	25.5	0.50
1973	16.7	5.8	5.3	27.8	0.40
1974	19.1	7.1	6.6	32.8	0.15
1975	24.4	7.6	7.4	39.4	0.20
1976	24.4	8.0	7.5	39.9	1.00
1977	25.7	9.1	7.9	42.7	1.20
1978[d,e,f,g]	28.3	10.7	8.5	47.5	2.85
1979[d,e,g]	30.1	11.5	8.8	50.4	2.70

Source: Federal Finance Law.

[a] Including national defense but excluding foreign purchases.

[b] Out of earmarked federal revenues.

[c] Including capital build-up.

[d] Estimated (basic budget).

[e] The projected stabilizers for 1978 and 1979 also include those of Table 5.

[f] Including expenditures for investment purposes of the reserve fund provided for in the Federal Finance Law of 1978.

[g] The use of other authorized financing makes the following additional sums available: for 1979, 1.4 billion schillings; for 1978, 1.3 billion schillings.

Table 5. Projected Stabilizers of Investment and Investment Support, 1978 and 1979 (in billions of schillings)

	1978[a]			1979[a]		
	Stabili-zation Quota	Business Stimulus Quota	Total	Stabili-zation Quota	Business Stimulus Quota	Total
Government invest-ment and mainte-nance costs[b]	2.5	1.9	4.4	2.5	1.9	4.4
Investment supports in the economic sector[b]	0.3	0.5	0.8	0.3	0.5	0.8
Total	2.8	2.4	5.2	2.8	2.4	5.2

Source: Federal Finance Law.

[a]The use of this sum requires approval by the Finance Ministry.
[b]Including national defense but excluding foreign purchases.

in gross plant investments between 1975 and 1978–1979 are viewed as constituting a government share or social quota in the growth-stimulating investment process of the total economy, then there exists a relatively constant quota of 40 percent that decreases only in its final phase. In a time of weak private investment this conforms to Keynes's contention in the *General Theory* that "a somewhat comprehensive socialisation of investment will prove the only means of securing an approximation to full employment; though this need not exclude all manner of compromises and of devices by which public authority will co-operate with private initiative."[3]

The final relevant point in this context concerns the internal direction of the different households and financial sectors—the side-by-side existence of various public hands. There is a difference between the central government and the lower bodies in their readiness and ability to take on indebtedness. As a rule the credit standing of even the poorest central government is superior to that of the wealthiest local community, particularly so if foreign and domestic credits are added together. A business-

Figure 3. The Federal Government as Loser: Decline in Tax Collection.
Final Share of Total Collection (in percent)

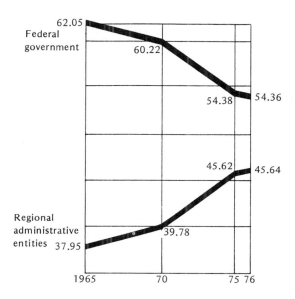

The federal government's share of the total tax collection has been declining steadily.
This pronounced decline is due only in small part to the federal government's falling
share of the tax proceeds; the greater factor is that the federal government has taken
over the costs of regional administrations, thereby easing the burden on their budgets.

and structurally motivated policy of deficit spending of the
public sector hence requires not only the equalization but also
the redistribution of burdens. Even if in time of recession federal
revenues decline more slowly than state or municipal collections, simply because boom profits do not figure as prominently
in the households of lower administrative entities, the central
government, because of its greater debt and refinancing ability
in time of recession, rarely if ever can avoid a cut-back in its
share of tax collection and a simultaneous increase in its share
of total public indebtedness. That is why extended depressions
always restrict the self-financing latitude of the higher administrative entities (central governments) more than those of states
and municipalities, even if those who profit from this cyclical
financial equalization never or rarely admit it. Figure 3 shows
that this trend toward the internal equalization of burdens
set in prior to the crisis of 1975, and it has continued at an ac-

celerated pace since that time, particularly if foreign indebtedness is included. The official foreign indebtedness of the Austrian government, which continued to decrease until 1971 (down to 9 billion schillings by the end of 1973) has since skyrocketed, especially in 1975, when the government refinanced almost its entire deficit, approximately 26 billion schillings, abroad. The foreign indebtedness by the end of 1979 is expected to stand at some 72 billion schillings, more than seven times that of 1973. In contrast, domestic public debt during that period "merely" tripled, reaching some 160.5 billion schillings at the end of that year (see Tables 6 and 7).

The problem of whether and how this domestic and foreign indebtedness can be erased and the likely consequences of such debt liquidation will be discussed in detail in Chapter 6. The policy of a high and constant "social quota" of the total investment activity introduced after the escalation of the worldwide economic crisis in 1973, and strengthened anticyclically in the weak years 1975 and 1978, is the crucial factor in Austria's net capital-formation rate, outstripping that of the Western industrial nations in a time of international economic crisis. While the anticyclical trend of most of the other OECD (Organization for Economic Cooperation and Development) countries (either spontaneous or forced by business policy) included and raised the share of consumer spending of the gross or national product, this held true for Austria only to a limited degree (and

Table 6. Domestic Effect of the Federal Budget Deficit[a]
(in billions of schillings)

1970	1971	1972	1973	1974	1975	1976	1977	1978[b,c]	1979[b]
0.11	1.88[d]	1.88[d]	2.98	5.78	26.13	26.53	23.12	26.3	27.37

Source: Working paper of the Federal Finance Law.

[a] Domestic effective spending surplus of the basic budget.
[b] Estimate.
[c] Including the management of the reserve fund mandated by the Federal Finance Law of 1978.
[d] Domestic effective income surplus.

Table 7. Federal Indebtedness

| | Domestic Debt | Foreign Debt | Total Debt[a] | Total Debt | Costs[b] | | | |
| | (in millions of schillings at year's end)[c] | | | (as percent of GNP) | Interest | Liquidation | Other | Total |
					(in millions of schillings)			
1970	33,582	13,489	47,071	12.68	2,727	4,979	215	7,921
1971	34,715c	12,132	46,847c	11.35	2,931	6,053	306	9,290
1972	39,554c	10,304	49,858c	10.62	2,999	6,249	334	9,582
1973	47,232c	9,019	56,251c	10.55	3,238	5,665	358	9,261
1974	47,855d	13,540	61,395d	10.01	3,640	6,880	209	10,729
1975	68,305	32,062	100,367	15.34	4,725	7,499	1,165	13,389
1976	98,824	34,958	133,782	18.36	7,868	10,687	1,153	19,708
1977	117,155	47,426	164,581	20.82	9,869	11,982	879	22,730
1978e	139,535	61,458	200,993f	23.96	13,632	16,063	1,218	30,913
1979e	160,494	72,036	232,530f	25.96	15,499	18,563	1,679	35,741

[a] Figures for 1970–77 are from the working paper of the Federal Finance Law; figures for 1978 and 1979 are estimates of the Federal Finance Ministry (as of October 1978).

[b] 1978 and 1979 federal estimates.

[c] This amount is 69 million schillings less in the federal budget due to an exchange difference in the calculation of the repayment, based on the transfer of the Austrian quota at the International Monetary Fund to the Austrian National Bank.

[d] Taking into account the findings in Federal Register No. 377/1976.

[e] Not including projected stabilizers.

[f] Estimate.

only for some sectors). Investment spending has remained the crucial demand, growth, and employment stabilizer of domestic spending, as Table 8 makes clear.

Austria's expansionary, domestic fiscal surplus policy does not conform to Kaldor's model of "consumer-led growth" nearly so much as is generally suspected or assumed.[4] Rather, given its situation and interests it has been behaving like a relatively late arrival among industrial nations: It has supplemented scarce domestic resources and real savings with imports of capital (goods) and financial instruments, which it used primarily even if not exclusively to build and expand an efficient industrial sector. In the course of this development the country's capacity to absorb more expensive and durable consumer goods (household appliances, passenger vehicles) continued to rise, but this is neither an aberration nor an undesirable by-product of an otherwise successful developmental process. It is a normal, unavoidable concomitant of an industrially expanding society that is not degenerating into, nor aspiring toward, the inhumane, unproductive expansion of East European society. On the contrary: the new consumer preferences that are part of the new prosperity conform to Engel's law,[5] the oldest and most "humane" of all laws of development, according to which the demand for goods that enhance the quality of life and raise the standard of living are the logical outgrowth of the increasing satisfaction of primary needs—food, clothing, shelter, and education. In countries that ignore or possibly even suppress this improvement in the standard of living, as is still the case in the planned economies of Eastern Europe and many perhaps even "wealthy" developing countries, internal and interindustrial dislocations are unavoidable; but worse still, this type of social management discredits itself. People forced to live under such systems where technocracy is an end in itself (and which they cannot understand) ultimately reject it politically, economically, and individually.

The qualitative improvement of the Austrian consumer quota and the consequent increase in the import- and exchange-financing component do not mean, contrary to what has been said in some quarters, that "overconsumption" has led to the deterioration of the balance on current accounts and blunted

Table 8. Comparative Economic Growth as Measured by Change in Real Gross National Product Compared to Previous Year (in percent)

	1960–1969	1970	1971	1972	1973	1974	1975	1976	1977	1978a	First Half 1979a,b	1970–1978
United States	4.1	-0.1	2.9	5.8	5.4	-1.3	-1.0	6.0	4.9	3.8	3.0	2.9
Canada	5.2	2.6	7.0	5.8	7.5	3.6	0.9	4.9	2.6	4.0	4.0	4.3
Japan	11.0	10.9	7.3	8.9	9.8	-1.0	2.4	6.0	5.1	5.5	4.5	6.0
German Federal Republic	5.0	5.9	2.9	3.4	5.1	0.5	-2.6	5.7	2.4	2.5	2.8	2.9
France	5.7	7.1	5.3	6.1	5.4	2.8	0.7	4.6	3.0	3.3	3.8	4.3
Great Britain	3.0	2.5	2.8	2.5	6.6	-0.6	-1.6	2.3	0.7	2.8	1.8	2.0
Italy	5.7	5.0	1.5	3.2	6.9	3.9	-3.5	5.7	1.7	2.0	3.0	2.9
Average for "big" industrial nations	4.9	2.7	3.7	5.6	6.1	-0.2	-0.7	5.5	3.9	3.5	3.3	3.4
Belgium	4.9	6.3	4.0	5.5	6.3	4.0	-2.0	5.5	1.8	2.8	—	3.3
Denmark	5.1	2.7	3.6	4.3	2.8	0.2	-1.1	5.4	1.9	1.0	—	2.2
Finland	5.4	8.3	2.4	7.0	6.5	4.3	0.9	0.3	-0.8	1.0	—	3.2
Ireland	4.7	3.2	4.1	5.4	4.4	1.3	0.2	2.4	5.0	5.5	—	3.5
Netherlands	5.4	6.9	4.4	3.9	5.9	4.2	-1.2	4.6	2.3	3.0	—	3.8
Norway	5.0	4.3	4.6	5.1	4.1	5.2	3.6	5.8	4.1	3.5	—	4.5
Austria	4.7	7.8	5.3	6.4	5.8	4.1	-2.0	5.2	3.5	1.5	—	4.2
Sweden	4.4	5.0	0.7	2.6	3.5	4.0	0.9	1.3	-2.5	0.5	—	1.8
Switzerland	4.4	5.6	4.1	3.2	3.1	1.5	-7.5	-1.3	4.3	1.5	—	1.4
Average for "small" industrial nations	4.9	5.8	3.5	4.4	4.7	3.4	-1.3	3.2	1.9	2.0	—	2.9
OECD total	4.9	3.0	3.8	5.5	6.1	0.3	-0.6	5.2	3.6	3.5	3.3	3.4
OECD Europe	5.0	5.3	3.6	4.4	5.7	2.1	-1.2	4.3	2.1	2.5	—	3.2

Source: OECD; for Austria: Austrian Institute for Economic Research.

aProjected value.
bFirst half of 1979: seasonally adjusted rate based on the second six-month 1978 rate.

the country's competitive edge. If that were true, the increase in the consumer quota would have substantially exceeded its capital-formation (or investment) quota. (Great Britain constitutes an almost classic example.) The exact opposite appears to be true: Thanks to its increased investment quota and the consequent high (real) growth multiplier, Austria was able to effect a rapid expansion of its real income (aggregate and per capita) and to increase spending for higher-cost consumer goods payable in foreign exchange. Thus the so-called overconsumption of the post-1975 years, even if it is reflected in negative figures in the balance on current accounts, is a result of desired economic growth, the persistence of higher income and job security, as well as an objective indication that Austria did not have to share in the fear of investment risk and unemployment that others were experiencing. Tracing how investments were used and looking at the newly created production capabilities— i.e., first analyzing capital formation and following this with a study of capital use—confirms this result.

Professor Kausel[6] has brought statistical evidence that Austria's high investment quota had not only considerable effect on income, but also positive structural as well as innovative and production effects. Amidst the crisis, Austria managed to modernize and diversify its industrial production. Aided by a high industrial capital absorption rate, it built up and rejuvenated its capital stock. In those years of crisis not only did Austrian industries strengthen their productive capacity and investment dynamics to a greater extent than the older industrial nations (particularly neighboring West Germany), but Austria's unprecedented spurt in technology and its greater access to sources of supply, coupled with its improved price and cost elasticities, also gave it a considerable competitive edge on foreign markets.

As Table 9 shows, domestic capacity expansion was concentrated primarily in industries with substantial future potential like chemicals, machinery, passenger vehicles, and a wide assortment of finished goods. This sort of "production intelligence" helped Austrian exports join the top rank of industrial exporting nations. The balance on current accounts by branches of industry shows more clearly than any other set of statistics or extrapolation the continuing activating trend (see Table 10).

Table 9. Austria's Technological Progress: Per Capita Exports of Chemical Products, Machine Tools, Passenger Vehicles, and Other Finished Goods (SITC 5, 7, 8, 9)

Year	Austria (in U.S. dollars)	OECD Europe (in U.S. dollars)	Austria (OECD Europe = 100)
1955	22	44	50
1960	43	72	60
1965	84	114	74
1970	167	205	81
1975	493	535	92
1976	559	590	95

Source: A Kausel: "Der Schilling ist nicht überwertet," in Wirtschaftsberichte der Creditanstalt-Bankverein, No. 5, Vienna, 1977, p. 8.

By introducing domestic and foreign planning data, fiscal policy prevents the innovative process launched by an enterprise from coming to a stop (as happened in developing countries) or from being interrupted because of domestic and foreign financial bottlenecks. Thus even amidst the crisis it was possible to increase production and to make available the requisite capitalization for essential plant improvements. Consequently, Austria since 1975 has witnessed an almost explosive increase in industrial investments. In that same period West Germany's employment picture darkened and its plant investments stagnated, whereas by the end of 1977 Austria registered a 30 percent increase in investments. Instead of reducing the number of available jobs, higher investments helped to safeguard and expand existing job opportunities.

If this leads one to conclude that Austria's capital stock is newer and more modern than Western Germany's and that this rejuvenation and modernization is continuing, that is only part of the truth. The whole truth is that this newer, more modern capital stock makes possible better planning for the immediate future, i.e., for the first half of the eighties—a considerable advance over the past in terms of domestic and foreign financing.

A newer capital stock with less real wear and tear reduces the need for new (replacement) as well as net investments, and at the same time allows for an increase in the income-based real- and nominal-savings potential. A greater balance between

Table 10. Covering Quota of Imports Through Exports (in percent)

Year	Raw Materials, Food, Energy (0–4)	Semi-finished Goods (6)	Chemicals (5)	Machine Tools, Passenger Vehicles (7)	Sundry Finished Goods (8,9)	Total of (5,7,8,9)	Sum Total (0–9)	Exports
1960	53	186	39	45	107	52	79	99
1970	52	141	46	62	114	69	80	103
1975	38	149	70	74	85	76	80	102
1976	41	137	60	65	77	68	74	94
1977	40	126	62	57	75	62	69	89
1978a	41	132	64	72	73	71	76	97

Source: A. Kausel, Beurteilung der nachhaltigen Wettbewerbsstärke der österreichischen Wirtschaft aufgrund makroökonomischer Tatbestände, Vienna, 1978 (manuscript), Table 2.3.

aEstimate based on the January–October 1978 figures.

marginal investment and savings tendencies eases the cost and price situation endogenously. This automatically diminishes the need for importing stability via a permanent policy of appreciating hard currency. However, it also means that the production and export potential that developed in the years when investment was building up can be marketed even more advantageously than before, because price and cost factors have enhanced the competitive position. In other words, the improved capacity and productivity attests to the effectiveness of the policy of underwriting development by balance on current accounts deficits and capital imports—in real terms because of the greater abundance and lowered cost of the available export potential, and also financially because of the inevitable increase in the rate of savings in which their domestic absorption quota declines, which makes for a greater degree of freedom in foreign debt liquidation and capital exports. For that reason the recently expressed concern about Austria's internal and external debt position and its prospective dangers, designed to influence investment and savings crucial to the country's financial future, is unfounded, if not downright irresponsible, so long as it is not supported by an overall economic (ex-ante) projection of future investment needs and future savings possibilities, let alone political action parameters available to a government and/or central bank aware of repayment obligations.

An entirely different—and open—question is how entrepreneurs spoiled by high "social" quotas of their (private) investments will react when such support is no longer forthcoming (because no longer necessary) or can no longer be justified (because not sufficiently productive of foreign exchange and socially tilted). It remains to be seen whether Austria's investors will be able to kick the habit of this financing drug without painful withdrawal symptoms. The expected increase in real savings will not only draw on the allocation of capital investments (from business self-financing to outside financing and participation in enterprises owned by others), but also lead to higher savings in the private (nonentrepreneurial) households and thus lead to lowered profits. Moreover, the side-by-side existence, or rather proliferation, of uneconomic global investment supports within the "social" quota, without any direction by the fiscal financier or any hint of the desired (i.e., sector- or project-oriented), selective, focused investment support cannot continue much longer. Too many growth, structure, and financing advantages are being given away by this mixed system, a point to be taken up in a later chapter.

3

BALANCE OF PAYMENTS
DICTATES THE MONEY SUPPLY

In no Western industrial nation have revised ancient monetary doctrines made so few waves as in the Austria of the seventies. The assumptions about banking theory that David Ricardo and John Stuart Mill had already refuted 150 years ago— according to which neither deflationary nor inflationary imbalances are to be feared from money left to the "free" disposal of money and credit consumers so long as the money supply (the basis of all financing processes) is kept under tight control— have never, either before or after 1973, guided official monetary or fiscal policy.[1]

Because no official body proclaimed any sort of monetary goal, Austria has been spared three problems:

1. confusion about the content and meaning of the various types of money, from central bank money to M_1, M_2, etc. (Table 11);
2. the humiliation and consequent loss of confidence about established economic guidelines that caused the cautious German central bank to retract all proclaimed monetary goals and retreat into nonbinding "variable corridors"— eloquent testimony to the inconstancy of the planning data in economic decision making (from investment planning to price and wage policy);
3. extraneous social conflicts over who is the "guilty party" in this entrenched monetary misadventure—the price push of business, the wage push of unions, the public deficit that inflates credit demand, or a combination of

all three (that is, all except the central banks, of course)—
frustrating their own objectives on the rate-of-exchange-
intervention front.

This sort of thing never happened in Austria. Its policy mix
does not allow for the autonomous regulation of the money
supply by the central bank. As Table 12 shows, the currency-
reserve balance derives from the balance of payments (position II, 1) and the domestic budget deficit (position II, 2).
However, the net credit (or indebtedness) of the entrepreneurial
sector at the banks—the only financing source on which the
national bank has influence—plays no part in this whatever.
Even in 1973, 1976, and 1977, when the balance of payments
tended to restrict the money volume and the budget was the
sole expansionary influence, the economy was able to liquidate
its bank debts, a process that began in 1973 and has been under-
way practically ever since.

Thus Austria's liquidity is in principle more dependent on the
balance of payments and the budget than on the central bank.
If the total liquidity flow (M_1) to the Austrian economy in the

Table 11. The Definition of Money Amounts

M_1	Cash in circulation (exclusive of cash holdings of credit institutions) plus sight deposits of domestic nonbanks
M_2	M_1 plus term moneys of domestic nonbanks, with terms of less than four years
M_3	M_2 plus savings deposits with legally fixed cancellation terms
Central bank money	Cash in circulation (exclusive of cash holdings of credit institutions) plus 17 percent of the sight deposits, 12 percent of the term deposits, and 8 percent of the savings deposits of domestic nonbanks at domestic credit institutions. The central bank money includes term and savings deposits with terms of less than four years.

Table 12. Sources of Austria's Money Supply (M_1)

	1973	1974	1975	1976	1977	1973	1974	1975	1976	1977
	(in millions of schillings)					(in percent)				
I. Increase in the volume of money (M_1)	+6,227	+5,762	+20,243	+12,682	+6,685	100	100	100	100	100
II. Originating Source										
1. Central bank reserves (+ = increase; – = decrease)	–1,814	+6,311	+20,515	– 3,652	– 7,241	–29.1	+109.5	+101.3	– 28.8	–108.3
2. Domestic budget deficits	–2,980	–5,780	–26,130	–26,530	–23,120	–47.9	–100.3	–129.1	–209.2	–345.8
3. Debt liquidation of the economy vis-à-vis the banks	+4,548	+8,114	+24,810	+45,285	+45,495	+73.0	+140.8	+ 23.8	+357.1	+680.6
4. Foreign bank business (– = indebtedness; + = debt liquidation)	+4,207	–2,729	+ 1,995	– 6,941	– 5,426	+67.6	– 47.4	+ 9.9	– 54.7	– 81.2
5. Other factors	+2,266	– 154	– 947	+ 4,520	– 3,023	+36.4	– 2.7	– 4.7	+ 35.6	– 45.2

Sources: Annual Reports of the Austrian National Bank (Positions I, II, 1, 4, 5); *Doppelstrategie für Arbeit und Stabilität, Der Bundeshaushalt 1979* (Vienna, 1978), p. 205 (Position II, 2; Position II, 3; Difference of II, 2 and the surplus of credit extension and/or money capital formation).

five-year period 1973–1977 equals 100, the net foreign-exchange purchases of the central bank account for 27 percent of the rise in the liquidity level, and domestic budget deficits account for 164 percent. This enabled the domestic economy to grow without incurring (credit) debts. On the contrary, its permanent money-wealth build-up allowed the Austrian economy to act as the "banker" to the country's banking system, a claim no other industrial country can make (see Table 12, position II, 3, in every year since 1973). The debit balance of foreign-exchange purchases of the Austrian national bank increased the gross reserve position by 20 percent between 1973 and 1977, but this largely reflects the foreign refinancing of the domestic budget deficits.

The shift of public deficit financing to the foreign money and credit markets has contributed substantially to the money and credit supply of the Austrian economy, and the capital-balance deficits as a planned source of liquidity played a part similar to that of the largely (monetarily) unplanned balance on current account surpluses of the German Federal Republic. In both cases the preponderance of external liquidity supply reduced the domestic debt level of the economy vis-à-vis the banks, and that of the banks vis-à-vis the central bank. Without the comparatively strong spurt of liquidity supplied by external refinancing sources, the Austrian banking system would have had to incur far greater liabilities toward the Austrian national bank, which in turn would have affected the internal credit and interest situation. As we have seen, the inclusion of the foreign money and credit markets in the internal financing process eased the domestic money and credit markets. Now we also find out how the mechanism operates: because the state incurred greater foreign debts, the private sector (banking and economic) was able to reduce its domestic indebtedness.[2]

Fiscal debt management bore on internal financing directly through its impact on the changes in the money volume (M_1), and indirectly via its influence on the debt level of the banking economy and the resultant interest-rate structure. The public foreign-debt policy thus played a rather significant part in increasing the domestic credit-creating potential of the commercial banks and loosened the credit reins of the central bank, which are tightened only when the commercial banks are dependent on, not independent of, refinancing.

However, the Austrian banking community did not exactly rush to grant the economy credit or extend loans. Despite the unusually high real-investment rates of the economy, credit extension and financing levels from outside funds through the financial-paper markets (out of obligations and related fixed-interest-rate securities) remained comparatively low. Between 1971 and 1977, 568 billion schillings, or 44 percent out of a total (gross capital) investment of 1,157 billion schillings, was financed from outside sources—a very low level compared to the investment-financing rates of West Germany. This low level of investment financing underscores the great contribution of Austria's public debt policy to the self-financing capacity of the country's private sector.

While in West Germany both investment and self-financing have continued to decline since the beginning of the seventies, in Austria both have shown increasing strength. Even though West Germany's domestic capital market has grown and become more profitable, it still has been unable to absorb the decline in investments: in real-capital (asset) formation. Its financing capacity has been forced increasingly to curtail its commitments (investment and loans being lost to domestic investment financing) to help in the building up of a domestic public debt (to balance the deficit of federal and social insurance obligations) used predominantly for "consumer purposes."

In Austria, the upward trend of the real-capital (asset) formation was neither restricted by the relatively weak capital market nor blocked by public deficits. Entrepreneurial capital formation (or self-financing) was strong enough—and remained so, even during the crisis—to sustain and even accelerate domestic investments.

One of the reasons for this is already known to us: The treasury, by granting general and generous investment incentives, sacrificed a portion of its tax collection to stimulate business profits. The other reason is this: At the same time, the increase in the foreign public debt lowered not only the domestic indebtedness of Austria's banks but also that of its investors, for the treasury borrowed not only net liquidity from abroad, which helped reduce domestic debt, but also (foreign-financed) demand. By making use of the positive domestic spending multiplier, the government was able to sustain and even raise its spending level, thereby strengthening the international profit and self-financing position of its domestic investors via its active capital-import–financed business policy. This could not have happened if (as did happen in the German Federal Republic) the government had limited its indebtedness to the domestic sector. In that event there would have been a shift in potentially available liquidity—a change in domestic creditors, not a net debt-liquidation by the private sector (a point to be pursued later).

The budget, financially speaking, is the heart of the Austrian policy mix. Its liquidity chamber supplies and revitalizes the money supply, easing pressure on the banks; its demand chamber, by reducing investment risks, eases the burden on the economy—a constant flow of profits and lower debt (or outside financing) requirements. Because the treasury rather than the banks or domestic investors went into debt, the budget not only relieved these two sectors of potentially greater financing liabilities, but it also prevented an excessive demand for domestic credit from heating up domestic inflationary movements.

Of course, there remains the question of whether this fiscal policy of protecting the domestic money and capital market against the liquidity offers of the banks as well as the credit demand of the economy does not hamper its "natural" growth rate. If business did not have to resort to this degree of self-financing (which in the final analysis represents a forced saving by all consumers, via price), it would have had to compete much more actively for the available savings capital, i.e., ask for more credits and pay higher interest rates, which would have invigorated the capital market as well as the savings activity backing it up. Thus the possibility that the officially tolerated and supported high degree of entrepreneurial self-financing has negative effects on the extent, distribution, and productivity of capital and savings formation cannot be ruled out, nor that its future effects may be still greater, and this may turn out to be the Achilles heel of Austria's overall plan—a problem that will be examined in greater detail in Chapter 5.

Two questions must still be asked and answered in this context: To what extent is the unusual shape and technique of monetary fiscal policy tailored to the specific Austrian situation? What will become of this policy when its most important premise, the budgetary invocation of foreign (reserve-protective) refinancing, no longer exists?

Which aspects of this policy are and which are not specifically Austrian? We know that the role distribution between the central bank and the budget conforms to, or rather would have had to conform to, the role perception of the Bretton Woods era. According to this concept, balance-of-payments equilibrium via capital imports instead of internal (deflationary) adjustment is always right and advisable as long as it does not overstep the international credit framework. In that respect Austria's deficit and monetary fiscal policy is not the exception but the rule of a "classical" strategy combining internal with external stability goals.

The crucial factor—the volume of foreign indebtedness that determines the external and domestic balance—of course remains the same in both instances. In the classical concept the private sector goes into debt, while in the Austrian model the state eases the burden of its private enterprise not because it enjoys being in debt but because there exist objective doubts about the readiness of the private sector, the guarantor of domestic full employment, to take on debt. And in that context all conservative critics of the "ballooning" government debt must ask themselves whether they would rather see "excessive" private than public indebtedness, and if so, why? To that extent the "new" Austrian fiscal policy merely translates a proven classical approach into current usage—a policy that other countries in a like situation could certainly afford.

But what happens when the budget can no longer be refinanced abroad? When instead of foreign credits one would have to resort to available domestic credit lines? At this point the actual base of Austria's credit adjustment emerges in all its clarity: the balance-on-current-accounts deficit. It protects the country against unplanned and undesirable liquidity imports: Austria never came up against the German situation, in which 100 percent and more of domestic liquidity depended on foreign-exchange factors. All that Austrian fiscal policy had to do was to keep the domestic liquidity level from sinking too much because of the import surplus. For domestic demand and money flowed out, not in, via the balance-of-payments deficit. The balance-on-current-accounts deficit enabled, or possibly even compelled, the household to pursue surplus liquidity policy if it wished to prevent an excessive decline in domestic activities. The monetary fiscal policy, looked at more clearly and against the background of the deficit balance on current accounts, is not one of supplementary liquidizing but one of defensive reliquidizing: a return of Austria's money supply and liquidity level to that of a balanced, nondeficit balance on current accounts.

Is such sustained activity on the deficit side of the balance on current accounts, if pursued over a period of time, perhaps irresponsible, and does it escalate the danger that inheres to a deficit? And with the passage of time does mistrust inflate the danger of even bigger outflows due to capital-balance deficits? This is a problem that, except for a brief period in 1977, has never become acute, and when it did, only because for no discernible reason rumors began to circulate that the schilling was about to retreat from its hard-currency position. It was a setback based on a hypothesis, not on reality, but it did teach the lesson that a policy committed to the reliability of its planning data must be concerned with the underlying assumptions of its success and must never cast doubt on them, certainly not publicly. And so there remains the astonishing and indisputable fact that Austria's deficit balance on current accounts has neither impaired its international credit standing nor launched a flight from the schilling.

But even if a premature or unexpected financing bottleneck— self-caused or not—should develop on the international money and credit markets (such as a discrepancy between the planning data of creditors and debtor), the impact on Austria could be calculated, and substantially alleviated—even in case of a total collapse of the financial markets à la 1929–1932.

First of all, the volume and due dates of Austria's foreign debts move within narrow and known limits. The maximum burden that could be imposed by a possible reduction of terms of the outstanding foreign debts (57 billion schillings at the end of 1978) to half their stipulated repayment term in say five years from now would amount to 9 billion schillings annually, i.e., 5 percent of the gross foreign-exchange receipts out of current exports, or 13 percent of the present gross reserve holdings of the Austrian national bank. Even in the event that these figures should turn out to be inaccurate—exports could rise and reserves melt away more rapidly—they still give an approximate picture of the response time available to the government.

Second, inherent in the financing techniques used is a strong insurance, if not to say resistance, against any premature credit termination; Austria's foreign debt is largely long term, not short term (the average length of foreign loans contracted before 1978 is twelve years). A premature liquidation or reduction of this outstanding debt (if contractually feasible at all), would impose substantial interest or discount losses on the creditor, certainly in excess of the remaining loan sums, for the market would strike off not only the interest loss but the future risk (in the interim greatly increased). Both represent losses that the creditor can avoid if he adheres to the agreed-upon time schedule.

In other words, Austria's technique of consolidated long-term indebtedness shifts the risk of premature debt liquidation largely to the creditor; he bears the full (interest-rate and value-change) cost risk, while all the debtor has to do is be responsible for a liquidating commitment using instruments whose prices have in the meantime come down.

The third and crucial factor in the case of a decline concerns Austria's potential behavior as a debtor. If Austria were to decide on a strategy of depreciation (relinquishing the hard-currency policy that makes possible and brings down the cost of its foreign credits) it would gain nothing, even in the absence of denominations in foreign currencies, because as the schilling depreciates, more would have to be liquidated than was originally contracted for in schillings, and everything—namely, Austria's foreign credit—would be lost. But if it were to decide on an interest-adjustment strategy (by making an "erosion promise" in the shrinking foreign-credit market), it would, despite the crisis, hold on to everything—its liquidity and its foreign credit—

and would have to pay only the difference in the interest rate, and that would have been lost anyway in the depreciation difference.

In other words, in view of today's foreign debt and incomparably more "weatherproof" financing structures, Austria could survive an international payment crisis with far less damage to its domestic liquidity and demand than was possible at the end of the twenties and early thirties. It would "only" have to take into account the additional interest on its outstanding and still needed new credits. Interest adjustment would give it a weapon that would help it withstand any liquidity crisis.

Therefore, the deficit tendencies of the balance on current accounts made possible the monetary countersteering through fiscal policy that, together with foreign indebtedness, prevented the balance-of-payments deficits in the private sector from drying up the national money and credit markets—a deflationary liquidity squeeze and cooling-off of business activity with all the negative growth, profit, and employment effects.

The long-range problem of this monetary fiscal policy is thus neither the drying up nor the exhaustion of foreign credit and debt sources (which will be discussed in detail in Chapter 6), but rather the very opposite. The question we have to deal with is: What will become of the active domestic fiscal policy when its underlying assumption, Austria's sustained balance-on-goods-and-services deficit, ceases to be? In that event, Austria could not resort to foreign indebtedness to compensate for the loss of liquidity—not without noticeable inflationary consequences. This question, which perhaps cropped up sooner than anticipated, will also be discussed in Chapter 6.

4

BALANCE OF PAYMENTS
DICTATES INCOME POLICY

Austria is among a handful of Western industrial nations whose social climate has remained benign in the face of world-wide economic crisis. That alone would be reason enough to look more closely into the methods and results of Austria's income policy. Without a doubt, the institutional interlocking relationships of Austria's economic partnership have become far more broad based than those of most other Western industrial nations and function more efficiently than, for example, those of West Germany.[1] We need only compare the sad fate of West Germany's Concerted Action program with the work of Austria's Commission for Economic Partnership, in which the spokesmen for unions, business, and agriculture meet to iron out their differences. There can be no doubt that their nonpartisan, disinterested discussions about the problems of economic, monetary, and fiscal policy have helped neutralize ideological ferment more successfully than anywhere else. Austria's trade unions recognize the real limits of income redistribution via wage policy more clearly than their colleagues in, say, Great Britain; and because Austria's employers are far more aware of the essential advantages of stable full employment than their West German counterparts, they have, out of enlightened self-interest, refrained from acting like a Fifth Column pressing for a monetary policy that would affect employment stability.

If the achievements of these economic partners—their rejection of primitive methods in the pursuit of possibly conflicting goals (the class struggle, it is said, is being fought not in the streets but around a conference table)[2]—should ultimately turn out to be of little value, it still would not detract from the truly typical Austrian income policy. It would merely put it into proper perspective, for even the Commission for Economic Partnership can do nothing more than carry out its official mandate: to arrive at a consensus and peaceful solution to disagreements. This perhaps is no small feat, but it is no substitute for the development and binding agreement on overall policy.

Therefore, in looking for an answer to the question about the "success" of the income policy, we must assess the real as well as psychological pressures being exerted by the spokesmen for the special and legitimate interests of the groups they represent. Seen objectively, there appears to be no reason for this pressure, at least not since the early seventies. Full employment amidst the crisis was not won at the expense of job and work conditions or business stagnation (which even Keynes thought to be inevitable at times),[3] or even the relative deterioration of the real wages of workers compared to the real profits of employers. Whatever the basis of comparison used, before and since the growing world crisis the basic trends of the real income of all social groups have shown almost unparalleled symmetry.

The real gross national product and real aggregate income of workers before and after 1973 have risen at the same rate: 46 percent between 1970 and 1973, and 23 percent since 1973. This means not only that the purchasing power of one hour of work or unit of money has increased and now (1978–1979) is some 50 percent higher than at the beginning of the seventies, but also that in the course of this continuous and real growth no shift in real income distribution has taken place. In contrast to Great Britain, where the real-wage share of workers has declined, and in contrast to the German Federal Republic, where the real-profit share of employers has declined (as compared to previous years and to the income share of employed persons and retired workers), in Austria real wages and real profits over a ten-year period increased at approximately the same rate: 4.5 percent.

All social groups, and of course the nation as a whole, have profited from this policy of continued growth. Austria's per capita income at the beginning of the seventies stood at 22 percent below the Common Market average; by 1976, the middle of the crisis, it had caught up to the Common Market average, and at the end of 1978 it apparently exceeded it by 3 percent. This catching-up process is even more dramatic if the comparison were to be based on the OECD rather than the EEC averages, for then it would show that by 1973 Austria had moved up to the OECD level and subsequently exceeded it by some 12 percent. In the course of ten years Austria joined the top ranks of the prosperous nations of the West, and unlike most other members of that elite group it has done so without any erosion of its income structure.

To what or whom do we owe this stabilization of income distribution, so vital a factor in the preservation of social peace in modern industrial societies? In times of crisis weak spokesmen for industry and labor involved in bargaining, under pressure (or subject to pressure) from their constituencies, invariably allow themselves to be pushed into power plays of inequitable income distribution. Even when the tactical appraisal of the superiority of their positions (albeit temporary) is correct, they tend to misjudge the limits for any redistribution of real incomes that are the sole determinants of any long-range strategy. Thus every downward swing that accompanies a reduction in profits may initially appear to strengthen the bargaining power of unions, because employers may persist in the optimistic belief that they will regain their old market and profit positions and that they therefore can continue to roll over the higher real wages paid to their workers. But once these business and profit illusions begin to fade or, rather, once the crisis enters into its "secondary" phase, employers, faced with what they now see as an inflated real-wage position, are forced into a defensive call for greater efficiency, thereby transforming production wage costs into economic social costs. The trade unions, taken by surprise by this new "toughness" of the employers, see this stiffening of the fronts not as the result of an objectively more accurate evaluation of planning data bearing on (deteriorating) investments but rather as a power struggle. And so income policy leaves the bargaining table and takes to the streets. Once under way, this process changes the capital and labor intensity of the economy, and the longer the fight lasts the more profound is the change. What most observers fail to see and take into account is that the bigger and the more capital-intensive the industries, the more the elimination of jobs pays off—not only in saved "labor costs," which society now shoulders as social costs in the form of unemployment payments, but increasingly in the "saved" (outside) financing costs as well. How?

Every big business that budgets its cash flows looks on the wage bill not only from the perspective of cost but also of liquidity, for the wage bill represents a loss of liquidity; capital use and write-offs are permanent assets, and thus represent liquidity returning with the cash flow. In times of crisis employers learn that although they must pay out wages, write-offs can be stretched.

The substitution of write-offs for wages resulting from labor disputes during the crisis does not necessarily mean the reduction of an employer's per item costs. It serves its purpose if it improves his price and cost elasticity (through time extensions of the write-offs) and the balance position of the business (by strengthening the internal or self-financing possibilities). The only thing the union achieves by its effort to strengthen the real-wage position of its workers is to have the employer change fixed production costs (wages) into fixed social costs (unemployment compensation), with the additional bonus of higher variable production costs (write-offs) and cheaper refinancing sources (increased cash flow).[4]

Unfortunately, this employer strategy of enhancing plant price cost and financing elasticity (which over the long run yields much more than the one-time wage saving of the first efficiency measure) cannot be countered by an adjustment of work hours. Even supporters of a full-employment job-sharing policy (through the reduction of the work day, week, or year) base their model on a constant demand for labor, something that does not exist in normal times, let alone in times of crisis. Employers will—and must—minimize costs via substitution of input factors and relate this to their planning. Consequently they will always substitute capital for labor, whose aggregate cost remains fixed even when unit or (wage) rate costs are flexible, because they can manipulate aggregate capital costs and they can decide the time period of regeneration (or write-off). The only, and only interesting, question is whether and how this process mapped out by competition and technological progress can be "steered" so if it is too rapid—e.g., substitution-caused unemployment—or too slow (thus impairing the competitive ability of the entire economy), it will not cause structural unemployment.

The second illusion holds that the shortening of the work day costs nothing. Even without wage adjustments for the time not worked, the new free time costs that portion of the social or national product that is no longer produced, and irrevocably so, because there can be no return to the former time norm. Because the price paid for this shorter work week is a loss of potential real income and wealth formation growth (investment as well as savings), the shorter work week, instead of being an equalizer of existing underemployment, becomes the source of yet greater future underemployment.

An economic policy of full employment therefore does not offer much latitude for reducing the work day, and this scope becomes even more restricted in times of existing or threatened unemployment. The only choice open to a society dedicated to full employment is that of consuming its growing productivity (the real increase in per capita production) in the form of either higher real income or more leisure time, a margin that even in good years in most Western industrial countries amounts to 3–5 percent per capita annually—not too much elbow room for speculative programs, let alone new ventures.

In times of actual or threatened unemployment there is no latitude to speak of for the expansion of leisure time. Those involuntarily unemployed already consume the biggest part of the economic leisure-time potential and receive real income created by others. Adding voluntary unemployment (that is what a mandated reduction of the work week means) must, because it reduces the rise in real-income of all who are gainfully employed, sooner or later turn economic growth into economic shrinkage, with the logical and fatal consequence that the up-to-now gainfully employed would now have all the leisure time imaginable, but no one working and paying for it.

This law incidentally holds true equally for market and planned economies, with one striking difference to which the opponents of market economy seem to have given little thought.

In a market economy the ultimate stage—total unemployment—would always be postponed through the permanent entrepreneurial substitution of capital for labor. Although this destroys jobs, it does not destroy the real income increments needed to feed and support the unemployed (the product of rationalization). In planned economies, on the other hand, everything is simpler and quicker: when sufficient real income is not being created, all go hungry. So Malthus turns out to have been right after all.

The role of the economic and social partners in modern Western industrial societies in the determination of income policy boils down to this: They can either interfere with or support the goals of official economic policy (substantially), but they can never become a substitute for policy. If Austria in the seventies succeeded in attaining the productivity and prosperity level of its European neighbors, and in part even exceeded it without endangering domestic full employment and domestic and external monetary stability, credit is due to its economic policy. That policy is responsible for creating a social climate in which workers and employers talk to each other rationally without pressure from their respective constituencies. This in no way detracts from the achievements of Austria's economic partners, who succeeded in removing the roadblocks that obstruct government activity in most other countries. However, two exceptions must be noted: (1) this applies to the past, and (2) it only concerns the support of the government's economic policy in its domestic goals—full employment and price stability. But what about the effects of the income policy on Austria's foreign trade balance?

In the past this problem was somewhat peripheral since available foreign credits were able to balance the current accounts deficit. Austria earned its imports and currency reserves not only through its own production (exports), but also through foreign advances and prefinancing. Not that the sources of foreign exchange and credit were indifferent to, or unaware of, the behavior of their trading partner; it obviously entered into their appraisal of Austria's credit worthiness. Only so long as Austria is able to balance a substantial part of its external balance of payments out of credits rather than exports is it less dependent on making the most of its international competitive capability than it would be if it had to or wished to repay these foreign loans. If Austria is to change from a net-capital import to a net-capital export country (and if this process is to be as free of friction as the safeguarding of its internal stability), its income policy must tilt more toward the balance of payments.

What is at issue? In a world union of integrated national economies every (relative) national wage inflation (measured against the real-wage level of the other trading partners) affects that country's foreign competitive position, regardless of whether the rates of exchange remain stable or not. In the case of stable exchange rates such a wage increase leads to greater position adjustments via direct foreign investments, i.e., the use of overvalued foreign securities (as happened in the United States up to the beginning of floating in 1971). In the case of flexible exchange rates the same effect is achieved by floating, which spreads inflation and instability. Great Britain "balanced" its national wage rise by depreciating its currency, and West Germany continues to enforce its national wage policy by appreciation. However, despite the assumptions of the fiscal and monetarist textbooks, British depreciation did not make the British market more attractive to foreign investors. On the contrary, the risk certainty of bigger depreciation losses against the prospect of current investments in the sterling area led to the permanent capital flight of domestic investors and a similar reluctance of foreign investors, with the result that job opportunities had to be exported to other countries.

As far as the job market is concerned, West Germany's DM appreciation also did not work. The prospect of quick appreciation profits attracted only short-term, profit-oriented money and capital speculation to the DM area, not the kind of real and capital asset investments that translate into jobs. On the contrary, the higher costs of making position in that area sent domestic and foreign investors in search of better opportunities outside Germany.

The short-term, expectation-contingent German capital balance with foreign countries became an asset because the German commercial banks that acquired these foreign instruments financed the DM appreciation, but the long-term capital balance with foreign countries (contingent on portfolios and direct investments) became a liability. As a result, job opportunities had to be ceded to other countries—a process that could become even more destabilizing once the upward movement of the DM (which in this respect is still thought to be undervalued) comes to a stop.

If setting a ceiling to national nominal wages calls for restraint on the part of employers as regards the introduction of labor-saving processes, the international ceiling is linked to preventing the excessive export of jobs, a danger which even flexible exchange rates cannot eliminate. Therefore the voluntarily agreed-upon income policy of the social partners to preserve and upgrade the competitive position in foreign trade and investment positions is a crucial factor. It would appear to be obvious that the role of income policy in foreign trade is of far greater significance in small economies that are dependent on world markets than in large areas in which outside competitive and investment factors play only a marginal part.

Kausel recently discussed the relative abatement of the "wage inflation" component in Austria's upward movement of the seventies, particularly compared to the major hard-currency trading partners and competitors (West Germany, Switzerland, and the Benelux countries).[5] Although his figures are certainly correct for the past (and, moreover, prove our thesis that the flexibility of the parties to a wage agreement does not derive from their autonomy or market power but from the realistic ability to increase total production), they must be interpreted cautiously and accurately for future use. Austria's fairly substantial labor costs are still below those of other hard-currency countries, as are its wage levels. But this is a lead that is neither natural nor likely to last forever—and, moreover, one that, except for West Germany, has narrowed significantly since 1975. Given Austria's fixed exchange rates, the rise in the relative and effective foreign labor costs and foreign prices—a crucial factor in Austria's growth and stability—determines its present and prospective international competitive position or, to put it differently, determines the extent to which it can exploit (in terms of foreign exchange) the export potential that has been created.

What does this mean? Fixed exchange rates limit the flexibility and range in the redistribution of nominal wages. To the extent they do exist, they are confined to balance-of-payments objectives. The real balance on current account surpluses needed for the liquidation or reduction of foreign debts determines the scope of domestic (nominal and real) wage increase and redistribution. Consequently the wage policy agreed upon by unions and employers must be oriented toward the balance of payments. Unions always find this easier to do if it involves a cutback of export surpluses; employers find this easier to do if it means the piling-up of export surpluses. For example, in West Germany, which has an export surplus, the unions would have economic logic on their side if they were to base their wage demands (in excess of productivity) on balance-of-payments considerations (as their contribution to the reestablishment of external equilibrium and the requisite export substitution). Austrian employers can argue that any wage policy that impairs the nation's international competitive standing and export capability threatens both internal (real) growth as well as the external (financial) credit position. If in the possibly near future of greater export dependency the hard-currency policy should fail to stabilize Austria's competitive capability, the need for a wage policy, or more broadly, an income policy attuned to the new foreign-trade situation (if not to say requirements) would be more compelling than ever.

Austria's industrial build-up, productivity, and favorable foreign price structure—the basis of its competitive edge and export capability—can be maintained only in the absence of the sort of high-wage policy that has grown up among the other international trading nations. With accelerated foreign debt liquidation, real productivity growth coupled with the utilization of the external rate of inflation—above all rising prices in the hard-currency countries—set the ceiling on any future nominal wage hike. If Austria's wage increases were to be based solely on domestic real productivity increases, given the fixed schilling rate, the export sector would be substantially undervalued: involuntary (and real give-away) export surpluses à la West Germany would put the economy under steady (imported) inflationary pressure, while flexible interventions on the other hand would subject the schilling to dangerous pressure to appreciate. The goal therefore must be externally stable real-wage and real-labor costs that take into account the rising prices of their most important foreign competitors.

An open economy dedicated to the liquidation rather than the continuation of indebtedness guided by such an income and wage policy can assure this in three ways:

1. *Foreign trade.* The desired export (surplus) position can be reached and sustained without fear of disequilibrating adjustment problems (imported inflation) or retaliation of irate partners, for no terms-of-trade advantages in favor of the expansion and profitability of the domestic export sector are being "given away."

2. *Social and distribution policy.* This strategy prevents undervaluated (inflation) profits—that accrue only to business and investors—from being created from the difference between the foreign export prices stabilized by the fixed rate of exchange and the external rate of inflation. The just allocation of the unavoidable (external) rate of inflation that is beyond the control of domestic economic policy protects both sides of the bargaining unit—workers against a creeping redistribution and adulteration of their real-wage position through imported inflation, and employers against erroneous decisions based on the (nominal) overestimation on their investment returns and the (real) underestimation of labor costs in the export sector.

3. *Structural policy.* If foreign and domestic returns are correctly calculated in real as well as nominal terms, future structural disproportions that are not readily correctable, or correctable only at great expense, can be avoided. These disproportions can be seen as overinvestment and overproduction in an export sector overrationalized first because of the overestimation of its profit potential and later because readjustment of its high capital intensities and (fixed) costs are no longer possible, turning it from a growth leader into a protection- and support-seeking sector (or one trying to turn the state into a "repair shop of capitalism").

5

A CATALOGUE
OF MISSED OPPORTUNITIES

Success, too, has its price. Behind the impressive high, stable, largely self-financed Austrian investment rate stands a very modest savings rate for private households. The gross investment quota of 29 percent of the gross national product in 1973–1977 is matched by a private sector savings quota of only 12 percent of the gross national income. Austria's next-door neighbor, West Germany, invested only 22 percent of its gross national product during that same period, while saving 12 percent of its national income. Thus almost half of West Germany's macroeconomic investments were covered by savings, as compared to one-third of Austria's (see Table 13). In view of Austria's leadership among OECD nations in real per capita income of private households (see Figure 4), this lag in savings cannot be ascribed to either a lack of savings potential (due to low average income) or a lack of savings capability (due to inequitable income distribution). What then is the explanation for this "underdeveloped" level of savings?

In the underinvestment countries of the Third World savings exceed investments, and that portion of savings not visible at home could probably be found in accounts outside the country were it not for bank secrets and similar protective screens. In an overinvestment country like Austria private savings are also missing, but even in the absence of protective screens they cannot be found either abroad or at home. This savings deficit is the more surprising in view of Austria's real interest rates, among the highest of all Western industrial countries (see Table 14). The answer becomes clearer if we refer to Chapter 1.

Table 13. Investment and Savings Quotas

Year	National Product (Social Product)	Gross Investments		National Income (NI)		Savings[a]
	AUSTRIA					
	(in billions of schillings)	*(GNP = 100)*		*(in billions of schillings)*		*(NI = 100)*
1973	535.7	159.8	29.8	392.0	46.3	11.8
1974	613.1	186.9	30.5	450.2	50.4	11.2
1975	656.3	171.0	26.1	480.4	69.8	14.5
1976	727.6	206.3	28.4	534.5	86.1	16.1
1977	792.5	231.8	29.2	583.1	53.3	9.1
1973–1977	3,325.2	955.8	28.7	2,440.2	305.9	12.5
	GERMAN FEDERAL REPUBLIC					
	(in billions of DM)	*(GSP = 100)*		*(in billions of DM)*		*(NI = 100)*
1973	920.1	232.6	25.3	720.9	82.0	11.4
1974	986.9	221.9	22.5	772.3	94.9	12.3
1975	1,033.9	212.2	20.5	805.6	113.5	14.1
1976	1,121.7	241.6	21.5	874.8	107.7	12.3
1977	1,193.7	258.2	21.6	929.3	105.5	11.4
1973–1977	5,256.3	1,166.5	22.2	4,102.9	503.6	12.3

Sources: Statistisches Handbuch für die Republik Österreich 1978 (Vienna, 1978); Austrian National Bank, Vienna, Annual Reports; German Federal Bank, Frankfurt am Main, Monthly Reports.

[a]For Austria, development of the most important forms of savings; for GFR, private households.

The fiscal incentives for domestic investments in 1978 in privately owned enterprises increased profits by 6 percent on the average.[1] Even if this figure should turn out to be accurate only as an indication of a trend, it still shows that every investor with a business of his own is able to create effective additional returns if he does not put the money he earns into outside businesses or the capital market or banks (savings).

Figure 4. A Comparison of the Per Capita GNPs of Austria, the EEC, and the OECD-Europe (in U.S. dollars)

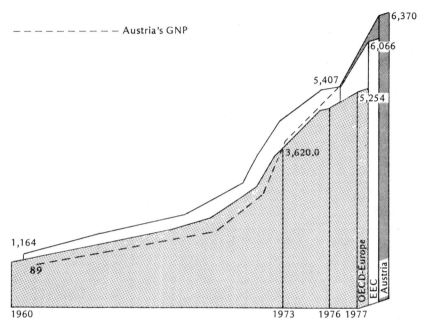

At the beginning of the seventies, Austria's per capita GNP was still 22 percent below the EEC average and 8 percent below that of the European OECD countries. In 1973 Austria overtook the OECD countries, and in 1976, the EEC. In 1977 Austria's per capita GNP was 12 percent above that of the European OECD average and 5 percent above that of the EEC countries. *Source:* Austrian Institute for Economic Research.

Stating the problem in these terms it immediately becomes clear where these "missing" savings have gone: into self-financed overinvestment. And looking at this more closely we find that this overinvestment encompasses a double component of reversed forced savings, for businesses finance their "self"-investments only pro forma. They get the major portion of their savings through the prices they charge for their products, and so they obviously are responsible for a forced savings by the customers paying these prices. The second, and smaller, portion of

Table 14. Price Increases and Interest Rates in Summer 1978

Country	Rate of Inflation (annual cost-of-living rate)	Long-term Interest (in percent)	Real Interest[a]
Denmark	10.6	16.5	5.9
Belgium	3.9	8.75	4.8
Austria	3.0	7.75	4.75
Great Britain	7.8	12.5	4.7
German Federal Republic	2.5	7.0	4.5
Netherlands	3.4	7.5	4.1
Japan	3.6	6.3	2.7
Switzerland	1.1	3.4	2.3
Canada	9.2	9.4	0
Italy	12.3	11.4	-0.9
United States	10.5	8.5	-2.0
France	12.5	10.5	-2.0

Source: K. Richebächer, Währungen und Kreditmärkte (Frankfurt/Main, August 28, 1978).

[a] Long-term interest, allowing for rate of inflation.

their savings is paid for by the treasury, which also has the financial backing of the taxpayer. Business self-financing consequently is possible only because other sectors, the private and public households, do not save. And that brings up the question of why not.

The strong support of self-financing in Austria clearly has a pernicious effect on the savings accounts of the private and public households. The sums that business is able to reinvest out of its own account cannot appear on the accounts of the other sectors. And conversely, if both the private and public sectors were to keep their savings for themselves—the private sector by buying less and the public sector by refusing to pay investment incentives—the investors would either have to do without the now missing "self-financeable" investments or look to other sources, such as the now visible savings of the private and public sectors.

In contrast to the typical development country, Austria's savings—self-financed overinvestment—remain in the country, and therefore Austria is spared all growth-restrictive withdrawal effects. On the contrary, the fiscally supported forced transformation of potential savings into certain investment is a sort of growth insurance, for if possible savings of the private and public households were to turn into genuine savings, the investors would have to choose between investing less than before or accepting outside financing and credit offers.

The policy of fiscal investment incentives is spurred by the desire not to let growth and full employment go down the drain because of investor reluctance to go into debt and thus from this angle as well avoid any possible destabilization. But the price of this sort of growth insurance apparently not only puts asset formation ahead of money wealth, but also puts the money wealth of the entrepreneurs ahead of the money wealth of the nonentrepreneurs. This obviously is a serious social problem. Conceptually and effectively, socially balanced real-income development is completely at odds with socially imbalanced real-wealth development. Austria's modernized capital stock has not only increased dramatically, but thanks to government support and a 40 percent "social" quota in its financing, it developed largely into private special business capital that is missing from the base (and real cover) of the savings of private households. Opponents of private enterprise find little consolation in the fact that one-third of this reprivatization of real wealth takes place directly, or indirectly via bank participation, in the area of nationalized industry, and hence remains under public control. The crucial point, however, is not that the one (business) gets too much, and the other (non-business) gets too little, but rather whether or not the productivity results of this socially skewed investment support offset and justify the obvious social costs.

*   *   *

In addition to the inadequacy of private household savings, the underinvestment countries of the Third World and the comparatively wealthy overinvestment country of Austria have yet another thing in common—a relatively weak capital market. The developing countries use that weak market in support of the argument that besides foreign-exchange help for their structural balance on current accounts deficit, they also need capital aid to "cover" their domestic investment-financing deficit. In Austria the weak capital market is cited in support of the argument that investors must not be scared off by high interest and outside financing rates, and that therefore, for the time being, fiscal investment incentives are essential, for they combine additional returns (i.e., interest) with higher profits for the investor, and hence constitute capital and interest subsidies. In that respect the fiscal investment bonuses play the role of fiscally directed capital aid at preferential rates.

Yet despite all the protection, the strange part of this story is that neither a quarter century of outside capital assistance to the developing countries nor domestic capital assistance to outside (investment) sectors of industrialized Austria substantially expanded the domestic capital markets. Why?

Every ad hoc intervention in the capital-yield and capital-interest sectors blocks not only the capital-forming and -raising mechanism, but also the capital-using or -distributing mechanism. In the developing countries the inflow of massive capital imports at (low) foreign, not (high) domestic, conditions means that domestic investors and savers no longer consider domestic investments worthwhile. In view of the depressed domestic real interest rates, the result of competition with subsidized foreign capital (i.e., development aid) rates that do not meet the realistic or unrealistic subjective expectations (i.e., risk threshold) of investors, they prefer to invest abroad—insofar as they have or can gain access to the foreign-exchange accounts built up by assistance to their countries. In that event capital assistance involuntarily helps to finance capital flight. Or if that avenue is closed to them they invest their money in lucrative "bazaar" enterprises whose real profit yield is higher than real interest yield. The question we must reluctantly ask ourselves is whether, given these negative feedbacks on investment and savings, the type of aid given by the West to the developing countries has not served the export interests of the helpers more than it has the development interests of those being helped.

And what about Austria? The only choice open to the enterprise-owning investor is to reinvest his real earned profits at a plus-6 percent fiscal bonus in his own business, or minus the

6 percent fiscal bonus somewhere else, e.g., the capital market. With a single stroke the selectively distributed additional return and capital subsidy for capital use or investment have made the (sectoral) real interest level of all other types of investment and savings unacceptably low. Investors who own businesses must necessarily see the returns offered elsewhere as below their realistic or unrealistic subjective expectations, and so they give the capital market a wide berth. But private households without their own businesses, seeing the second-class interest rates being offered them, will weigh their choice between savings and the possibly higher real return of household investments, i.e., putting their money into labor-saving and durable consumer goods like cars, refrigerators, washing machines, dishwashers, audio equipment, etc. The booming imports that burden the Austrian balance on current accounts are in part due to the mishandling of the capital-yield and interest sectors—a telling example of how interventions in one area can have undesirable consequences in other areas where they are least expected.[2]

Austria's surplus of real investment-capital formation over the simultaneous nominal savings or money-capital formation might be considered an artificial contraction, or more properly "amputation," of its money economy. This is a counterpart to what is taking place internationally on the Eurodollar markets, where, as shall be seen in Chapter 9, the amounts of available money and credit are divided between a "too big" finance or speculation cash drawer and a "too small" transaction- or income-financing cash drawer. In Austria the opposite is happening: the amount of available money and credit is being used up at too high a percentage rate for real income or profit (i.e., wealth accrual) financing of the business sector, and consequently too little is left for the financing of savings. Austria's money and capital markets can thus accomplish very little because most of the capital formation takes place "real" in business, but "inflationary" in the prices paid by the consumer to business. Therefore, because Austria's money and capital markets are not needed they are not forced to perform—very much like those of the developing countries.

The fiscal investment supports block the liquidity flow to the Austrian capital market from two directions and so cut it off from the most important and abundant refinancing sources available to industrial countries: the entrepreneurial cash flow. Despite real high interest rates the supports also paralyze the domestic savings capability of the private households, a sector that is concerned not only with the level of returns it receives but also with the level of returns it does not receive: those of the fiscally supported business households. So they too invest less in the capital market than they otherwise might, with the inevitable result that the offering volume of the Austrian capital market remains smaller than it could be. It has to make do without potentially available loanable funds. Because there is more involuntary than voluntary saving, domestic costs and prices are higher than they would have to be. The "false" investment support, because of its inflationary consequences and also its deficit effects on the balance on current accounts, compels a still "harder" hard-currency policy than would otherwise be necessary. But that, alas, is not all. The additional fiscal advantages enjoyed by one form of investments and savings but not by others diminish not only the pool of real possible investments and savings, and with it a potentially still bigger economic growth rate, but also dissipate possible real productivity and structural effects.

*   *   *

Interest-rate sclerosis and circulatory disorders of the money and capital markets not only deprive both investors and savers of investment opportunities but also make for different yardsticks of evaluation for investment alternatives that are or should be of equal value. They block the "law of the equilibrium of profit rates" basic to capital use and distribution in united monetary economies (currency areas). The refraction of the interest and yield structures between business and nonbusiness households gives rise to socially explosive property concentrations not only in and of the expanding economic capital stock, but also in its sectoral structure and magnitudes.

In the case of profit- rather than project-contingent investment incentives, the biggest premiums are collected by those who reaped and wrote off the highest profits, in absolute terms, in the preceding fiscal year. In times of lagging investment and capital intensity, this can accelerate the catching-up and making-up process in undercapitalized sectors and branches whose domestic and foreign markets permit high write-offs and reinvestment rates. Kausel showed this convincingly in his study of the chemical, machine-tool, electrical, and automotive industries. But what happens once these lags are eliminated? In that event the fiscal interest and capital subsidies permit the carrying forward of the old write-offs and reinvestment rates and plans, even if these sectors have in the meantime become "oversubscribed." How? Because compared to other forms of investments a 6 percent tax-financed additional return is still more profitable than most. The tax savings feed and finance an illusion about a profit and competitive capability that threatens to become fatal once there is nothing left to catch up with, if not sooner. Kausel's optimistic assertions and conclusions are therefore relevant and reassuring only in terms of the past.

For the future, given the fiscally financed illusory returns and profits, overcapacities and ill-advised investments in the former growth and industry leaders are much more likely, as is the possibility that the profits of these successful sectors are due to highly developed skills in the art of the write-off.

A completely "exogenous" factor, unanticipated by investors and policy makers alike, and certainly not calculable, takes on crucial dimensions: If the technical-economic innovative process within and outside Austria accelerates, the capital and interest subsidy that is geared to the profits and write-offs of the past constitutes an unplanned negative premium on future projects that, even though they are promising, are not yet ripe for investment. Since the subjects of this kind of support are not only future expected profits of such projects, but also the profits and investments realized in the past, the profits and investments of the future are automatically encumbered by those of the past by not being credited to tax savings.

From whatever angle and whatever aspect one looks at the business- and investment-linked tax support, it has the fatal effect of an internal tariff on the domestic economic capital transaction that promotes capital endogamy, both intersectorally and intertemporally. It clusters capital use in the successful sectors of the past whose future may be uncertain, and at the same time it restricts the time and investment scope of investors by reducing the risk of old investments and offering no premiums for new investment risks (that must yet prove their worthiness).

It is hard to decide which of these disturbances are the most onerous: entrepreneurial ownership overconcentration in the capital stock, the shrinking overinvested undersaved capital market, or the blocking of the profit-rate equilibrium with its dangerous illusions about profit, competition, and the future. One thing stands out clearly: The promotion of socially explosive and productivity-dissipating business-oriented fiscal investments changes from a reward for growth to one for holding fast or even for regressing once the gap in capital formation and capital intensity is closed—a stage that Austria seemed to have reached in 1978–1979. Once the gap is closed and an accelerated innovative process has turned into a slowed up (exogenous) one, what is to be done?

To begin with, Austria should be turned into a tariff-free zone of domestic capital transactions, intersectorally as well as intertemporally, either by extending existing fiscal incentives equally to all forms of investment and savings, wherein the additional costs of this extended support could be absorbed by a drastic reduction of the strike-off rates, or by doing away with all tax support of investments and savings, for reasons of social justice. Once all intersectoral and intertemporal refractions have been eliminated—the internal tariffs on capital transactions either equalized or abolished—the bill for tax-supported investment and savings capital formation (even the most neutral) is being footed by noninvestors and nonsavers. And these are more likely to be the poor than the rich. The unequivocal removal of tax and fiscal policy from the promotion of investment and savings thus becomes not only a technical dictate of economic policy, but an overriding postulate of social justice that no democratic government can afford to ignore.

There remains only the question about the right type of (farsighted) support of innovation. Its parameter of action is a selectively focused promotional policy. The Austrian public household presents a rather checkered picture of partly publicly financed, partly guaranteed paratreasuries (see Tables 15, 16,

Table 15. The Development of Guarantees by the Federal Government (in millions of schillings)

Year	Total Liabilities[a]	Export Support[b]	Specific Liabilities				Construction Sector		
			Electric Power Industry	Investments in Agriculture	Nationalized Enterprises (excluding electric power)	Highways	Housing	Water Conservation Fund	Others[c]
1970	43,296	19,210	13,792	1,229	2,169	3,490	2,072	725	609
1971	49,506	23,415	14,020	1,281	2,191	4,195	1,772	1,069	1,563
1972	55,051	25,316	14,594	1,321	3,600	5,426	1,481	1,512	1,801
1973	62,738	30,141	15,960	1,331	3,520	6,847	1,225	1,798	1,916
1974	74,348	38,570	15,321	1,278	4,071	9,316	989	1,767	3,036
1975	104,084	58,297	20,818	1,357	4,623	12,508	778	1,626	4,077
1976	140,610	89,162	22,626	1,398	4,979	15,089	579	2,261	4,516
1977	176,734[d]	118,278	25,378	1,465	5,705	17,518	380	3,100	4,910

Source: Working paper, Federal Finance Law, Section C, Para. VIIIb.

[a] For capital amounts at the end of the year. As a rule the federal obligation is also assumed for interest and costs. Therefore the actual guarantee incurred is and was higher than is shown in the table by the amount of these hard-to-estimate additional costs.

[b] In accordance with the Export Support Law and Export-Financing Support Law.

[c] For example, guarantees for other enterprises in which the government plays a part, for savings and credit premiums, and for duty-free zones.

[d] The government is legally responsible for the obligations of the Austrian postal savings bank, which on December 31, 1977, amounted to 40,311.14 million schillings.

and 17). If economists have a problem finding their way through this array of numbers with its overlapping supports (central government, private wealth, state banks, and subsidizing offices), types of financing (incentives, interest subsidies, credits, liability assumption), and application (investments, infrastructures, research, social costs), and translating it into a functional equilibrium of fundraising and spending, how are those who are looking for assistance going to do so? What Austria's selective structural policy lacks more than anything else is clarity. As long as all these activities and programs are devoid of a comprehensive development and structural budget spanning at least one legislative period, the danger persists that only insiders will know and be able to make use of the programs that exist. Moreover, the even greater danger exists that the government itself will be unable to plan and coordinate its structural policy efficiently because its many heads and hands have lost sight of what happens where and to what effect. The incorporation of all selective (project- and preference-related) structural activities in one focused development budget is not simply a matter of yet another set of statistics. A capital budget (a vital necessity for poor developing countries, even if it does not make them any richer) is indispensable for Austria as a yardstick of its success and as a control device—not to mention its contribution to letting the public and legislature know what is going on. It is essential for Austria to begin to draw up economic, monetary, and fiscal estimates of the future chances of domestic development and structural programs, and to do so promptly; for only then will it be able to tell for how long it must continue with its policy mix of increasing foreign indebtedness, how soon it can begin to liquidate these debts, and how this decision will affect the balance of payments and the budget.

If Austria hopes to avoid the "German" problem of a deadlocked policy of fiscal stability following the normalization of its foreign position, a policy whose restrictive effects are needed to counteract the inflation-importing export surpluses—which in effect means the renunciation of a domestically oriented fiscal policy (promoting export substitution and domestic restructuring)—it must secure its future balance on current

Table 16. Measures in Support of Trade, Industry, and Tourism[a] (in millions of schillings)

Year	Trade and Industry			Tourism					Grand Total
	Subsidies Authorized by Trade Regulation of 1969	Other Subsidies	Total	Subsidies Authorized by Trade Regulation of 1969	Subsidies to League for Austrian Tourism	Subsidies Authorized by Finance Regulation	Other Subsidies	Total	
1970	66	77	143	6	52	—	34	92	235
1971	69	85	154	7	50	—	49	106	260
1972	71	80	151	11	60	—	107	178	329
1973	116	81	197	31	72	30	107	240	437
1974	120	128	248	50	90	30	108	278	526
1975	130	109	239	58	105	30	139	332	571
1976	149	60	209	68	120	35	160	383	592
1977	152	147	299	75	132	35	205	447	746
1978[b,c]	205	519	724	96	145	35	271	547	1,271
1979[b,d]	232	882	1,114	114	148	34	189	485	1,599

[a] Excluding mining.
[b] Estimate (federal budget).
[c] Including an additional 530 million schilling subsidy authorized by law in 1978 for promotional activities.
[d] Including an additional 610 million schilling subsidy.

Table 17. Public Guarantees: Claims and Refluxes[a] (in millions of schillings)

Year	Export Support[b]		Nationalized Enterprises		Others	
	Claim	Reflux	Claim	Reflux	Claim	Reflux
1970	34.9	6.5	22.1	—	3.4	1.2
1971	56.6	10.7	34.6	—	1.1	1.4
1972	94.1	25.2	35.8	—	0.5	2.2
1973	202.1	52.9	—	—	2.9	1.9
1974	339.3	44.1	—	—	0.4	2.5
1975	288.1	46.3	—	—	7.0	2.1
1976	728.9	35.4	—	—	12.1	2.6
1977	595.8	65.9	3.9	—	7.0	0.1

[a]The guarantees for the electrical power industry, agricultural investments, and the construction sector by the federal government did not result in any liability claims.
[b]In accordance with the Export Support Law and Export-Financing Support Law.

accounts surpluses over capital exports from its own and possibly also from outside sources. But to do so it needs above all a vital, not sclerotic, capital market—a theme discussed in greater detail in the next chapter.

6

THE LIMITS OF
GOVERNMENT INDEBTEDNESS

Does Austria live above its means? Does the present generation impose an almost unmanageable debt burden on its chil-
dren? How can a budget change its deficit into a surplus if
86 percent of its expenditures are fixed by legal obligations and
long-established political practices, making a reduction of
spending, let alone debt liquidation, in our time seem like a pipe
dream (see Table 18)? And what will happen on the day the
borrowing stops, when foreign and domestic creditors ask for
their money? When that happens, will this sort of debt-based
prosperity in the midst of energy crisis have to collapse? Moreover, despite all the built-in guarantees (see the section on debt
consolidation in Chapter 3), the day of reckoning can be moved
up. The history of money is filled with accounts of panicky
creditors, thought of as safe bets by their debtors, who overnight cut off the credit lifeline. Comparing the situation of
today's free dollar money and capital markets not covered by
any final liquidity guarantee with Charles Kindleberger's account
of the collapse of the world capital markets after 1929,[1] at
least half a dozen examples exist that could touch off such an
explosion: unexpected balance-of-payments deficits and the
sort of egotistical export offensives launched by the Soviet
Union; agricultural surpluses that led the United States (like
the Common Market today) to strengthen its protectionism;
expectations of currency depreciation that led France to its
gold "blackmail" of Great Britain; the decline of the raw material markets that knocked out the countries of that era's
Third World (in Latin America and Southeast Asia) as balancing

79

Table 18. Fixed Government Expenditures (in millions of schillings)

Year	Legal Obligations (excluding personnel)	Personnel and Administration	Highways and Administrative Expenditures of Government Enterprises[a,b]	Total	Percent of Total Expenditures
1970	37,071	38,780	11,741	87,592	86.2
1971	42,006	43,255	13,578	98,839	87.8
1972	47,565	48,274	15,448	111,287	87.0
1973	59,139[c]	46,392[c]	16,396	121,927	86.4
1974	70,511[c]	49,001[c,d]	18,368	137,880	82.5
1975	84,489[c]	56,196[c,d]	21,874	162,559	82.6
1976	99,948[c]	62,482[c,d]	24,402	186,832	84.2
1977[e]	109,392[c]	66,938[c,d]	24,893	201,223	85.0
1978[f,g]	128,319[c]	75,113[c,d]	28,946	232,378	86.8
1979[g]	139,011[c]	79,214[c,d]	31,413	249,638	86.6

Source: Working paper, Federal Finance Law, Section C, Para. I.

[a]Not included in first two columns. Highway construction expenditures in accordance with earmarked funds.

[b]Up to 1977 this includes only administrative costs of the regular business of government enterprises.

[c]The teacher payroll of the states is a federal responsibility. Since 1973 this item no longer appears under the federal personnel but is budgeted by the states. The federal government reimburses the states out of its administrative government enterprises account.

[d]As of 1974 administrative expenditures do not appear separately but as part of general expenditures.

[e]Result.

[f]Estimate.

[g]Inclusive of reserve fund mandated by employment insurance regulations.

markets; or a super-OPEC of all strategically vital raw material suppliers, etc. It almost does not matter where the match is lit— on the corn exchange in Winnipeg, the stock market in New York, the gold market in London, the international raw material trading posts—nor does it matter when—whether half a year sooner or later. If the creditors become nervous, and in such a situation this may be only a matter of time, a credit-contracting chain reaction has as much chance of being stopped as a chain reaction in a nuclear installation.

The legitimate concern about Austria's overindebtedness leads us to the consideration of where the debt limits lie. Those who deny that debt limits exist or try to minimize the problem by arguing that they cannot be calculated with any degree of accuracy make the age-old error of believing them to be more remote than in fact they are. Precisely because these limits, like most burdens of this type (whether taxes, foreign, or interventionist burdens), cannot be estimated with any degree of precision, nor over time do they even approximate a constant, they are psychologically far more tightly drawn than they appear to be. Their subjective lack of precision reduces the limits of financial capacity far below their objectively calculable level. That is why politicians operating with public debt must navigate like seamen in a fog who change course long before approaching the shoals shown on their maps. Once word gets about that the country may have relied too heavily on debt, circumspection is indicated, for yesterday's financing markets may no longer be here today, particularly if their own structure is unstable. The time horizon of the economic and fiscal policy controlling the foreign and domestic debt is thus substantially more limited than the existing financing and debt potential would normally allow. If we want to know how long or how short this time horizon really is, we must look at the controlling factors.

In trying to determine the degree of responsibility or irresponsibility of public (i.e., overall economic) indebtedness processes, analogies of proper individual economic behavior—e.g., the archetypical good family man who predates the invention of consumer and personal credit—are of no help. The only analogy that does apply, within limits, is that of the eternal (i.e., nonbankrupt) big business whose external financing (or credit debt) determines the final balance or postings of its cash flows—the difference between the investment and renewal programs essential to survival and the earned financing means (profits plus write-offs reflected in prices). The credit line used marks the amount of financing that is still needed to keep the enterprise running as planned. How do creditors or banks measure the credit framework of such an enterprise with available internal and external financing sources? Ultimately they do so on the basis of the (also subjective) picture that they paint of its future profit potential and repayment ability—its foreign balance on current accounts and payment surpluses after covering all domestic payments essential to production such as wages and write-offs.

If we subject to closer scrutiny the time horizons of the domestic and external financing and credit worthiness of national economies and the public households that represent them, we must, in analogy to the big individual enterprises, ask: What are the chances and time frames of changing existing foreign balance on current accounts deficits and domestic budget deficits into surpluses?

The question itself, even before it is answered, flies in the face of the beliefs held by the majority of conservative critics of the budget. Whether Austria stays within its foreign and domestic credit framework or steps beyond it cannot be determined on the basis of its individual positions, either from its balance on current accounts or its domestic budget, not even in only a single year. Therefore nothing can be concluded if in one year (1977) the balance on current accounts deficits increased because of preemptive buying (for example, purchasing passenger vehicles in anticipation of higher prices) or if in 1978 the budget shows the same fixed spending relationships as obtained in the beginning of the seventies.

And not even the most farsighted budget critic can calculate in advance whether the debt commitment based on the existing debt situation (interest rates and amortization) will constitute a progressive or degressive burden on future generations. Neither the future costs of wealth being formed now (it will undoubtedly be higher than today) nor the real income of the future beneficiaries of these fortunes (which undoubtedly will also be higher than today) can be determined with the evidence now available. The experiences of our economic history, which incidentally are being repeated in the developing countries of the eighties, rather point to the opposite: highways, railroads, cathedrals, and pyramids that attract tourists burdened those who built and financed them, but benefited later generations, and in most instances spared them expenses they could not have afforded.[2]

What we need to know are all the economic real factors that

objectively determine the productive ability of "Enterprise Austria" and based on that—like a "good" (i.e., cautious) banker—make our necessarily subjective, careful deductions. The future state of Austria's balance on current accounts and Austria's budget balance depends on three factors each:

The future balance on current accounts depends on:

1. The real growth difference between the gross national product (GNP) and internal demand. Only when domestic use (absorption) of the GNP for private and public investment and consumption declines instead of rises can the accumulation of the real (export) and financial (foreign exchange) surpluses needed for the liquidation of foreign debts begin to take place.
2. The real cost and price neutrality of domestic production vis-à-vis (and in the currency prices of) the so-called hard-currency countries with which Austria's foreign trade capability stands and falls.
3. The availability (volume) and conditions of the credit facilities (the so-called capital-export potential) needed for the financing of balance on current accounts surpluses.

The future budget balance depends on:

1. The real income growth and distribution, the two important yardsticks of tax collections.
2. The inherent income elasticity (or tax productivity) of the tax system.
3. The spending plans of the government, which should fix its sights on obtaining the moneys needed for debt liquidation from not spending the moneys it collects (planned surplus or reserve formation).

Thus the rate of real economic growth is the common denominator and underlying base of any future balance on current accounts and budget surpluses. It is also the most important consideration with regard to both. The bigger the gross national product or gross domestic product, the "simpler" (and without policy intervention) it is to get the foreign exchange as well as tax revenues needed for this surplus formation. This may seem a trivial point, but it is ignored by those who look at the problem of indebtedness and debt liquidation from the vantage point of civil (i.e., sectoral economic) morality instead of in the context of more or less automatic economic development processes whose tempo can perhaps be regulated—good policy accelerates it and poor policy slows it down—but whose direction never can be.

If we summarily designate future gross national products as dY, and future increases of domestic (public and private) investment and consumer spending as dA, then $dY - dA$ becomes the factor that "determines" the monetary and fiscal policy of the coming years. If dY increases more than dA, only a moderate amount of governing will be necessary. After satisfying its domestic demand for investment and consumer goods, Austria's economy in its role as a big one-man business will yield enough balance on current accounts surpluses to be able to do without additional foreign credits, and perhaps will even be able to embark on debt liquidation.[3]

If, on the other hand, dA rises more than dY, much intervention will be needed. The government and central bank must then coordinate their activities and reduce dA more than dY. How? If they weaken investment activity they gamble away the future growth rates of dY, which means they are solving a current problem (debt liquidation) at the expense of the future. What the authorities must do is accomplish the miracle of curbing consumption without at the same time curtailing investments. Finally, every economy has one, and only one, quantity that possesses the remarkable facility to act like an investment and still reduce domestic consumption—export growth (dX).[4]

The question of the future scope, direction, and course of policy interventions that bear on economic processes, as simple as it is crucial, is this: How much voluntary dX can be expected in the course of the next few years, or, how much involuntary dX must, if necessary, be created without the help of economic policy? The answer to this, in turn, depends on how many voluntary helpers (i.e., prospective customers) the government can marshal to reach this goal.

The second factor in any future balance on current accounts surpluses—Austria's competitive capability in the hard currency

markets—is the responsibility of the economic and social partners. In Chapter 4 the "iron income law" for Austria's balance-
of-payments neutrality was examined. If this were to become
the premise of the economic partnership agreements for the
next few years the government would not have to be so concerned about its dX. Moreover, neither employers nor the
unions would have to fear excessive government intervention:
the employers could in all good conscience equate the favorable
(export) activity with profits, and the unions, with equal
justification, with guaranteed jobs. Whether this all-important
consensus of the autonomous economic partners can be reached
or not will determine not only how well they have learned
the lesson of peaceful solutions of conflicts even under
changed, more trying circumstances, but also whether they
have taken the long-range goals of social equality of their
government's economic policy to heart. If the government has
to intervene restrictively, jobs would be endangered even more
than possible wage increases (as seen in the German Federal
Republic).

The third determinant of future balance on current accounts
surpluses—the dX financing volume and conditions—falls within
the purview of the (somewhat) underdeveloped capital market.
Its "midget growth," essentially the fault of fiscal policy rather
than savings or banking behavior, is the real troubling factor
in the future direction of the current accounts balance. If it
should prove impossible to cover the accumulating dX surpluses either out of real domestic savings or (alternatively) out
of outside borrowed savings (capital transfer), deflationary
tendencies abroad and inflationary tendencies at home will
develop. Sooner or later this policy will have to be discarded,
most likely because of protectionist retaliation by other countries—measures more easily invoked against a small country like
Austria than, say, West Germany. One way or another, fiscal
policy is needed in the promotion and opening up of capital
markets. The impending era of inescapable debt liquidation
merely "updates" the systematic (timeless) analysis of the
arguments presented in Chapter 5.

*   *   *

The time has come to draw up an interim balance sheet. As far as Austria is concerned there is no alternative to a consistent policy of growth, now or in the future. As a matter of fact, this growth policy is even more important for the future, since it acts like a built-in regulator of a debt liquidation inherent in the development process itself, with respect to both foreign and domestic debt. On the other hand, a falling growth rate of the real social product, whether for external or domestic reasons, would make literally everything more difficult and would force economic, monetary, and fiscal policy to intervene sharply, creating disequilibrium in the private sector and automatically increasing the danger of further decline in growth, and with it new disturbing interventions.

The result of this is that contrary to the opinion of conservative critics of the policy of "borrowed prosperity" (which rests on false analogies), the imminent, unavoidable debt liquidation does not call for less but rather continued growth, and, if need be, the investive multiplier (dI) effects would have to be exchanged for similarly convincing export (dX) effects. Consequently nothing could be more ill-advised than to try and force a balance on current accounts and budget surplus through domestic investment curbs and a hard-currency policy based on domestic high interest rates, as was done in the German Federal Republic. It is possible that this sort of austerity policy might open an export outlet for some domestic products that can no longer find a good investment market at home, but at what cost? An export surplus won by emulating West Germany not only means the renunciation of domestic (real) investment and consumption, but the more dangerous alignment of balance on current accounts and budget surpluses as well. Such a growth reduction through restrictions could hardly yield the budget surplus that, in the form of "domestic proceeds" (or financing), makes possible the acquisition and transfer of foreign exchange through export and its utilization in debt liquidation.

At this point the flaw in the analogy between the big one-man firm and the economy based on the division of labor becomes obvious. The firm earns its domestic and external (foreign exchange) profits in one and the same balance sheet and profit-and-loss account and consequently liquidates all accrued credit debts out of the same income drawer. But in the economy the private sector (including the government and government-operated enterprises) earns foreign exchange from exports, while the public sector gets its surpluses in domestic currency.

The economy is faced with the problem of "double" accounts and finances. The privately earned foreign-exchange surpluses must somehow be channeled into the public sector so that the state may repay its foreign debts. In free and open financing systems private foreign-exchange offers and the state's demand for foreign exchange must meet somewhere for the treasury to liquidate its foreign credits.

Of course this domestic Austrian meeting of two market prices could be organized outside the country, on the Eurodollar markets, for example, even if they are not an exactly safe place (see Chapter 9). Since the limitation or collaboration of these markets cannot be ruled out, and since Austria must be concerned with its economic continuity, the foreign-exchange acquisitions of the treasury should be limited to transactions with the Austrian National Bank (transactions that, incidentally, grow out of the business and legal position of both these agencies).

The private sector sells its foreign exchange to its domestic banks, the Austrian National Bank gets it from these banks, and the treasury in turn gets it from the National Bank. The only thing that matters is that the treasury's foreign-exchange purchases from the National Bank are cash transactions. The household thus must channel the money needed for the liquidation of foreign debt from its domestic tax collections.

Why is that important? Every internal deficit or even National Bank financing of dX surpluses, regardless of whether these are needed "only" for the reduction of balance on current accounts deficits or for foreign-debt liquidation, makes these surpluses extremely inflationary at home. The money income earned in the export sector is not matched by any real income. So if real savings brought about by the income surpluses of the treasury are replaced by an increase in domestic money supply (from the National Bank credits to the treasury), demand and liquidity see to it that the price-neutral fiscal savings are not replaced by either price- or income-distributive-neutral forced savings. The combined cost and tariff effects would destroy the real competitive base of the export industries. Even if the first five factors relevant to the external and internal debt liquidation (export potential, foreign trade capability, export financing facilities, tax-rate base, and income elasticity) deliver optimally, the sixth economic and economic-policy factor is the one that determines the role of the budget in the synchronization of private balance on current accounts and public income surpluses.

The catastrophic history of the payment of the German and Austrian war debt and reparations after World War I shows what does or can happen when this synchronization of domestic collections and external (foreign-exchange) transfer does not take place, or takes place too late. Because neither country had budget or export surpluses, the process of permanent domestic and foreign indebtedness continued undeterred to the bitter end— until the first international creditor decided to go on strike and set off the chain reaction of credit recalls, with the results we all know only too well.

At first glance it might seem, though this is not necessarily true, that a debtor nation like Austria can choose among three possible strategies:

1. To create export surpluses but not budget surpluses. In this event the Austrian export economy would have to use its "overearned" foreign exchange on the free markets: the schilling, like the DM, would become a currency in (too) short supply. The public sector would not liquidate its foreign debt, although private foreign wealth would build up.
2. To create budget surpluses but not export surpluses. In that event the foreign exchange needed to liquidate the foreign debt would have to be obtained on the free markets. The schilling (even though hard at home) would depreciate abroad, and this would increase the cost of the debt services (in proportion to the depreciation rate), but it still could take place.
3. To create both budget and export surpluses. In that event the budget would be in a position to "buy up" regularly accruing foreign-exchange surpluses out of current schilling surpluses. The debt liquidation would be exchange-rate- as well as price- and job-neutral.

Because the third choice is the only rational economic solution, fiscal policy must seek to make available the reserves needed for debt servicing. In principle this means that, in the case of growing indebtedness, the balance of payment will continue to define how much domestic elbow room there is for spending. The balance of payments surplus tells the budget at the start of debt liquidation how much foreign-exchange liquidation is affordable in view of the balance on current accounts and balance-of-payments surplus.

This anatomy of economic indebtedness and debt liquidation, of the built-in regulators and the important policy difference between "process-dependent" and "intervention dependent" (real) financing latitudes, raises three equally important questions with regard to fiscal fine-tuning.

1. How much process-dependent foreign exchange and revenue-surplus formation can be expected in the next three to five years? This will decide what consumer curbs, if any, and what tax increases, if any, will have to be imposed.

2. Given the inevitable and desired turn-around of its double deficit of the balance on current accounts and the budget into a double surplus, is Austria heading toward the "German situation," where the domestically restrictive budget surpluses ultimately turned the desired export surpluses into a highly undesirable (and unproductive) disproportionate reserve formation?

3. Given the unfavorable international economic climate, has Austria selected the worst of all possible times for a reorientation? At a time when domestic demand compensated for the lacking foreign demand, Austria turned its back on the world economy. Now that it is forced to try and keep its domestic absorption quota (dA) below that of its domestic gross national product (dY), it is turning to an increasingly feeble world economy. It must try to sell more instead of fewer goods on world markets that tomorrow might atrophy. Perhaps Austria is tilting at economic windmills, for just as Don Quixote could not make the windmills stop, Austria cannot unclog stopped-up, blocked world markets—not even in the neighboring hard-currency countries.

Let us begin with the first question. Kausel's structural analysis[5] refers to the rapid growth of the rejuvenated Austrian industrial capital stock and its substantial export capability, or rather that of its modern, technologically advanced sectors (machine tools, chemicals, automotive industry, and finished goods), and shows that this sectoral core of export-led growth is representative of an overarching trend in all industrial sectors. Kausel re-examined his "old" theses and supported them with newer findings and data.[6] Among the many factors he cited that are not yet generally known three seem highly relevant in this context:

1. The overall economic (real) productivity possibilities growing out of the strengthening and rejuvenation of per capita capital intensities.
2. The internal strengthening of Austria's export position through the qualitative improvement and variety of products and cost easement due to capital rather than income factors.
3. Austria's greater revenue production and real procurement elasticity, particularly by comparison with the German Federal Republic, whose lead continues to shrink.

In the "crisis years" 1970–1978 Austria topped the industrial real capital formation of West Germany by 18 percent, thereby creating for itself a higher (+6 percent) as well as a more youthful capital stock per industrial workers. "Of the real capital holdings created since 1960 in Austria, 57 percent are less than eight years old, compared to 52 percent in the German Federal Republic (where the volume is, moreover, smaller). With this, Austria has already created the basis for a superior industrial dynamism in the eighties."[7]

What does this process mean for all branches of industry in Austria? The real depreciation quotas decrease (physically) but are nevertheless earned in reinvestments and write-offs, thereby strengthening the cash-flow financing and liquidity of business. Business has the choice of either making greater net investments without having to go into debt or—in case the internal tariff walls referred to in Chapter 5 collapse—of venturing into the money and capital markets. But even if the overdue change from fiscal investment incentives to nondiscriminatory capital neutrality and (selective) program and project ties instead of (linear) business ties should not come about, the inevitable rising liquidity level of Austrian industry would compel a tendential shift from a (real) investment to a (financial) savings quota. A youthful capital stock (because of the lower loss quota) requires smaller additional investments, a process also supported by the calculation of the inevitable decline in real returns in the event of increasing capital intensity. If, however, real interest remains high (a likely possibility in view of the financial demand backlog of Austria's money and capital markets), then the (re)investments saved in the business area more or less automatically change into money-wealth formation fed by the cash flow. This could finance not only money and capital market growth, but also the building up of an industrial balance on current accounts surplus and the expected export surplus.

The real capital-use consequences (which can be derived from the capital stock) thus anticipate—at least tendentially—the building up of an efficient money and credit system, as outlined in Chapter 5. But that is not all. The tendency toward a falling rate of real domestic investment or toward a rising rate of real savings or outside financing potential not only affects the money and capital markets, for in that event the rising domestic prices and costs (which necessitated the permanent "cooling off" via a hard-currency policy) begin to taper off by themselves. With growing outside financing (or indebtedness), the recovery of investment costs via prices (self-financing by courtesy of the buyer) becomes increasingly more difficult. This contributes to the growing export efficiency and competitive ability of all branches of Austria's industrial sector, not just the technologically most advanced.

The savings and productivity potential rooted in the over-investment of the 1970–1978 period can be utilized in the restructuring of the domestic and foreign markets. Nobody can say with certainty whether the favorable capital output ratio inherent in the youthful capital stock can by itself bring about the swing from a domestic-oriented to an export-oriented economy, but the groundwork has been laid. This is shown very definitely by the second criterion selected from Kausel's study: the clearly discernible tendency toward an industrial balance on current accounts surplus. The sectoral balance on current accounts according to covering quotas (of goods imports through exports) not only strengthens Kausel's thesis of an expanding export market for future products (chemicals, machine tools, and automotive products) whose former deficits are rapidly melting away, but also shows that the competitive data (of productivity and labor costs) underlying them deserve a closer look.

*   *   *

Austria's capital intensity, i.e., plant equipment, throughout the entire industrial sector is not only superior to West Germany's, but is also concentrated (and surely this is no accident) in the most dynamic export sectors: chemicals, machine tools, and automotive products. A study by E. J. Horn of the Kiel Institut für Weltwirtschaft (also referred to by Kausel)[8] clearly leads to this conclusion. His list of "research-intensive industrial goods" includes chemicals (exclusive of raw materials and fertilizers), special machinery, electronics, and special automotive vehicles (excluding passenger cars and trucks). It is surely no accident that the recent list of major foreign industries with direct investments in the schilling area is composed almost exclusively of firms with export-, capital-, and research-intensive branches, among them Philips, Grundig, Daimler-Benz, and BMW.

This high capital intensity in all sectors of industry, though to different degrees, allows for greater flexibility in costing. As already shown in Chapter 4, the traditional ideas and classifications of fixed and variable plant expenditures and costs of enterprises budgeting their cash flow are no longer valid: at least the costs and reserves of capital conservation and regeneration within a broad spectrum are no longer fixed but elastic with regard to time and allocation. That holds true particularly where the capital stock is new and capital equipment per worker (or job slot) high. If a business decides to write off its capital over five years rather than four, as in the past, it can reduce its capital costs by 20 percent in five years, and have the additional flexibility to concentrate these 20 percent on the later (perhaps more critical) years or to distribute 40 percent annual average capital costs throughout the entire period.

This additional capital cost elasticity (based on variable time spans) allowed Austria's leading export industries to maintain their international competitive position and even expand in all the hard-currency markets, including West Germany, despite more rapidly rising wage costs. As Kausel points out, in the meantime Austria has overtaken its next-door neighbor and rival, West Germany, in real (productivity-related) export output. In real export output per capita Austria drew equal with the German Federal Republic in 1975, and since that time has widened its lead by 4 percentage points, as Table 19 shows, and at an accelerating pace.

The strong showing of Austria's export industry—its full effects are yet to be felt—is undoubtedly due to the (inherently strong) productivity potential of the capital stock and capital intensity. In its export race with the German Federal Republic, Austria has enough breathing space to widen its lead still more, provided it does not dissipate its savings or productivity gains.

Table 19. Austria's Exports Compared to Those of the German Federal Republic

Year	Export (Real) of Goods and Services Per Capita (1960 = 100)			Comparative Level[a] G:A (100)
	Austria	German Federal Republic	$\frac{A}{G} \cdot 100$	
1960	100	100	100	113
1970	238	211	112	101
1975	316	279	113	100
1977	376	322	117	97
1978	400	339	118	96

Source: A Kausel, *Beurteilung der nachhaltigen Wettbewerbsstärke der österreichischen Wirtschaft aufgrund makroökonomischer Tatbestände*, Vienna, 1978 (manuscript), Table 3.9.

Note: A = Austria; G = German Federal Republic.
[a] 1960 at official rates of exchange.

The overinvestments retained in the old structures and locked behind the business tariff walls discussed in Chapter 5 contain a negative savings effect that puts a burden on innovative planning (and consequently on long-term higher capital-output ratios) as well as on more efficient money and credit management.

The disproportionate increase in both nominal and real industrial labor costs is having (perceptible) negative effects on productivity. Kausel is, unfortunately, wrong when he minimizes this point. It is simply not true that "labor costs in [Austrian] industry fell by about a quarter [24 percent] between 1960 and 1970 as a result of the twice repeated decision not to go along with the DM [1961 at 5 percent and 1969 at 9.3 percent]," and that "today's parity with the DM . . . is still 9–13 percent higher than the development of Austria's wage level since 1960 would justify."[9]

The truth of the matter is that in terms of productivity and competition Austria's industrial wage increases were in line with West Germany's in the sixties but not in the seventies, as Kausel's figures clearly indicate (see Table 20).

Table 20. Labor Costs in Industry (1960 = 100)

Year	Gross Wages			Productivity			Labor Costs		
	A	G	$\frac{A}{G} \cdot 100$	A	G	$\frac{A}{G} \cdot 100$	A	G	$\frac{A}{G} \cdot 100$
1960	100	100	100	100	100	100	100	100	100
1970	218	234	93	172	162	106	127	145	88
1975	415	388	107	202	189	107	205	205	100
1977	493	454	109	226	215	105	218	211	104
1978	523	481	109	235	222	106	223	217	103
Annual increase: 1960–1978	+9.6	+9.1		+4.9	+4.5		+4.5	+4.4	

Source: A Kausel, *Beurteilung der nachhaltigen Wettbewerbsstärke der österreichischen Wirtschaft aufgrund makroökonomischer Tatbestände*, Vienna, 1978 (manuscript), Table 3.3.2.

Note: A = Austria; G = German Federal Republic.

Austria's dubious wage margin for 1978 would have been 16 percent, not 9 percent, higher than Germany's had Kausel based his figures realistically on the 1970 index rather than on that of 1960. The fact that up to now Austria has not suffered any competitive set-backs on the hard-currency export markets is due first to its internal absorption through reduced capital costs, and second to its external neutralization by the external inflation rate of the other hard-currency countries—two allies that can be counted on occasionally.

Austria would have done still better in 1961 and 1969 had it followed the hard-currency policy of the seventies in tandem with West Germany. Kausel becomes the victim of his own exchange-rate illusion if, on the basis of two missed schilling appreciation opportunities—one eighteen and the other ten years ago—he concludes that the real greater margin of the Austrian labor-cost growth rate of 13 percent in the overall economy and 9 percent in industry as compared to the German Federal Republic (margins which would be still greater if the index were based on 1970 instead of 1960) was the result of the since apparently perpetuated exchange-rate differential between the DM and schilling.

The fact of the matter is that the hard-currency policy instituted in 1971 equalized the purchasing power of the two currencies (aside from some minor differences due to inflationary factors). Thus if nominal and real labor costs in the schilling area rise more rapidly than in the DM area (in relation to the respective rates of productivity), without any perceptible effects on the profits or competitive position of Austrian industry, this merely demonstrates the extraordinary advances in productivity, not because of its income policy but because of the rate of capital formation.

The trend away from industrial balance on current accounts deficits and toward surplus can continue in the eighties only if Austria's autonomous economic partners adhere more rigidly than they did in the seventies to the model of a "balance-of-payment-neutral," less burdensome income policy (shown in Chapter 4). Unless labor-cost neutrality can be attained, Austrian industry will not be able to perform as expected—i.e., secure the foreign-exchange surpluses that keep foreign debt liquidation free of all extraneous restrictions and that at the same time make it into the biggest, most reliable source of foreign exchange in the country.

This is the major structural product, not merely a by-product, of the debt-liquidation process: Austria needs a reliable supply source of foreign exchange since its old one, tourism, has become somewhat shaky. When floating opened up worldwide disparities in the domestic and foreign purchasing power of one and the same currency—the U.S. dollar now is worth more at home than outside the country, the Austrian schilling more outside the country than at home—the income from tourism became subject to monetary fluctuations and turned into an unpredictable economic factor. Ever since Austrians have stopped playing host to foreign visitors and have begun to visit other countries and other cultures, they have also had to make a choice as consumers: industry, the source of "their" foreign exchange (which they need if they want to travel) must have labor-cost stability.

What does this mean in terms of Austria's fiscal policy? Austrian fiscal policy of the seventies is a textbook example of the fact that outside of the works of some economists a "neutral" budget formation does not and cannot exist. Being an instrument of economic policy the budget always serves a purpose: to protect price stability in times of inflation, and full employment in times of depression. Since the first requires surpluses and the second requires deficits, it is obvious that a "balanced" budget belongs to a world that knows neither the threat of inflation nor the danger of depression (therefore, not our world)—a macroeconomic rule of thumb that would be even more "correct" if the multiplier effects of every initial outlay and every outlay mentioned in Chapter 3 were taken into account. Thus the initial multiplier effect of public consumption on investment would be smaller than on savings and imports, but in the later rounds the effect on indirect investment would be substantially greater.[10]

Even though the demand-equilibrating function of the budget is a more effective allocator than, say, the export and import vents as far as domestic demand deficits and surpluses are concerned, and although it avoids the inevitable (according to

Kaldor) structural distortions and conservations of unilateral export-led growth (a major reason why the German Federal Republic in the eyes of its critics both of the left and the right has become an interventionist state on behalf of sectors that only yesterday were growth leaders but today are losing world markets), a steady stream of new theories seeks to commit the state to so-called budget neutrality.[11] However, neither the monetarists who want to confine fiscal policy to instrumental nonaction nor the game plan supported by the majority of the German Economic Advisory Council in 1974 go so far as to demand the classical balancing of annual expenditures and income— an understandable reaction, historically and politically, to the spending excesses of the *ancien régime* that shocked Adam Smith when he visited France and that led him to refer to the state as a "trader."[12]

Both monetarists and the German Advisory Council accept the demand for a debit quota at a percentage of the gross social and national product. At any rate both "permit" budget deficits when these restrict growing public demand to the limits of the increase in private demand while magnanimously ignoring the fact that a fiscal policy oriented toward full employment would under these circumstances tend to turn into a relative surplus policy. Here, too, so-called theoretical and political liberalism (particularly when prefixed by "neo") turns out to be nationalism. That portion of the domestic production potential that remains unused because of inadequate support of public demand, just like the secret and open wage, price, and currency dumping connected with it, will always be exported at the expense of the world economy.

*　　*　　*

This incidentally is also the weak point of the expert opinion offered by Professor Seidel in his report on the financial condition of Austria. According to his calculation of demand,[13] which echoes that of the German Advisory Council, Austria (except for 1977) had steadily been building up a domestic trade surplus, or rather, was protected against a slide into recession and unemployment. Still, this push of deficit financing was not enough to sustain the production capacity of the early seventies. On the contrary, it continued to regress (see Tables 21 and 22). Instead of drawing the only possible conclusion, that from the perspective of the available production reserves a still bigger budget deficit would not have been "excessive," Seidel arrives at the opposite conclusion: "In the long run . . . it is not possible to neutralize employment risks that grow out of balance on current accounts deficits through budget deficits,"[14] nor, he continues, can a budget deficit of this size be financed for too long even if the present rate of economic growth continues. "With a deficit quota of 4 percent [of the gross national product] and a nominal economic growth rate of 7 percent, the government debt quota would rise to 60 percent. . . . Based on these assumptions, the government debt quota after only five years would amount to one-third of the gross national product."[15] Therefore, "one of the most important social and political tasks of the future is to reduce the *excessive demands on the state* [italics in the original] and to strengthen the responsibility of persons and groups."[16]

However, if the real supply margins allow more, not less, demand, one does not have to worry about their financing, and certainly not about excessive demands on the state. If domestic private or public demand is not strong enough to absorb possible overproduction, foreign demand sooner or later will close the gap, and financing by the Austrian National Bank would be a lot more inflationary than the budget approach which we are told should be discontinued to protect the state against excessive demands. In 1914 E. Von Böhm-Bawerk, the Austrian classical economist whom Seidel quotes in this context, warned his successors against cutting the budget. He made clear that every domestic demand margin ultimately depended on "self-earned" or "borrowed" balance-of-payment surpluses, which is why even at that time he did not oppose financing full employment at home by foreign credits as long as (1) they were available, and (2) their domestic marginal utility was greater than the real burden that interest payment and liquidation would later impose.

It is therefore wrong to base growth calculations on constant government deficit quotas. At a nominal economic growth rate

Table 21. Budget and Trade

| Year | Gross National Product Growth Rates | | Net Budget Expenditures[a] | Budget Receipts Validated | Budget Balance Levels[a] | | Production Potential Capacity |
| | Nominal | Real | | | Net Balance Validated[b] | Effective Domestic Balance | |
	(in percent)		(in billions of schillings)		(in percent of GNP)		(1956-1977 = 100)
1971	11.17	5.28	8.78	10.85	0.02	0.46	103.52
1972	13.74	6.35	14.80	14.17	-0.12	0.40	104.60
1973	13.61	5.79	10.94	6.86	-1.02	-0.54	103.30
1974	15.04	4.13	16.54	14.81	-1.39	-0.95	101.66
1975	6.68	-1.99	20.41	7.59	-4.39	-4.03	97.81
1976	11.35	5.22	11.61	11.80	-4.35	-3.64	97.54
1977	8.48	3.45	6.93	10.15	-3.58	-2.92	96.61

Source: H. Seidel, Bericht über die Lage der Finanzen in der Republik Österreich, Vienna, June 1978 (manuscript).

a- = deficit
bWithout debt liquidation.

Table 22. Trade Effect of the Federal Budget as Projected by the German Economic Advisory Council (basis, 1960–1969)

Year	Net Expenditures	Trade-Effective Revenues	Net Deficits	Net Expenditures	Trade-Effective[a] Revenues	Net Deficits
	(in billions of schillings)			*(in percent of GNP)*		
1971	+ 0.59	+0.18	+ 0.77	+0.14	+0.04	+0.19
1972	+ 2.97	−0.25	+ 2.73	+0.63	−0.05	+0.58
1973	− 1.42	+7.66	+ 6.23	−0.27	+1.44	+1.17
1974	− 2.12	+9.10	+ 6.98	−0.34	+1.48	+1.14
1975	+12.21	+8.39	+20.60	+1.87	+1.28	+3.15
1976	+13.53	+8.65	+22.18	+1.86	+1.19	+3.04
1977	+ 9.49	+6.48	+15.98	+1.20	+0.82	+2.82

Source: H. Seidel, *Bericht über die Lage der Finanzen in der Republik Österreich*, Vienna, June 1978 (manuscript).

[a] Validated magnitudes without debt liquidation; deviations from the trade-neutral expenditures (26.675% of production potential) and revenues (25.009% of GNP).

of 7 percent and a real growth rate of 4 percent, the government deficit quotas cannot over time remain "constant" at 4 percent, even in the case of extremely unfavorable assumptions about (or according to Seidel because of the high indirect tax component of) Austria's steeply declining tax-yield elasticities. *They must fall*, not because the government has quite properly decided so, but because the investment and export multipliers of a real-growth capital stock (even if only 96 percent utilized) heat up private demand permanently and thus would make Seidel's constant 4 percent deficit quota of the public households (apparently independent of trade and growth) immaterial.

Regarding the much publicized "excessive demands on the state," the fact is, this so-called overburdening of the state really benefits all citizens. To a large extent it equalizes, and inexpensively at that, burdens that most people could no longer carry on their own—the care of the sick, the old, the indigent, the education of the young, the preservation of farms and villages and all those romantic idyls of a rural past that everyone would like to conserve but whose real costs, once borne by the private sector, no one wants to assume any more. The budget of a society composed of large families living on farms that support themselves (with food, infrastructure, education, amusements) can be small; the budget of an urban industrial society of small families and "socialized" education and costly infrastructures unfortunately has to be bigger. But that does not mean that it is more expensive. Are excessive demands really being made on the state if it takes real burdens off families and thereby increases the productivity of the private sector of an industrial society? The conclusion would seem to be that those who analyze budgets and the available financing capacities (indebtedness and debt liquidation) must also evaluate the social role and scope of that budget. Their figures and conclusions add up only if measured against the yardstick of our time, not of an agrarian past when most states, because of the (largely forcibly extracted) social contributions of their subjects, were able to make do with a "small" self-financed (if not necessarily fair) government budget.

That the calculations ignore reality financially as well is shown also by the projected budget for 1978–1982 prepared by the Commission for Economic and Social Questions headed by Professor K. Socher.[17] It is a "projection of the presently discernible income and spending trends" of the federal household, and sets itself the goal to present "proposals for solutions" for "identifiable middle-range problems." What this projection believes itself to be identifying is stated quite clearly: the continuing proliferation of internal and external deficits, which calculated in two variants up to 1982 will absorb between 3.9 and 3.3 percent of the gross national product.[18]

If Seidel reduces the real-growth margins of budget policy and sees excessive demand by the state on the gross national product where none exists, the commission takes the opposite tack: its spending projections (which, being projections, presuppose an underlying spending-effective budget policy) reduce the financial margins of budget policy by ascribing spending and debt intentions to the state for which, apart from the technique of projecting past magnitudes as "constants" for the future (see the comment on the multiplier in Chapter 3), there exists no objective or policy reason. This projection creates the financing problems the committee points out and then sets out to solve. Because the projection puts the nominal gross national product increase at 33.5 percent by 1982, state expenditures "must" (as in the past) follow at that same rate. And apparently the state therefore "must" also build up its foreign and domestic debt, from 165 billion schillings at the end of 1977 to 353 billion by the end of 1982—i.e., by 120 percent. To make the parallel work (again)—if possible according to the old financing forms and categories—they project 27 percent foreign loans, 21 percent treasury notes, 19 percent government obligations, 33 percent loans—even including a detailed outline of the capital markets and their interest rates until 1982.

Why such an indeed irresponsible bigger public debt, which does not meet any discernible political objective to justify this projection, should be at all necessary neither the analysis nor the commentary tells us. It is therefore confusing to find that every entry bears the stereotypical annotation that it does not of course "represent any economic policy recommendation."[19] Those who want to enlighten us through prognostications (which as we know are more binding than mere projections since they do not rule out policy) about attainable and feasible ways of balancing current accounts and the budget must also tell us what the policy ought to be and what effects it is likely to have. Assertions like "these magnitudes [of a balance on current accounts that will continue to decline until 1982] would in themselves not be dangerous and could be financed, but they presuppose corresponding and continuous [?] policy efforts and certainly a measure of confidence in the flexibility of the Austrian economy [?]," if they mean anything at all, tell us that their authors either mistrust their own prognosis or the policy on which it is based.[20] At best, this sort of thing contributes to the instability of an economy that depends on the reliability of its planning data. For the sake of preventing misunderstandings and misdirection, what cannot be stated objectively should not be asserted, and certainly not in the form of a prognosis whose "explanatory" annotations put its main thesis in question. Unfortunately, this is a fairly common practice, and more than any other must be held responsible for depriving economic policy and theory of credibility.

What the economy must and can have, without any restrictions, is a budget policy that has as its aim the reduction of foreign credit financing (since it determines domestic financing). The graphic presentation submitted to the government with the 1979 budget (see Figure 5) should have contained guidelines for at least the next three to five years, the average span of a "private" economic planning period. Since a government budget must spell out and commit itself to a definite fiscal

Figure 5. Reduction of Credit Financing as a Middle-Range Goal. Share of Net Deficit in the GNP (in percent)

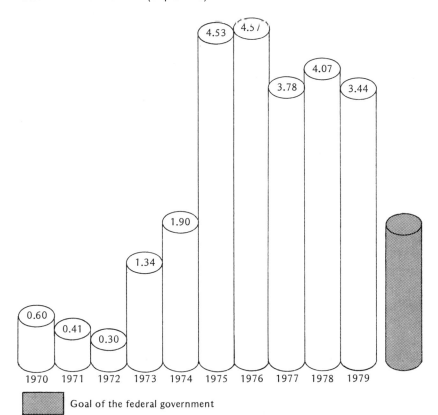

Goal of the federal government

The net deficit is the most meaningful reference point for the gross national product. During the recession, the budget was used to stimulate trade. The share of the net deficit in the gross national product rose accordingly. The low growth rates since 1975 make a rapid reduction of the deficit very difficult. The goal of the federal government, however, is to reduce the share of the net deficit.

policy, it must also cite and make public the relevant data. The sooner it remedies its failure to have done so, the sooner can business respond by making the structural changes and allocations needed for the implementation of the policy recommendations, a process that in the future will be no different than in the past—even if its market direction and financing change.

The economy needs such an orientation. The budget and the plans submitted by the government for how it is to be financed indicate more reliably than any dubious (monetarist) money amount goals and growth rates what aggregate demand at what price, interest, and exchanges, and what income distribution and social conditions the investing and exporting sector can and cannot expect in the foreseeable future.

The inquiry should have posed the following question: If, on the basis of the expected real growth rates of the gross national product and of the expected tax-collection elasticity, higher revenues will accrue while the need for public spending will level off (because of the continuing "stabilization" of domestic—though not necessarily foreign—trade), does this call for greater measure of flexibility in the design of a budget based on these factors? In the event of stable domestic trade, "domestic-effective deficits" will not be needed. Hence funds must be "freed" and rechanneled into foreign-debt liquidation.

How much latitude is there for this rechanneling? Let us look at the only relevant calculation. In line with economic insights restricted to probable development of trends, where even pseudo-accurate models are not of much help (see the comments on the multiplier in Chapter 3), and also in realistic awareness of the limited calculation capability of individual experts, the following outline for such an overall economically reasonable budget-capacity estimate is sketched in broad outline. The projection in Table 23 is based on the following goals, alternatives, and assumptions.

Austria's foreign and domestic financing debt of approximately 200 billion schillings at the end of 1978 (based on the projection of the 1978–1982 budget proposal of the Advisory Committee for Economic and Social Questions of June 1978) is not carried forward but reduced. By 1983, within the space of five years, the foreign debt, which at the end of 1978 stood

Table 23. Budget Projections of the Federal Government of Austria
to 1983: A Model

	1980	1981	1982	1983
I. Tax receipts[a] 1979: 223.8 billion schillings at an annual GNP growth of + 3.5% and a tax collection elasticity[b]				
1. + 3.5%				
(a) η = 1.0	231.6	239.7	248.1	256.8
(b) η = 1.1	254.8	263.7	272.9	282.5
(c) η = 1.15	266.4	275.7	285.4	295.3
2. + 4.0%				
(a) η = 1.0	232.8	242.1	251.7	261.8
(b) η = 1.1	256.0	266.3	276.9	288.0
(c) η = 1.15	267.7	278.4	289.5	301.1
3. + 4.5%				
(a) η = 1.0	233.9	244.4	255.4	266.9
(b) η = 1.1	257.3	268.8	280.9	293.6
(c) η = 1.15	269.0	281.1	293.7	306.9
II. Total spending 1979: 288.1 billion schillings at an annual GNP growth of:				
1. + 3.5% resp. + 4.0%	298.2	308.6	319.4	330.6
2. + 4.5% and an annual spending increase of + 3.25%	297.5	307.1	317.1	327.4
III. Built-in financing latitudes: difference of I and II				
1. + 3.5% GNP				
(a) η = 1.0	−66.6	−68.9	−71.3	−73.8
(b) η = 1.1	−43.4	−44.9	−46.5	−48.1
(c) η = 1.15	−31.8	−32.9	−34.0	−35.3
2. + 4.0% GNP				
(a) η = 1.0	−65.4	−66.5	−67.7	−68.8
(b) η = 1.1	−42.2	−42.3	−42.5	−42.6
(c) η = 1.15	−30.5	−30.2	−29.9	−29.5
3. + 4.5% GNP				
(a) η = 1.0	−63.6	−62.7	−61.7	−60.5
(b) η = 1.1	−40.2	−38.3	−36.2	−33.8
(c) η = 1.15	−28.5	−26.0	−23.4	−20.5

Source: Doppelstrategie für Arbeit und Stabilität–Der Bundeshaushalt 1979, Vienna, 1978.

[a] Based on the federal government's estimated share of total income.
[b] See note 21.

at 57 billion schillings, should be wiped out completely and the domestic debt of some 132 billion schillings reduced by half. According to this assumption the budget would have to liquidate a debt of 123 billion schillings (of which 57 billion would be in foreign exchange) within this five-year span. The interest accruing in that period would add another 25 billion schillings (6 billion in foreign exchange, 19 billion in domestic currency). The question thus is whether a total of approximately 148 billion schillings (63 billion for foreign exchange and 85 billion for domestic payments)—or 30 billion schillings annually—can be raised in the next five years. And if so, from where—higher tax revenues or reduction of government spending? To answer this we must know the answers to the following questions. What higher tax collections can be expected with a fair degree of certainty in the next five years, assuming economic real growth of between 3.5, 4, and 4.5 percent, respectively, and a tax flexibility (η) of 1.0, 1.1, and 1.15 percent, respectively?[21] What (normal) government expenditures, excluding outlays for debt liquidation, can also be expected with a fair degree of probability during the next five years?

A 3.5 percent growth rate of the gross national product is the critical threshold for a trade-neutral rise in spending. Any rate below that level demands a progressive rate of increase in government spending, and any rate above that demands a degressive rate. At a 3.5 to 4 percent GNP growth rate, the rate of increase in government spending should be set at 3.5 percent, and at a gross national product growth of 4.5 percent, it should be brought down to 3.25 percent.

By carrying forward the crucial income and outlay data of the estimated 1979–1983 values, and assuming cautious as well as theoretically and empirically plausible developments, Table 23 shows only a moderately rising budget deficit tendency, and at 4.5 percent even a slightly declining trend. This relative debt liquidation process accelerates the more stable and the higher the overall economic growth rate. And it can be assumed that the continued favorable trade outlook will have a positive effect on tax collection flexibility and reduce the need for increased government spending. Given both these assumptions, the year 1983 could have an almost balanced budget (with a remaining deficit of 20 billion schillings) without additional dispositive interventions (tax increases or government spending cuts).

This is no conjurer's trick but the logical outgrowth of the real contribution of the capital stock expansion and rejuvenation that took place in the seventies documented by Kausel, which prefinanced the effective domestic budget deficits of this period. Foreign countries and the budget played only the role of the "good banker" who believed that its client (Enterprise Austria) would achieve domestic and foreign balance on current account surpluses.

But what is the significance of these "theoretical" budget surpluses based on assumptions of higher real tax receipts and rising government spending in terms of the debt magnitudes? The extrapolation of the trends bears out what economic common sense tells us: In the event of bigger tax receipts and somewhat degressive government spending, both the domestic and foreign indebtedness will continue to decrease substantially until 1983. The debt liquidations included in the plan (repayments and interest) will reduce the still outstanding total domestic and foreign debt by a greater amount than is added by newly entered-into debt commitments. Or in figures of the model calculation, the liquidation of 150 billion schillings by 1983 can be achieved without any difficulty; the amount could even go up if the high liquidation figure for 1979 (35.7 billion schillings) could be accrued. The total amount allocated to liquidation and interest of 150 billion schillings to be raised by 1983 could be more than fully covered by the existing reserve holdings of the central bank if "only" the growth rate of the gross national product could be stabilized at the seventies level of approximately 4.5 percent.

As the model further demonstrates, at the maximal liquidation rate of 35.7 billion schillings in the next five years, new domestic debt in the amount of 98.4 billion schillings would accrue. If the liquidation were held to the 30 billion schillings annually required on the basis of our assumption, the 1983 public domestic debt validation would be reduced to 69.9 billion schillings, a little more than the 50 percent of the indebtedness at the end of 1978—a calculation that moreover is "inflation-proof." The calculated financing capacities freed by 1983 contain no inflation profits based on expected, or more properly, inevitable price increases between now and 1983, which, experience teaches us, is reflected more quickly in the receipts than in the outlays. The financing proposal thus contains a few added-on inflation costs as a silent, even if not planned, reserve.

Given the present income, outlay, and distribution structure of the Austrian economy, a still more rapid and more far-reaching (even if unnecessary) debt liquidation out of the built-in financial reserves of the central household could easily be undertaken without any additional interventions if either the future growth rate of the gross national product would be raised above 4.5 percent or if the Enterprise Austria would decide to broaden its debt liquidation horizon by projecting a ten-year liquidation span instead of the five-year term outlined here.

Quod erat demonstrandum.

There is no substance to the contention that fiscal policy acts to restrict budget policy or that it is putting an excessive burden on the present generation. On the contrary, the projections show that Austria's domestic and foreign public debt in fact was nothing but an anticipatory financing of future balance on current accounts and budget surpluses that lay within the realm of appropriate policy. Moreover, our calculation is hedged in with policy reservations with regard to the subsidy households, and also with regard to the open and hidden additional subsidies to state-owned enterprises.

Subsidies have three fatal flaws: first, they tend to get bigger, but rarely if ever are revoked; second, they become obsolete (a subsidy that initially may have made sense may become counterproductive once the needed adjustments have been made); and third, subsidies, like internal tariffs, are fiscal bonuses on capital transactions. To keep them the recipient will do anything at all—including the wrong things. Subsidy households therefore always contain financial reserves that could be put to greater advantage some other place—for example, the liquidation of public debt.

The inclusion of publicly owned enterprises (e.g., railroads and the postal system) in the public household not only inflates it unnecessarily and adversely, but also burdens it with the running losses to the tune of 20 billion schillings shown in Table 24—

Table 24. Budget Development Excluding Publicly Owned Enterprises (in billions of schillings)

Year	Expenditures	Receipts	Balance "Validated"	"Not Validated"
1970	69.8	73.5	+ 3.7	- 2.2
1971	77.0	82.9	+ 5.9	- 1.7
1972	88.8	46.2	+ 7.4	- 1.4
1973	94.4	102.8	+ 3.4	- 7.2
1974	120.3	119.3	- 1.0	-11.7
1975	140.7	128.1	-12.6	-24.7
1976	155.7	140.8	-14.9	-33.3
1977	165.8	156.0	- 9.8	-29.9

Source: Finance Ministry, Vienna.

deficits that as other countries have shown could easily be cleared by a cost-covering price and financing policy.

If these two household factors—the net deficits of the two public enterprises and the conservation subsidies that block an effective selective structural policy—could be validated, the desired fiscal savings balance could be achieved without either a raise in taxes or painful cuts in spending.

A number of questions still remain: First, might a resourceful finance ministry not be tempted to institute a partial rather than a total surplus policy by combining a "foreign-debt liquidation budget surplus" with a continued "domestic debt budget deficit," i.e., to finance foreign loans by taking on new domestic loans? Second, has Austria decided to enter the export market at an inauspicious time—is the era of international economic growth during which West Germany became a major world trader irrevocably over? And would a budget surplus policy of foreign-debt liquidation, once the export gap has been closed, lead Austria into the dead end of a one-sided export dependency? Should Austria, once it liquidates its foreign debt, really become the creditor of other countries by building up its own (net) foreign holdings that can only be invested in "public" reserves of the central bank or in "private" foreign investments (growing out of capital export demands)—on the model of England after World War I and the United States in the post–World War II era?

As to the first question, we know the monetary consequences of every temporal and volume-related division of domestic finance and external foreign-exchange real transfer. The economy could sell its total foreign-exchange surplus to the state, except that the state borrows its internal collection and does not save it. Thus neither a (temporal) desynchronization nor a (volume-related) underfinancing of the two transfer processes takes place. The only thing that would be lost would be the public savings effect. We already know from Chapter 5 that public debt strengthens the private savings potential, but unfortunately of the "wrong" account: the forced savings of the nonbusiness households created by the price and profit structure of business. Therefore a divided budget strategy would structurally aim in the wrong direction for two reasons. First, like a non-neutral balance-of-payments (i.e., too expansive) income policy, it would burden the competitive capability of the economy and require a further balancing schilling appreciation (i.e., involuntary appreciation)—an excessively hard hard-currency policy. Second, it would also thwart the building-up of efficient domestic money and capital markets, since those markets would now be put under double pressure: the intensified domestic borrowing of the state and the diminished supply of loanable funds, since the private households now would have less, not more, funds available for savings in the money and capital markets. The lack of fiscal savings triggers crowding out effects that drive up interest rates. The only thing fiscal policy was allowed to do after the oil crisis was to plan its effective domestic total deficit and present it to the private sector as a guideline, and the only thing it can do now, after the basic reorientation designed to lower its foreign debt level, is to determine its effective domestic total surplus. Just as in the case of the entrepreneurial cash flow and burden allocation, its only flexibility is that of time and term adjustments. It can plan its debt liquidation for five, ten, or fifteen years, depending on which "certain" foreign-exchange income—and which imponderables—it can (cautiously) count on as a basis of developments in the domestic money and capital markets on which it has no influence.

As to the second question: If the world economy is not as vital as it was before the oil crisis—as is quite obviously the case, even though the majority of the nations of the world are not part of the affluent society but rather of the society of (in part unimaginable) want—it must be assumed that the decline in world trade is due not so much to satiation as to problems of financing. Because most poor countries lack domestic savings potential—not because too little is being saved but because too little is being produced (their dA is still far greater than their dY)—the export opportunities in our world economy depend not only on price, cost, and productivity, but above all on available financing. Whether Austria wants to or not, in an economy of many poor and only few rich nations it can broaden and secure its export market only to the extent and at the pace it can finance its future balance on current accounts surplus out of domestic real savings. This concept would from the very outset avoid two things: the overexpansion of exports, as happened in neighboring West Germany, which derives its strong export position from its delivery, not financing potential—though it remains to be seen how strong this position in fact is—and a lopsided dependence on the (restricted) cash (i.e., foreign-exchange) payment abilities of other and poorer countries.

The financing of the desired and needed export and foreign-exchange surplus must be defiscalized and reprivatized. Not the budget but Austria's money and capital markets must insert themselves as the purchasers of the foreign exchange earned by the exports of the private sector. Its financing capacity would decide how much current export surplus and how much new foreign capital the economy can still afford, and how much "development aid" it will return to a world economy that at one time had also helped Austria through its foreign loans.

What would the structural effects of a reversal of this development policy be? The state would liquidate its debt and burden the economy with a decrease in publicly financed domestic demand. That is to say, its budget surplus would destroy the domestic demand potential and force the economy to look for substitute markets abroad: the fiscal withdrawal effects would accelerate the trend toward balance on current accounts surpluses.

But how is this to be financed? Once one discards the (monetary) illusion that additional loans could be created to finance these export surpluses (which of course could be done, but not without debilitating inflationary consequences), the only thing that remains is to fall back on the existing (real) savings potential. As we have already seen, this is nourished not only by the shift from real investments to real savings—the investment and capital market reforms discussed in Chapter 5 can accelerate this process considerably and mobilize additional means. Furthermore, an efficient money and capital market performs a multiplicative accumulation and turntable function. Not only does it lend its own assets, but it increasingly also soaks up foreign assets and moves them forward. Therefore Austria, once it breaks out of entrepreneurial and sectoral capital endogamy and the self-created ghetto of its internal capital transaction tariffs, could relatively quickly and painlessly become a transregional capital market. The visible good will of its hard currency and good credit and debt policy offer the best prospect for this.

Opening up Vienna as an international banking center for well-capitalized foreign banks experienced in international finance would be a step in this direction. Another, and no less important one, concerns the possible internationalization of the government's surety practices and policy. If the official risk premiums on foreign investments and credits were extended to foreign money suppliers financing Austrian export or foreign investments, the reluctance of domestic banks to finance what they believe to be excessive obligations would cease to be a consideration. Tying the financing of the domestic money and capital markets to domestic real productivity would, more effectively than anything else, prevent Austria from facing the problems of another one of its neighbors, Switzerland, which in its role as banker to the world has put undue stress on (re)-financing and too little importance on its real supply ability.

*   *   *

In the eighties Austria must draw the right conclusions from the real capital formation of the seventies. The desirable equilibrium between balance on current accounts surpluses and capital balance deficits (capital exports) at the beginning of the new age should not only lead to a private foreign capital formation, it should also counteract the unproductive (and tax-financed) public reserve hoarding of the central bank. Moreover, the country must continue to steer clear of unproductive goal conflicts. Austria, unlike the German Federal Republic, does not have to fear involuntary balance on current accounts and capital balance surpluses it neither can nor wants to finance; nor like Switzerland does it have to ward off involuntary (super)capital balance surpluses it neither can nor wants to use as investments; nor like both of these neighbors does it have to live locked in discord, in permanent goal conflict between a restrictive policy aimed at domestic stability and full employment and a continuous flow of imported inflation and depression—the result of the disequilibrium of the balance of payments as well as unneighborly attempts to get rid of these problems by exporting them.

*   *   *

The policy mix Austria developed in the seventies thus also deals with the problems of the eighties. Given a favorable balance on current accounts and a general budget balanced through long-range capital exports, monetary policy can continue to defend the hard schilling abroad, and fiscal policy can remain in charge of full employment and price stability at home, except that in the event of foreign activity on the balance-of-payments front, the task of both these instruments and guarantors of Austria's prosperity will have been made easier, not harder. What outsiders apparently see more clearly than the people of Austria is that Austria's future, thanks to the real and policy accomplishments of the seventies, looks more promising than ever, better than that of most other countries including those who only yesterday were among the most prosperous. Austria can only lose the opportunities others still have to gain or regain. Examples of that also exist. This analysis of Austria's situation is an attempt to make a repetition of such errors more difficult.

PART 2

THE THEORETICAL BACKGROUND: IS ECONOMIC INDEPENDENCE POSSIBLE?

In a nationalistic world everything is difficult to achieve except an international economic crisis, which of course is very easy to get into.
—Michael A. Heilperin, 1969

7

DEMAND
(OR MONEY) ILLUSIONS

Western economic policy once again must draw on the experiences of a world economic crisis. At the beginning of the thirties the (classical) thesis of the autonomous downward adjustment of flexible costs and prices failed. The United States, following the market crash of 1929, gave up its role of world creditor and reversed its capital-balance deficit via its domestic high-interest-rate policy; the decline in demand and liquidity resulting from the calling-in of loans of debtor nations like Germany and Austria depressed their domestic cost and price levels and affected their profit, investment, and employment structure. The changes in (relative and intersectoral) prices and costs caused by the money and capital shortages in the deficit economies, to the utter amazement of textbook-trained theoreticians and policy makers, were at complete variance with established theory: The "imported depression," by dislocating the price and cost structures, changed the data on which business had based its production, investment, and employment estimates. Because selling prices fell even more than labor costs, profits shrank. The question was whether this was due to the stubborn refusal of trade unions to accept a like-reduction in the wage income of their members, whose now inflated real-wage position had to be adjusted to the already diminished real profits of employers.

What almost all analysts failed to see was that another adjustment process was taking place: Employers and workers reacted similarly to the deteriorating profit and job expectations by cutting back on their spending. Within the framework of their still existing (real) income possibilities all social groups sought

117

to strengthen their financial reserves: Contrary to expectations they saved more than ever, to the surprise and chagrin of the members of the business community, for they had based their production, investment, and employment plans on "old" spending patterns, namely no rising (panic) savings tendency (or degressive demand development).

It was John Maynard Keynes who after many preliminary exercises arrived at a distillation of the actual cause of the "theory-defying" crisis. There were obvious shifts between active money (which he dubbed M_1) and inactive money held in reserve (M_2). The fear-induced (rather than speculation-induced) increase in liquidity preference (which is nothing more than a decrease in the money-circulation rate of the old quantity theory) destroyed the underlying assumptions of the classical working hypothesis of money circulation, according to which nothing is lost—in which saving does not mean the nonspending of money but the spending of money somewhere else (i.e., investment). To show this and at the same time to refute Say's theories of closed money circulation, which do not provide for total crisis, Keynes wrote his *General Theory of Employment, Interest and Money.* Keynes showed that the highly realistic (and rational) "prudent" savers endanger the operational stability of every free, value-backed economy, because no stable volume of real demand can develop to guarantee the full employment that makes possible the balancing of all goods, money, and labor markets via price, interest-rate, and wage movements— even downward movements if necessary.

In his timeless work Keynes made clear that economic behavior and reaction can never be precisely "calculated" but only "stochastically" surmised, which is why all those who interpret Keynes's model econometrically are guilty of misinterpreting it. (In this context see note 1 of Chapter 2 on the misinterpretation of his multiplier theorem.)

Since market as well as planned economies must always be prepared for unexpected developments, surprises are always possible; hence old textbooks should not be thrown out, but they should be read with caution.

Keynes's *General Theory* draws the only logical conclusion from the basic unpredictability of the reactions and choices of economic subjects seeking to protect themselves: to safeguard our economically unstable universe by setting up policy guidelines. What kind of guidelines? If the economic world, unlike the physical universe, does not have a law governing the preservation of available (demand) energy, then economic policy must fill that role. In the absence of the aggregate demand needed for full employment and the desired real income distribution, anticyclical demand equalization must fill that void. When free enterprise and credit markets become too much of a good thing and create inflationary overdemand, anticyclical skimming is indicated.

Once the people become convinced that their economy functions predictably and calculably their reactions will again become predictable and calculable as well, and the economy will really function. This is the basic (sociopsychological) keystone of the Keynesian structure. But when (because of faulty policy) we find ourselves in a crisis or beset by inflation and thus overreact, be it out of fear or euphoria, any merely value-oriented steering is bound to fail ultimately, because the basic equation underlying the constancy of demand and supply—that investments absorb planned savings—does indeed describe an equilibrium norm but not a (permanent or self-fulfilling) reality. In times of crisis prudence dictates greater savings rather than investment, and in times of high inflation rates investments exceed savings. In the first instance underdemand (because less M_1 money than expected is being spent) creates underutilization of available capacities, ergo unemployment; in the second instance (because more M_1 money than expected is being spent), overutilization of the available capacities results, ergo inflation. Both processes reinforce themselves through the self-protective reaction of those involved. The army of prudent savers is reinforced by old investors turned new savers.

One of the statistically as well as politically most profitable and most widely ignored sources of "fear" savings in times of depression are the uninvested (no longer invested) business profits, particularly of the depression-endangered private small and medium-sized business sector. As we have seen in Chapter 1, in the post-1972 crisis years private small and medium-sized businessmen in the German Federal Republic took more out of their enterprises than they earned. Where was that money invested? Given the overall regressive investment rate and rising rate of savings, it can be assumed that instead of reinvesting their money, these businesses sought out "risk-free but secure" savings, such as government securities, which in times of crisis always chalk up record sales. Investors turn into savers, and this intensifies the crisis "endogenously" (see Figure 2).

What happens in inflation? Since investors and savers learned that when prices rise they get back less in real coin than their current asset and money wealth investment, they calculate the depreciation rate of their anticipated income and wealth into their anticipated returns and interest. In other words, they anticipate the inflation rate (regardless of whether their calculations are right or wrong) of real profits and interest and thus, precisely by these efforts to protect themselves against it, set the rate of inflation. We will examine the consequences of this process of self-protection in greater detail when we discuss the "free" international (Euro) money and credit markets and the threatened danger of their collapse.

To the delight of post-Keynesian economists, the calculations of the overwhelming majority of investors and savers turned out to be realistic after the fading of the money illusions, and the social partners also are settling their disputes over the distribution of the social product in a thoroughly modern fashion by establishing the real profit and wage shares of the national product. But, according to Keynes's discovery and underlying assumption of the *General Theory*, the trickling down of needed demand (in liquidity "hoards") and the inability of prices and costs to compensate for this demand deficit through downward adjustment, unfortunately persist. But if (national) cost and price levels can only rise, not fall, and if wealth and income determinants orient themselves on real (i.e., price-validated) data and goals, then all attempts at anticyclical and demand stabilization are bound to fail. This is so because the skimming of inflationary overinvestments (compared to simultaneous real savings) only works when the real interest of the savers exceeds the real profits of the investors, which (as we can see in the German Federal Republic) leads to the permanent change of investors into savers, and thus to crisis. But the incentive of investment shortages (in comparison to real savings) also does not work because the "nominal" expansion of demand (in M_1 money expenditures) is either absorbed "factually" (through price increases) or nominally trickles away in fear-induced greater money savings. Or the incentive does not work because of a combination of the two when fear of inflation and crisis coincide, which has long been the case in almost all Western industrial countries.

Thus the alleged failure of Keynesian demand or global direction can be explained by a sort of self-protective reaction of the economy to uncertainty. If in addition there are oligopolistic market strategies—something the monetarists are unable to detect—according to which not only "expectations" but also the "policy data" (such as interest rates, taxes, and other supposedly anti-inflationary financing costs) are calculated into the selling price and rolled over to the consumer, the fight against inflation itself becomes the cause of further inflationary thrusts and depressions, for every monopolistic price increase destroys demand in other places for other products—a mechanism described elsewhere by this author.[1]

None of the above relegates Keynes's *General Theory* to the junk heap; on the contrary, it makes all those who do not know how to apply it to the conditions of today and tomorrow into junk dealers.

8

TERMS-OF-TRADE (OR EXCHANGE-RATE) ILLUSIONS

Keynes's successors (the fiscalists and their adversaries, the embattled monetarists), faced with the rigidity of national prices and costs, found a way out that, despite their strong disagreements, unites them more than they seem to realize: If the internal adjustment process of price and demand levels in an economy is blocked, it can be "replaced" by an external adjustment process (in the relation between national economies). The decline in domestic (absolute) prices and costs is replaced by external (permanent) currency appreciation, and instead of domestic (global) rise in demand we have a permanent currency depreciation. If an economy should pursue a dual strategy of fighting off both imported inflation and depression, relative depreciation and appreciation can even be combined. How? By the permanent appreciation of the local currency vis-à-vis the competing foreign currencies, but never at the full rate of the world rate of inflation—a game that the German Federal Republic has continued to play with consummate skill, as this author has elsewhere demonstrated.[1]

Since the dismantling of the Bretton Woods monetary system and the introduction of floating this adjustment process has become part and parcel of the economic policy of almost every Western industrial country—including those that have joined together in the European Monetary System (EMS). How does it work? After being dethroned as the monetary yardstick between currencies, the rate of exchange is now determined on the foreign-exchange markets like any other normal market price and acts like a protective heat shield between

domestic and foreign temperatures: if the price levels abroad are
higher than at home, the lower domestic prices do not adjust
to the higher foreign prices; instead, the too low foreign worth
adjusts to the domestic currency. The undervalued currency
continues to appreciate until the domestic monetary unit at-
tains the same unrefracted real purchasing power in domestic
and foreign markets. The currency appreciation thus compen-
sates for the otherwise inevitable (imported) inflation, a process
that grows out of the rational consumption behavior of domestic
and foreign money users without any policy intervention. And
as long as the domestic consumers get more for their money
abroad than at home, they will substitute domestic purchases
for foreign goods (imports), and as long as foreign consumers
get more for their money at home than abroad, they will substitute foreign goods (imports) for domestic purchases, until
all import deficits (i.e., export surpluses) and import surpluses
(i.e., export deficits) have been wiped out.

The restoration of real purchasing power parity of domestic and foreign money use or spending (thus of a "sensible"
buying pattern of the domestic and foreign money users) in
one stroke also restores the equilibrium in the balances on
current accounts and in exchange-rate relations. If, on the
other hand, there is a decrease in international trade demand
because one (or a group) of the international big creditors
insists on import deficits (or export surpluses), then a declining external value of the domestic currency makes it possible
to compensate for the decline in international trade by additional foreign as well as domestic demand.

How is this done? The disequilibrium of exchange-rate relations growing out of the disequilibrium of the balance on current accounts (which appreciates the creditor currency and
depreciates the debtor currency) automatically reduces all
sources of income in the depreciation countries, both at home
and abroad. The higher real foreign purchasing power of foreign
currencies (in the depreciation countries) permits the substitution of imports for domestic goods, and the lower foreign purchasing power of the local currency (in the appreciation countries) permits the substitution of domestic goods for imports.
The depreciation thus mediates an additional demand stimulus

between foreign and domestic goods, wherein the former result in exports while the latter cut down on imports. Depreciation, by improving the balance on current accounts of the deficit country, becomes a substitute for the otherwise inevitable (imported) depression or unemployment.

If Keynes in his *Treatise on Money* (1930) still believed that this exchange-rate strategy "merely" creates balance on current accounts equilibrium, his monetarist adversaries of the sixties and seventies (with H. G. Johnson in the lead) rightly pointed out that the exchange-rate fluctuations necessarily must affect the capital (balance allocation) of the international trading partners. An overvalued currency (i.e., one not depreciating according to its real domestic purchasing power) makes the domestic currency area too expensive as a position for foreign investments and brings down the cost of all foreign currency areas as the position for one's own foreign investments. An undervalued currency (i.e., one not appreciating according to its real domestic purchasing power) brings down the cost of the domestic currency area as a position of foreign investments and makes all foreign currency areas more expensive for one's own foreign investments.

Keynes explains his balance on current accounts and capital balance strategies that differentiate between rates of exchange and interest-rate elasticities "instrumentally." The commodity markets belong to the entrepreneurs, and the money markets to the banks. Thus price fluctuations induced by exchange-rate fluctuations enter into the balance on current accounts via the trade balances, while exchange-rate–induced interest-rate fluctuations enter into the capital balance via the bank balances. In other words, Keynes saw the floating he encouraged on the foreign-exchange time (not cash) markets as a continuation of the short-term interest-rate policy by other means. "By varying these rates they [the central banks] would be able, in effect, to vary the interest offered for *foreign* balances, as a policy distinct from whatever might be their bank-rate policy for the purpose of governing the interest obtainable on *home* balances."[2]

After World War II, this swap policy was rediscovered by B. Hansen.[3] Harry G. Johnson, in his pioneering study *International Trade and Economic Growth* (1958), traced the domestic

and external terms-of-trade effects on exchange-rate fluctuations, though under the only partially correct assumption of
exchange-rate illusions on the part of at least one of the trading
partners.[4] Still, Johnson had some tangible evidence for his
theories in the form of the long-term U.S. capital balance deficit—
the result of the dollar overvaluation—and the long-term balance
on current accounts surplus of the German Federal Republic—
the result of the undervaluation of the DM. However, this is not
necessarily related to the "accidentally" firm cash rates of
exchange.

On the other hand, the deficit capital balance of the United
States and the surplus capital balance of the German Federal
Republic before the energy crisis are textbook examples of
Johnson's thesis. Before 1971, the United States bought up
foreign industries and shares at bargain-basement prices and
thereby strengthened the capital-formation rates of the under-
valued-currency countries, but at the cost of domestic disloca-
tion. The United States lost domestic effective growth and
employment potential. The "overvalued" U.S. dollar did not
allow the U.S. economy to grow at its full potential and full-
employment level.

On the other end of this spectrum, the German Federal
Republic before 1971 sold its domestic goods (exports) and
domestic participations (capital demands) at bargain-basement
prices and thereby gave away domestically produced means of
production (export surplus). It financed this effective loss
through a higher real foreign debt—foreign direct investments
and other capital imports. The undervalued DM made it possible
for the German economy at that time to grow beyond its potential and beyond the full-employment level, but at the price of
major structural disproportionalities, which are likely to exert
even greater pressures than they already do: a hypertrophic
export sector and above-average "foreign penetration."

Considering the miraculous effects of the "free" floating
that began in 1973, it should have been possible to discharge
three of the most troublesome economic burdens that arose in
the development of domestic and international markets.

First, cushioning the shock waves of imported inflation and
depression, and refashioning the painful adjustment process of

of national cost, price, demand, and employment levels into comparatively harmless and equilibrating fluctuating exchange rates, would have turned harsh prosperity sacrifices into symbolic exchange-rate losses or gains on the boards of the currency markets.

Second, self-regulating exchange rates (in terms of real purchasing power parities) would necessarily have had far-reaching effects on national equilibrating trade, employment, and restructuring policies. Exchange-rate and balance-of-payments equilibrium achieved through the real (i.e., effective) goods- and capital-transfer relations would have stabilized prices and full employment via market processes at a minimum of tax interventions.

Third, the parity equilibrium between domestic and external real purchasing power of the currencies circulating in world trade would ultimately have led to a restructuring of world-trade and capital movements, in keeping with the natural productivity and position income of the world trading partners, free of all the misdirection and imbalances arising out of the overvaluation of a currency—an international economic and monetary order based on *quid pro quo*, in which no country derives special advantages from currency manipulations, let alone from its position as a world reserve power.

*   *   *

A comparison of ideal (model) and reality since 1973 shows that none of these three potential effects of floating occurred. Ever since international demand lost its earlier dynamicism, most of the Western (and Eastern) industrial nations and almost all developing countries have had to wage an uphill fight against inflation and depression, floating notwithstanding. In that respect the establishment of realistic exchange rates apparently has not become a substitute either for the domestic adjustment of the economies to the changed situation of international trade or for a domestic equilibrating (or stabilizing) policy; i.e., depreciations were not a valid substitute for decline in domestic demand, nor was appreciation a valid substitute for holding the fort on domestic prices and employment.

On the contrary, the old goal conflicts not only continued;
they intensified. Because the balance-of-payments disequilibrium reached unprecedented peacetime proportions, world
trade purchasing-power disparities persisted. Optimal trade and
payment structures and balanced domestic growth, employment, and stability goals also were not achieved.

Why these failures? To begin with, consumers faced with a
choice between domestic and foreign goods apparently reacted
contrary to theoretical expectations to exchange-rate fluctuations (depreciation and appreciation) by making price adjustments rather than quantitative adjustments. In the depreciation countries they did not substitute relatively still inexpensive
domestic goods for higher-priced foreign goods (imports) until
such time as the price relationship between the domestic and
foreign markets brought down domestic overdemand for
foreign goods and with it the balance on current accounts
deficits (import surplus). Domestic overdemand and balance
on current accounts deficits continued, but why? Because the
domestic producers and entrepreneurs used the greater latitudes
for raising prices that the higher prices of "their" imported
goods had opened up to raise the prices of their domestic goods
as well: the deflation-induced cost push of the imports had a
direct inflationary effect—via the so-called international price
connection (according to Wolfgang Stützel)—on domestic prices
and costs.

Conversely, in the appreciation countries consumers did not
substitute relatively more expensive domestic goods for imports whose prices had been brought down by the new foreign-
exchange rates. Here, too, domestic producers and entrepreneurs with market strength used the opportunity offered by
higher world market prices and refrained from lowering domestic prices as much as might have been expected in view of the
oversupply of favorably priced foreign goods. Therefore in the
appreciation countries there was neither price equilibrium between domestic and foreign goods (imports) nor a reduction of
balance on current accounts surpluses. On the contrary, the
appreciation-induced cost push of exports, via the direct international price relationship, had an inflationary impact on the
import prices of the purchasing countries, and, via the Keynesian

income mechanism of higher money and real incomes in the selling, or export, countries, on their domestic price and cost structure as well.

It took a long time for this well-known vicious-circle theory of the inflationary (not deflationary) feedback of all unilateral depreciations and appreciations to resurface in the short memory of modern monetary theorists. Otto Viet is among the earliest, and theoretically most perspicacious, refuters of the macro-economic exchange-rate illusion, according to whom appreciation in the surplus country acts as a substitute for demand stabilization in the deficit country. In 1961 he proved[5] that appreciation in the surplus countries opens up new inflationary demand and price-increase latitudes in the deficit countries, and that therefore a cumulative process of reciprocal inflationary thrust effects were more likely than even moderately successful stabilization.

Only in certain areas, such as the professionally managed travel and capital transaction sectors, does the exchange-rate mechanism of the float theoreticians work: greater numbers of vacationing and capital "tourists" made use of the real domestic and foreign purchasing-power advantages opened up by the depreciation or appreciation of their respective currencies. Thus the travel and capital-transaction balances of the hard-currency nations (e.g., German Federal Republic, Switzerland, the Benelux countries, and, at least in terms of its development trend, Austria) tended toward deficits, but being relatively insignificant they had no substantial effect on the balance of payments.

The forces behind the capital account balance also reacted contrary to theory, although "sensibly." Because nominal position costs of foreign production declined in the depreciation countries and rose in the appreciation countries, a worldwide shift of foreign industrial plants to the soft-currency countries might have been expected—a shift of massive capital imports and direct investments into, for hard-currency owners, less expensive monetary areas. Following the example of the United States prior to 1971, the export producers of the German Federal Republic, for example, should have shifted their production to a far greater extent than they did to the new soft-currency countries with attractive domestic markets (such as the United States, for example), replacing old-fashioned exports with "higher-grade" capital exports (or rather "exports in place"). In fact, however, this movement did not go beyond a few spectacular, overpublicized attempts. A regional analysis of the German long-term capital-transactions balance deficit since the beginning of the seventies (before floating began) shows a reverse trend. The hard-currency countries continue to be of interest as positions for German foreign direct investments, even though the nominal cost of investments in soft-currency countries has declined substantially.

There can be only two rational explanations for this dissipation of investment advantages: either the foreign producers do not believe that their nominal exchange rate returns will last too long, or they count on a real absorption of the exchange-rate advantages they have enjoyed because of a higher rate of inflation in the country to which they are tied for the duration of their foreign investment activities. Regardless of which of these two incidentally complementary motives dominates, if further depreciations or appreciations are expected, no foolproof calculations can be made, either real or nominal. But this sort of thing, as has been seen in the analysis of investment behavior in the presence of unstable planning information (Chapter 1), must inevitably lead to adjustments in the form, terms, and positions of investments.

The analysis of the capital-account balances of almost all Western industrial countries in fact gives ample evidence of this adjustment process. While volume and balances of the long-range capital transactions between countries since 1973 increased only moderately, short-range transactions practically exploded. The inescapable conclusion is that since the beginning of floating, the balance-of-payments (and reserve) equilibrium has shifted from the so-called basic balance sheet to the short-term capital account. This tendency becomes still more apparent if one quite properly sees the statistical "inconsistencies" of every balance of payments—its time spreads between lags and leads— as a not-included short-term capital transaction between firms and banks. Only what looks like a statistical fluke is the product of rational allocation. Since the professional financial players on

the international money and credit markets do not share the
exchange-rate illusions of their governments and central banks
but count on further depreciations and appreciations as well as
on the persistence of different inflation rates in hard- and soft-
currency countries, they "invent their own protection" against
fluctuations. Their calculations, like those of domestic investors,
savers, and trade unionists, from the very outset include a deflation rate of their capital investment in foreign currency: a real
exchange or retransfer rate.

But how is this done, and above all, where? The free international money and credit markets that have come to be known
as Euromarkets are nothing more than a stock market for currency valuations (regardless of whether "false" or "correct"),
and at the same time an insurance pool for currency risks. Their
option markets receive all offers for appreciation and depreciation of the currencies traded there and set an appreciation sur-
charge or discount, considered "real(istic)" by the respective
parties, for which every investor receives a reimbursement in
addition to the "normal" (cash) rate and interest. But this
swap-cost balancing is nothing but a new floating- and inflation-
validated real-exchange-rate system, which the Euromarkets
not only establish through valuation, but also finance by making available currency credits to the debtors—a process discussed
in greater detail in the following chapter.

The question that arises is: How real(istic) in fact are the
fixed rates arrived at in this way—validated by the exchange-rate
fluctuations and inflation rates expected by the market participants? They obviously can be correct only if the Euromarket
partners, who in the case of floating determine the value of all
currencies among themselves, have all the data bearing on the
determination of these values (until the next balance on current
accounts and also price and purchasing-power index) and also
enjoy identical voting rights and weight.

In fact, however, neither case is true. The international
money and credit market "freest" of all control is at the same
time the one farthest removed from all official information, as
well as the most unequal among partners. The growing exodus
to banking centers in Europe, Asia, and the Pacific and Caribbean
areas that in the past were the province of financial outsiders

and adventurers brought not only freedom from onerous controls, but also a growing estrangement between central and commercial banks. The undisputed market and price leadership of this market of unequal partners is exercised by a handful of U.S., European, and Japanese syndicates on whose flawed or correct judgment everything depends in the final analysis. With all due respect to these firms, most of whom also have to answer for the post-1929 crisis, the daily revaluations and new valuations of the currencies on the Euromarkets simply mirror the subjective expectations and oligopolistic and market structures of the voting members, not the objectively observed real purchasing power or nominal interest-rate disparities, which are largely unknown to the valuators. The float system, invented to help a currency valuation gain an international foothold free from domestic and foreign money illusions, resulted in a pernicious and equally dangerous self-deception—that a handful of private commercial banks by timely projection of real economic processes in practically the entire world, or at least in twenty-five of the most important Western industrial countries, could arrive at a comprehensive view of currency-exchange costs and "finance them away."

What actually happened was this: The Euromarkets bear the full responsibility for the uninterrupted flight of the sellers (exporters and importers) into price adjustments instead of quantitative adjustments; thus in one stroke they continued to finance world inflation and the growing disequilibrium of the balances on current accounts. They bear the full responsibility for the worldwide inflation and balance-of-payments disequilibrium and the intensified exchange-rate volatility—a vicious-circle effect. The insurance against currency risks and unforeseeable currency exchange costs in fact turns out to be a fire department which—for a fee—puts out the fires the carelessness of their governments allowed them to set. The Euromarkets also bear full responsibility for the intensification of the battle for better real terms-of-trade and real work income positions, which, since floating began, has also moved to the monetary front.

The way in which this process works can be shown by an actual example: In 1973 the OPEC nations, by exploiting their near monopoly on the crude oil market and raising their prices, improved their real terms of trade by nearly 400 percent, but they annually lose a portion of this advantage (albeit hard to quantify) to their customers, who skillfully manipulate their nominal rates of exchange. Every price-validated currency appreciation in the hard-currency countries reduces the real value of their oil imports, and every rate-of-exchange validated price increase in the soft-currency countries also reduces the real value of their oil imports. In the final analysis the OPEC states, as nominal world creditor, suffer annual losses of their money and asset investments in soft-currency countries and currencies, which they prefer to keep in U.S. dollars and Eurodollars. Since the OPEC states have to accept the exchange-rate and inflationary policy of their customers as a hard-to-estimate planning datum, their efforts to keep the real value of their oil prices and the consequent real terms-of-trade position from dropping below the 1973 level appears to be defensive rather than offensive. Of course, in order to maintain the position they won overnight in 1973, they would have to plan and succeed in keeping the nominal rate of their oil price increase independent of the simultaneous (and related) changes in the worldwide inflation and exchange rates of their clients, a squaring of world economic circular processes.

The dividing panel of the exchange rate has long since turned into a heating panel against which protection is needed just as it was needed against the earlier overheated domestic situation. If the dividing panel were abolished, neither the magnifying glass-house effects of external overheating nor the high internal temperature would present a problem, for in that event every domestic overdemand would (as in the old model of official, fixed exchange rates) cool off sooner rather than later because of the unavoidable consequent reserve loss. The early monetarists knew this. Walter Eucken, decades ahead of his epigones in his perception, left us with a highly practicable and realistic concept for mastering the crisis of the seventies, which, had we listened to him, would not have come about in the first place. Eucken had sketched the "minimal requirement" of a world monetary order appropriate to a market economy:

1. It must function automatically so as to prevent the central bank head from making arbitrary individual decisions based on changing perceptions.
2. The mechanism must be geared to the stabilization of exchange rates.
3. A powerful stabilizer designed to avoid deflation and inflation must be built into the mechanism.[6]

In other words, only the worldwide (not merely regional, as in the EMS) restoration of reliable currency parities can stop the drift toward an overdemand of international credits as well as currency-profit-sustaining and loss-inhibiting "hot" capital movements—the result of exchange-rate policy as well as of protective measures against currency speculation. Only then will "predictable" productivity and investment return patterns rather than unprovable expectations guide international capital transfers. Tying the unpredictable credit potential of the Eurobanks, which have degenerated into international mints (according to Eucken), to the real growth potential of a price-stable expanding world economy will contribute to the cure of worldwide inflation and balance-of-payments disequilibria by imposing international controls and restrictions on the money supply. Contrary to monetarist illusions, this does not happen by itself; it is the result of effective liquidity management, whether of cooperating central banks or of an IMF elevated to the rank of world central bank.

9

FACT AND FICTION
OF THE EUROMARKETS*

What Keynesianism does do and monetarism (of the Friedman and Hayek type) fails to do becomes clear when we apply
the M_1 and M_2 concepts of both to the international money and
credit markets (here referred to simply as Euromarkets). Keynes
(in Chapter 15 of the *General Theory*) differentiated between
that part of available money and credit needed for the payment
of real income processes, among which trade is included—
transaction drawer M_1—and the part needed for purely financial
purposes such as savings, investment, and speculation—speculative drawer M_2. The only error Keynes made, understandable
(and thus forgivable) in view of his time and circumstances, was
that he considered M_1, the part dependent on real national
income, real employment, and prices, as the determining factor; and of the always smaller M_2 he expected only easily correctable dislocations, under normal conditions in stock market
prices and nominal interest, and only in exceptional cases dislocations in prices, employment, and national income.

He wrote the *General Theory* at a time when the exception
became the rule, when a merely speculation-caused crisis that
began on the day of the New York stock market crash, October 24, 1929, spread concentrically and, helped along by wrong

*Nothing shows the illusion (as opposed to the reality) of the Euromarkets enter-
tained by theoreticians better than the collection of essays edited by Carl H. Stem,
John H. Makin, and Dennis E. Logue entitled *Eurocurrencies and the International
System*, published by the American Enterprise Institute for Public Policy Research,
Washington, D.C., in 1976. The elite of international monetary experts gathered
therein agree on hardly a single important question. See all the comprehensive
bibliography (pp. 377–413) of that collection.

countermeasures, degenerated into a real depression of prices, national income, and employment. Governments and central banks should learn from the *General Theory* to neutralize shifts between M_1 and M_2 (money and demand losses through over-speculation and oversaving) in time through an activist domestic deficit fiscal policy and a similarly active monetary policy before a new M_2-induced real crisis arises.

The developments at the modern Euro-, Asian, Pacific, and Caribbean dollar markets followed a totally different pattern. According to reliable estimates, 92 percent of their 1977 transactions were of a purely financial nature, and only 8 percent went to the financing of real world trade transactions. The international M_1 became the appendix of M_2. Speculation became the determining factor and income financing the incidental factor of international money and credit movements.

Why? What are the inevitable consequences of a dominating M_2 and a dominated over M_1? The triggering mechanism is the boundlessness of exchange-rate expectations (described in Chapter 2) and the concurrent ability of the international banking system to "protect" itself and its clients against them. Let us look more closely into how that is accomplished.

If the foreign (non-American) owner of a U.S. dollar claim or investment fears that the current (U.S. dollar) interest yield of his capital will diminish because of a future depreciation of the U.S. dollar vis-à-vis his country's currency, or perhaps even turn into negative interest (because he has to write off nominal capital losses), he will insure himself by contracting a Eurodollar debt together with his Eurodollar claim, which will enable him to balance the depreciation losses of his U.S. dollar capital against depreciation profits of his Eurodollar debts. This brings up two questions: First, why does he not use the same currency—U.S. dollars—for this method of balancing exchange-rate losses and profits instead of using the parallel Euromarket dollar? And second, what does this reinsurance against feared currency risks and depreciation losses cost?

The answers to both these questions are closely related: The Euromarkets are thought to be cheaper and more efficient than their competing national money and credit markets, and for obvious reasons. The national money and credit markets are con-

trolled: central banks fix the interest rates and refinancing costs
of "their" domestic commercial banks, and via their domestic
liquidity (minimum-reserve and open-market) policy regulate
the credit-creating multiplier. Central bank controls oversee
the surety of their banks through binding coverage guidelines
between capital, deposits, and outstanding credits. Regardless
of how valuable this protection is, it is always at the expense of
bank profits. The Eurobanks enjoy an inestimable advantage
over their national home offices and competitors in that for
them money and credit, like water and air, are essential ubiqui-
tous, free goods over which they exercise a supply monopoly.
Because their refinancing costs are not set by any national bank,
and because their credit-creating multipliers are not burdened
by any official solvency or liquidity conditions, they do not
have to share their credit heaven with anyone. A Eurodollar
credit is always cheaper than a U.S. dollar credit, a Euro DM
credit is always cheaper than a DM credit in the German Federal
Republic, thanks to the sublime freedom from all national obligations its producers enjoy—which is why they can point with
such pride to their financing efficiency. If in the long run things
should change, the world will not come to an end but the Euromarket very well may. That is why all dyed-in-the-wool Euro-
bankers fear nothing more than the day when they may be
forced to become more expensive than their national offshoots.
And therefore, as long as Eurodollar interest rates are lower
than U.S. dollar interest rates, all covering activities that restrict
the exchange-rate risk are carried out at the Euromarkets and
not at the domestic U.S. dollar and DM markets.

What is the cost of an exchange-rate insurance premium of
the Eurodollar market and what does it look like? The Eurodollar debtor, like any other debtor, must (1) pay running interest costs, and (2) offer his Eurobank something in return for
a feared possible U.S. dollar devaluation. His repayment rate at
the end of the Eurodollar credit term will be fixed at the Eurodollar (cash) rate at the time the credit is granted. He thus ac-
cepts an exchange-rate differential profit of his bank, which
protects him against such fluctuations.

His insurance premium against a decline in the U.S. dollar
rate is made up of two components: (a) a current Eurodollar

credit interest rate, which is always lower than its realizable
U.S. dollar interest rate; and (*b*) an exchange (or swap) loss
calculated by the bank at a discount rate, which is added on to
his Eurodollar credit interest rate.

How big can (*a* + *b*) be? Almost as big as the secret depreciation fears of the clients or owners of U.S. dollar claim. If they
anticipated a 30 percent depreciation of the U.S. dollar compared to their hard currency, a 29 percent insurance premium
would still leave them 1 percent ahead, even though they would
of course prefer a 5 or 10 percent spread. This demonstrates
two points. First, a completely subjective pessimism about U.S.
dollar depreciation (possibly encouraged by some money coun-
selors) determines the objective swap or insurance premiums,
not the other way around. What is missing is the fixed premium
that is customarily part of reputable insurance arrangements.
Second, the depreciation expectations of the U.S. dollar carry
over to the Eurodollar and also determine its exchange-rate
tendency. The (expected) depreciation rate of the Eurodollar
(*b*) follows the (expected) depreciation rate of the U.S. dollar.

This of course was part of the system of fixed exchange rates,
but with one important difference: As long as the exchange rate
of the U.S. dollar could fluctuate only within limits of its
present (or cash) markets (at a margin maintained by the central banks), the exchange-rate insurance premium (*a* + *b*) also
could rise and fall only within limits; it had an always predictable
top and bottom price—the exchange-rate fluctuation range at
the cash markets tolerated by the central banks minus the current difference between the interest rate earned by the national
U.S. dollar or DM investments and the rates to be paid by their
corresponding Eurocredits.

If we designate the maximum depreciation rate of the U.S.
dollar as *D*, and the U.S. investment interest rate as *i*, we arrive at this fixed price of the exchange-rate insurance premium
(*a* + *b*):

$$D - i = (a + b)$$
$$D = (a + b) + i$$
$$b = D - (i + a)$$

It would thus be possible to balance a let us say 5 percent estimated U.S. dollar depreciation expectation (D) either via $i > (a + b)$, or via an increase of $a + b$ to the level of $D - i$. That means that the insurance premium would always cost $D - i$. Its highest cost (if it remained constant) would thus amount to 5 percent; its lowest cost, if i increased by 5 percent, would amount to 0 percent. Even if the U.S. government refused to raise the domestic interest rate because of currency speculation, the rate insurance costs of the Eurodollar markets $(a + b)$ would almost by themselves balance the weak U.S. dollar rate, because both the rising Eurodollar interest rate (a) as well as the rising Eurodollar swap rate (b) would make speculation against the U.S. dollar uninteresting. If the difference in the interest rate between U.S. money investments (i) and Eurocredits of the same term (a) amounted to 2 percent, for example, the Eurodollar time rate (b)—expressed as a swap rate—would rise by 3 percent. A 3 percent weakening of the Eurodollar on the time markets would make any further speculation against the U.S. dollar on the cash markets superfluous. The exporters' and U.S. claim owners' interests in the safety of their dollar profits would thus have insured themselves against loss at a premium of 3 percent, and the importers and new buyers of claim titles interested in cheap dollars would, via the 3 percent decline of the Eurodollar (its deferment rate on the time markets), have reduced their acquisition costs by 3 percent compared to the U.S. dollar cash rates. Beyond this barrier no covering transaction between U.S. dollars and Eurodollars would pay. The depreciation expectations for the U.S. dollar at the Eurodollar (term) markets would thus come to a standstill for long periods of time.

Why was this possible in the past and not today? Is it because in the past the control by the central banks over how much cash-rate fluctuation in U.S. dollars was tolerable put a damper on speculation? Or because the Eurodollar markets allowed themselves or took greater freedom? Probably the latter: Before the institution of worldwide floating (1973) the Euro- and other dollar markets lived in principle from the difference in interest rates $(i \neq a)$. The covering transactions, on which the

Eurobanks made the swap costs ($a + b$) they charged their customers, were likewise an interest-bearing, not a speculative, business—a technical appendage of their real turnover financing. Consequently, the financing volume of the Euromarkets (beyond the question that had already arisen then over whether interest-rate advantages gained through the circumvention of national order were not simply monetary piracy) were about 90 percent M_1-motivated: the Euro M_1-financed real world trade and world-capital transaction volume. M_2-motivated covering transactions dominated only periodically in times of acute currency crises and exchange-rate adjustments (until the end of largely short-lived currency disorders), and incidentally were of a clearly defensive character, propelled by the desire and necessity of protection against threatening imminent currency losses.

All this, however, was destined to change fundamentally with the onset of floating. Why? Because it had now become interesting to make money on the diverging exchange-rate tendencies on both sides of the rate-insurance front. Formerly anyone who wanted to avoid depreciation losses had to pay his premium; there was little or nothing to gain. Even if ex post facto the depreciation turned out to have been bigger than the insurance premium paid, one had (defensively) avoided a greater loss, not made a speculative killing.

Things look different when not only available—that is, already earned real foreign-exchange—but also real not-yet-existing claims can be sold on term. If a Eurobank enjoying sublime freedom opens a Eurodollar credit line for the purchase of other, strong Eurocurrencies like the DM or Swiss franc, the sum (not only the balance) of depreciation and appreciation determines what premium is affordable. Assuming the U.S. dollar in the next three-month period is figured at $D = -5$ percent, and the DM at $D = +5$ percent, then up to 10 percent for $a + b$ is affordable and speculation is still risk-free.

But because in such a one-way speculation the time discounts for the U.S. dollar increase substantially, the time surcharges for the DM also increase substantially, perhaps even more substantially than those of the U.S. dollar deferments, and therefore the domestic interest rates i between the two currency areas would (to refract the exchange-rate expectations) diverge even more than 10 percent. The bill of the nominal interest rate spread made possible and necessitated by the Euromarkets and their credit-financed exchange-rate movement thus must always be paid by the domestic markets and the (nonmultinational) small and medium-sized enterprises dependent on domestic loan interest rates—the real victims of such a refracted credit market. Because floating enables the monetary speculators to recover their loan interest payments via exchange-rate and differential profits, the Euromarket not only raises exchange-rate risk but also the national interest-rate fluctuation risk for the small domestic investor and saver—something to which governments pay too little attention.

A look at Table 25 and Figure 6 bears out our contention that since floating began the Euromarkets have in fact financed

Table 25. World Liquidity and World Trade (in millions of U.S. dollars)

Year	Currency Reserves	U.S. Balance of Payments	Euro-Credit Volume	World Exports
1965	70,719	− 1,280	14,210	
1966	72,300	+ 219	18,330	
1967	74,053	− 3,418	24,850	
1968	76,928	+ 1,641	31,830	214,300
1969	78,214	+ 2,739	58,330	245,500
1970	89,472	− 9,840	78,250	282,100
1971	124,976	− 29,739	100,130	316,600
1972	117,907	− 10,313	131,840	367,200
1973	118,343	− 5,353	188,600	524,200
1974	146,110	− 8,821	214,120	773,400
1975	158,415	− 4,712	442,400	794,300
1976	182,105	− 10,470	548,090	907,000
1977	204,287	− 22,512	657,300	1,030,000
Reported:				
1965–1972		− 49,991	+ 119,620 = 1:2.4	
1973–1977		− 51,868	+ 525,460 = 1:10.1	

Sources: IMF, International Financial Statistics, Washington, D.C.; Bank for International Payments, Basel.

Figure 6. World Trade and Eurocredit Markets (1970 = 100, logarithmic index)

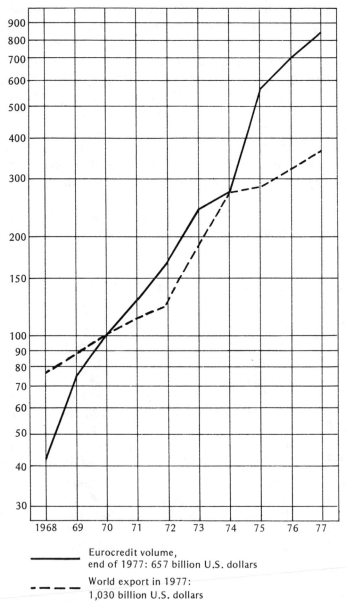

Eurocredit volume,
end of 1977: 657 billion U.S. dollars

World export in 1977:
1,030 billion U.S. dollars

Source: Figures for world export from IMF, International Financial Statistics, Washington, D.C.; for Eurocredit volume, from Bank for International Payments, Basel.

national exchange- and interest-rate disturbance and instability rather than real world trade and capital transactions. Both numerical values demonstrate clearly that since the beginning of floating the "financial" turnover rate (Eurocredits) have continued to increase more rapidly than the "real" turnover rate (world exports). Since 1974 nominal world exports increased by one-third (real exports by far less), while the Eurocredits rose threefold. These figures, better than all those more or less mythological bank models, clearly show that Euromarket self-financing is not only not declining but is on the increase.[1] But they also show that the once strict connection between the balance-of-payments deficit of the United States and the growth of these markets no longer exists. The assumptions by all the volume analysts of both the older and more recent schools about strict and constant relations between money base (i.e., U.S. balance-of-payments–contingent U.S. dollar drains) and Eurodollar credit increases no longer obtain. As Table 25 shows, the U.S. dollar drain due to current balance-of-payments deficits between 1965 and 1972 amounted to approximately 50 billion dollars, while new Eurocredits stood at approximately 120 billion dollars. Between 1973 and 1977 this relation went up, from a balance-of-payments deficit of 52 billion dollars to a Eurodollar credit creation in the 525 billion dollar range. The original relation of 1:2 of the sixties rose to 1:10 with a continuing strongly rising tendency.

The credit creation of the Euromarkets operating on the international scene thus emancipated itself from its source of primary dollar liquidity (from the United States). The federated system of the Euro-, Asian, Pacific, and Caribbean banks today works like an independent nineteenth-century private national or central bank system, which refinanced practically 100 percent of its credits through self-created bank deposits (interbank debts) and notes (certificates of deposit). This interbank system creates the previously described world financing framework that allows countries with balance-of-payments deficits to weather them and take their time about the necessary, painful adjustment. Thanks to this deficit-financing the surplus countries also can take their time; they can permanently export more as well as refrain from otherwise indispensable financing activities (capital exports). In other words, the credit-creating abilities of the free international money or credit markets preserve the reserves not only of the deficit countries but of the surplus countries as well. As to the deficit countries, they simply help them gain time, for they must repay their debts eventually. In the case of the surplus nations the flows remain a part of their reserve, for thanks to the Euromarkets they neither require as much monetary assistance as in the past nor do they have to finance capital exports out of their own reserves.

As Table 25 shows, the "official" reserves of all IMF members more than doubled between 1970 and 1977, from less than 93 billion dollars to more than 200 billion dollars, almost exclusively in foreign exchange (U.S. dollars) holdings, which more than tripled during that same period, from 45 billion dollars to more than 158 billion dollars. But even more important, the outstanding Eurocredit volume increased almost tenfold, from 78 billion to more than 657 billion dollars; both these amounts of international liquidity can legitimately be added, because they protect the reserves of both deficit and surplus countries.

The Euromarkets obviously have become a far more powerful inflationary mechanism than the Bretton Woods system in its late phase. If one compares the reserve growth of the sixties with that of the early seventies, the new inflationary mechanism shows a tenfold increase in the credit-creation multiplier. Moreover, this mechanism is no longer served by central banks that at least officially are not directly involved in purchasing. They allegedly still rely on the dividing effects of floating (however inconsistently they may handle it) and are literally blind to the inevitable inflationary consequences of the increase in reserves in surplus and deficit countries. Moreover, this permanent over-production of the alternative (or Euro) dollar and alternative reserves permanently finances its own slumps (in U.S. dollars) and booms (in strong Eurocurrencies)—ultimately because of the basically senseless, and for the United States dangerous, 1:1 relation between Eurodollars and U.S. dollars, which makes it possible for every self-legitimating currency valuation to percolate through to the U.S. dollar with the economic speed of light. Those who continue to insist that the United States is responsible for its own dollar weakness are only half right. For

it is not generally U.S. domestic overdemand or inflation that
sets off an oversupply of U.S. dollars, which depresses the free
U.S. dollar rate vis-à-vis other currencies, but an oversupply of
Eurodollars that depresses the U.S. dollar. What is right is that
the U.S. government is itself at fault for allowing this link by
the private banking sector between the U.S. and Eurodollar to
continue instead of cutting it.

Perhaps the President of the United States or his successor
will echo the sentiment voiced by Hjalmar Schacht in the
thirties, and the next time a European or Far Eastern visitor
complains about the weakness of the Eurodollar will say to
him: "Why are you telling me about the weak Euro or Asia
dollar? That's your dollar, not ours. Ours is the U.S. dollar, and
since it, like all normal currencies, is floating via-à-vis the Eurodollar, you as well as we ourselves can tell more readily how
much it is really worth."

Is Austria with its foreign debt perhaps a small link in the
chain between ex-territorial credit creation and the inflated
effective domestic demand? This question would have to be
answered affirmatively if the debtor country Austria (1) through
its credit demand would substantially affect the credit-creating
multiplier of the Euromarkets and their banks; (2) through its
use of credit would add to the potential for inflation, e.g., the
financing of export surpluses; and (3) were to combine its growing foreign debt with a policy of depreciation and soft-currency
instead of one of appreciation and hard currency.

*   *   *

The credit-creating multiplier of the Euromarkets does not
depend on individual credit demand but on the credit-creating
capacity available to, or rather retained by, all credit grantors.
But this capacity increases with the "courage" of the Eurobanks
for reciprocal refinancing assistance (the increase in interbank
debts), in which the lack of controls over these credit lines, and
if need be their restriction, accelerates the process. Economists
agree that credit demand can be curbed, but that credit curbs
can be effective only if the flow of credit is regulated as well.
Money supply, not money demand, points the way to the shrine

of stable money—one of the few issues on which monetarists and Keynesians agree. When Henry Thornton, the father of modern credit and banking theory, asserted before the House of Commons in the great bullion debate in 1811 that there could be no monetary stability without money and credit controls, he was laying the groundwork for Ricardo's subsequent currency principle, the very foundation of all modern central bank constitutions up to Milton Friedman's money supply: " 'The regulation of coin,' said Sir T. Rose, 'hath been left to the care of princes, who have ever been presumed to be the fathers of the commonwealth. Upon their honours they are debtors and warrantees of justice to the subject on that behalve.' "[2]

But what Thornton believed to be even more reliable than the "honor of the princes" was an official central bank that would regulate the credit creation of the commercial banks. However, even that was not enough for his disciple Ricardo. He did away with all discretionary powers of the managers by tying the issuing of money to a gold cover and the refinancing scope of commercial banks to stipulated covers. These firm binding regulations for central and commercial banks have fallen by the wayside and the efforts to formulate new ones still continue—a quest that finds all schools and directions of the otherwise warring economic fraternity united.

Eucken in his previously mentioned *Grundsätze* asked for a strict limitation of the national as well as international credit-creating scope of commercial banks. In his first draft of his Bretton Woods plan (August 9, 1941), Keynes already touched on the theme for the control of international liquidity and a fair (symmetrical) equalization of burdens of creditor and debtor nations. He attributed the recurring poverty, social unrest, war, and revolution in the world to the inability to solve the problem of the balance of payments between nations. Tracing history back 500 years, Keynes stated that only two periods of 50 years each saw money used effectively for foreign commerce: in the first of these periods (the second half of the sixteenth century) an unprecedented increase in the availability of silver from the New World transformed deflation into inflation; in the second of these periods (the second half of the nineteenth century), the system of international traffic of capital, administered from London, transferred the burden of conformity from the debtor to the creditor nations.

Had Keynes lived another ten years until 1956, he would have been able to cite a third, short-lived case of inflation-free balance-of-payments equilibration: the behavior of the United States during the first twelve years of the Bretton Woods system, prior to the creation of the Euromarkets. It, too, as a creditor nation financed the deficits of the debtor nations with reserves "borrowed" from other nations: capital exports like Marshall Plan assistance, Export-Import Bank credits, and private investments.

What Eucken asked for and Keynes so perceptively observed are two sides of the same coin: If the creditor nations refuse to finance their running export surplus out of their own savings, the result will either be periodic crises, which will break out in the deficit countries under deflationary pressure (Keynes's normal example of the last 500 years), or runaway, uncontrollable worldwide inflation, if unexpected money sources should open up (e.g., silver from the New World or, today, Eurocredits).

It is not surprising that Eucken and Keynes arrived at the same solution of the problem, since this is the only possible one: Only if Eucken's banks-turned-mints are prevented from swamping the real financing needs of an expanding world economy with their overproduction of liquidity can the producers of export surplus be induced out of self-interest to finance their surpluses themselves. This would eliminate all inflationary deficit-financing out of "additionally" created credits, and also all unfair overburdening of debtors. Export-surplus and savings-transfer magnitudes would remain stable—the gap between credit and savings will have been closed. Eucken saw this as a problem of the relentless mechanisms (goods-reserve-currency, 100 percent minimum reserve position), while Keynes considered it the task of international liquidity controls through the refinancing world central bank whose mission he outlined in his final Bretton Woods draft (April 1943):

> We need a *quantum* of international currency, which is neither determined in an unpredictable and irrelevant manner as, for example,

by the technical progress of the gold industry, nor subject to large variations depending on the gold reserve policies of individual countries; but is governed by the actual requirements of world commerce, and it is also capable of deliberate expansion and contraction to offset deflationary and inflationary tendencies in effective world demand.[3]

Regardless of whether one decides to go along with Eucken or Keynes or still more recent proposals, it all boils down to this: the boundless international credit-supply potential of the Euro and other foreign dollar markets must be restrained.

*   *   *

But what does the solution—or nonsolution—of the great world's monetary problems have to do with the position of a small debtor nation like Austria on the international money or credit markets? As was pointed out earlier, Austria has no influence on the amount and application of the credit-creating multiplier of these markets nor on the defective creditor policy of today's surplus nations. However, with its hard-currency policy not tainted by any surplus position, it shows that it is possible to use the inflated international capital market without becoming infected and without spreading the virus of inflation.

If, like other deficit countries, Austria had blindly depreciated (downward floating), it would long ago have come to the end of the rope of its effective domestic economic policy. It would have imported inflation instead of stability and thereby forfeited the real foundation of its foreign credits. Without access to real and financial foreign capital the external financing of a much needed domestic development and restructuring process would have had to be broken off midway. The firm insistence on a hard schilling on the part of Austria's responsible leaders deserves the credit not only for Austria's full employment without inflation, but also for its economic development and modernization. It may not be possible to tell just how many development failures the country has been spared by this policy, but on the basis of a comparison between Austria and other soft-currency countries, the answer would have to be quite a few.

Because Austria via its capital imports and reserve growth imported stability rather than inflation it of course could not export inflation. Since receipts and purchases—thanks to the rise in the schilling vis-à-vis the U.S. dollar—were calculated at domestic rates, which were far below the U.S. dollar-denominated world market prices, this portion of international credit creation did not intensify either objectively demonstrable or subjectively expected price thrusts. On the contrary, the foreign financiers acquired their schilling claims because they saw future stable profits rather than inflationary losses—neither domestic losses due to higher prices nor external losses due to currency depreciation (which, given its debt, would also be far too expensive for Austria). As a result, Austria's foreign debt offers the rare example of a stability-conforming loan.

Austria has shown the countries of the First and Third World how to pursue growth amidst crisis—how, despite worldwide inflation, to build up a debt that enhances stability at home and abroad. For that reason we will briefly examine the policy content of the Austrian model in the following chapters.

10

SOFT OR HARD CURRENCY? IS THERE A SUBSTITUTE FOR FISCAL POLICY?

No single assertion has sown greater confusion among students of economic policy than Jan Tinbergen's that rational economic policy can never realize more goals simultaneously than the policy methods or instruments available for that purpose.[1] This is basically so, but the Tinbergen theorem leaves open the question of whether, within groups of "given" goals and "given" instruments, there are not certain optimal combinations, that is, whether certain goals might not be achieved more easily with one instrument than with another.

Robert Mundell in a study prepared for the IMF demonstrated that the criterion of the principle of the smallest expenditure of energy also holds true for economic policy.[2] If two stability goals—one external (balance-of-payments equilibrium with free capital transfers and firm exchange rates) and one domestic (price stability with full employment)—are being pursued, and if economic policy has two instruments—monetary policy and budget policy—available for that purpose, the relationship between the two is optimal and depends on which of the two reacts most strongly (or most flexibly). Do liquidity and interest-rate variations emanating from monetary policy bear more strongly on price and employment than on balance-of-payment equilibrium? And where is the leverage effect of budget deficits and/or surpluses greater—at balance-of-payments equilibrium or at price and employment stability?

Mundell proved that fiscal policy "always" enjoys a natural superiority in the regulation of domestic demand, and monetary policy is superior in the creation of foreign trade balance. The expansion or narrowing of public demand via budget expansions or restrictions is always a precisely fixable partial sum of domestic economic aggregate demand, while the domestic credit built into real investments is determined by the expectation-contingent investment trend of business, which is far more dependent on the "auxiliary yardstick" of the interest rate. But in this context the short-term capital transactions, the determining factor in the balance-of-payments equilibrium, shows an exceptionally high response to the interest rate, higher than any domestic credit-demand factor. Consequently, it is more economical to put monetary policy at the service of the balance of payments, and budget policy at the service of employment and price stability. Mundell did not neglect to point to the underlying assumptions of the optimal combination worked out by him: the presence of fixed rather than variable exchange rates.

Basically, Mundell merely confirmed what Keynes found out in two stages of his march through the crisis of the thirties. In his *Treatise on Money* Keynes "discovered" the higher interest rate response of short-term foreign credit vis-à-vis the comparable domestic credit:

> This high degree of short-period mobility of international lending . . . means . . . that even a small and temporary divergence in the local rate of interest from the international rate may be dangerous. In this way adherence to an international standard tends to limit unduly the power of a central bank to deal with its own domestic situation so as to maintain internal stability and the optimum of employment.[3]

From here it is only a small step to the functional finance of his *General Theory* of 1935–1936, smaller than most Keynesians tend to think: If the instrument of monetary policy should fail, fiscal policy must close the gap if there is to be any employment policy at all.[4]

However, what role does the "fixed" exchange rate play in this connection? As we know from the analysis of the Euromarket in the preceding chapter, it insures the effectiveness of interest-rate arbitrage. The international credit flow follows the objectively calculable interest-rate level rather than the subjectively expected exchange rate only if the swap costs stay within the framework of the international interest-rate differences, and not (as in the unlimited exchange-rate expectations) burst through it.

The fixed exchange rate therefore is literally the Archimedean principle of an economic policy free of the conflicts between the goals of external and internal stability. An active domestic as well as foreign economic policy—i.e., a two-dimensional policy—is possible only with calculable, not incalculable, exchange rates: With the help of monetary policy (thanks to fixed exchange rates) balance-of-payments equilibrium (external payment ability or domestic economic liquidity) can be attained via interest-rate and debt adjustment (capital-account balance). Consequently, fiscal policy can be instrumental in creating the aggregate domestic demand needed to assure full employment and price stability.

If—and this is the crucial point—the demand should be out of kilter with the balance-of-payments equilibrium needed to insure domestic stability, if it is either too big or too small, the capital-account balance will close the gap. For example, if domestic demand due to full employment considerations should exceed the "self-earned" balance-of-payments framework (the balance on current accounts), capital must be imported. If, on the other hand, domestic demand due to stability considerations should lag behind the balance-of-payments scope (balance on current accounts surpluses), capital must be exported.

If all nations were to pursue an economic policy based on this policy mix of hard (because exchange-rate–stable) currency and budget-elastic (because it avoids demand deficits) domestic fiscal policy, growing (and restructuring) national economies could manage their conflicts between domestic goals (stable prices and full employment) and external goals (balance-of-payments financing). Above all, there could be no goal conflicts between the domestic objectives of internationally intertwined national economies, for if a worldwide balance-of-payments equilibrium were established via capital exports of the surplus nations and capital imports of the deficit nations no international trading partner would be forced into "unde-sirable adjustments." Deficit countries would not have to re-duce their demand and surplus countries would not have to inflate theirs. Currency depreciation or appreciation would become necessary only if a country either had forfeited its international credit (therefore having to depreciate), or no longer wished to export its real savings, perhaps because of essential restructuring (hence choosing to appreciate its currency).

The diagram on the left of Figure 7 shows the policy mix that is domestically autonomous while conforming to the re-quirements of the world economy, which essentially was the basis of a properly understood and properly implemented Bretton Woods system. In the IMF annual report for 1948 is this prescription for that system:

> It is not the intention of the rules regulating exchange rates to obligate the Fund to establish permanent rates of exchange that are out of touch with economic reality [p. 19]. . . . Stability and rigidity are not the same. The Fund never insisted on the retention of an exchange rate that was not in line with the economy of a country. On the contrary, it has always recognized that the adjustment of exchange rates makes up an important part of the measures needed to enable a country to pay for imported goods and services without

Figure 7. Coordination of Economic Policy Goals and Instruments

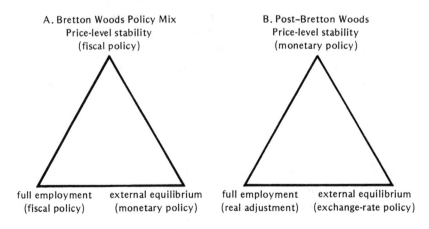

A. Bretton Woods Policy Mix
Price-level stability
(fiscal policy)

full employment   external equilibrium
(fiscal policy)   (monetary policy)

B. Post–Bretton Woods
Price-level stability
(monetary policy)

full employment   external equilibrium
(real adjustment)   (exchange-rate policy)

any untoward pressure on its monetary reserves. Stability includes
the idea that exchange-rate adjustments—should they become
necessary—are carried out in an orderly manner, avoiding all depreciation competition [p. 21].[5]

It is regrettable that a country like the German Federal
Republic, which was destined to play so vital a role in exchange-
rate policy, did not join the IMF until 1952, and that those
responsible for the unilateral and "illegal" cancellation in 1971
of Article IV, setting up these exchange-rate regulations and
adjustments, apparently never took the time to acquaint themselves with this important interpretation by the IMF of its pur
poses. They might have spared all concerned parties the float
excesses of the post-1973 era, the shoring-up of the disequilibrating and destabilizing international money and capital markets, and the no less dubious protectionism-inducing methods
of the regional floating blocks.

The change to floating not only destroyed the underlying
assumptions, nationally and internationally, of an economic
policy free of conflicts and contradictions, but also, as stated
earlier, its Archimedean principle. An economic policy unencumbered by external liquidity and exchange-rate commitments can shoulder the domestic task of securing price and full-
employment stability. When, in line with Tinbergen's theorem,
one problem (balance-of-payments equilibrium at fixed exchange
rates) is eliminated, a previously "tied" economic-policy instrument is freed, or more properly, becomes superfluous, and with
it the fiscal policy regulating domestic demand. Under favorable
circumstances it becomes the executive assistant or junior partner of a monetary policy whose natural (and by no means
purely ideological) interest is directed toward price stability
more than full employment or even essential economic restructuring. Monetary policy, except for historical traumas like the
two German superinflations produced by the profoundly irresponsible financing of two world wars, is always conserva-
tively drawn: It must put economic brakes on all the dynamics
that threaten money values. Therefore it was inherent in the
new role distribution that wherever monetary policy, freed of
its foreign entanglements, entered deeply into domestic trade,

stability was strengthened, but full employment and restructuring suffered, not only in the German Federal Republic but in all float countries, albeit to different degrees.

But what is the situation with regard to the economics of the internal and external policy mix, in which balance-of-payments equilibrium becomes a game of flexible exchange rates, and capital movements and monetary policy take on the main responsibility and burden for domestic price and employment stability while fiscal policy relaxes, i.e., more or less limits itself to the financing of public spending in the narrow (administrative) sense? (See the diagram at the right of Fig. 7.)

The new policy mix (whose techniques as practiced in the majority of Western industrial countries follows monetarist rather than fiscal directions) showed three diseconomies resulting out of inherent goal conflicts.

First, unavoidable internal friction exists between the achievement of stability and full employment. Since the changing of roles does not alter the tangible reaction and elasticity structures of an economy, and the greater rigidity of domestic investments observed and confirmed by Keynes, Mundell, and others in regard to financial incentives (greater money supply, low interest rates) compared to the highly reactive short-term foreign investments remains unchanged, the domestic monetary policy must resort to the big guns to achieve comparable results. That is true with regard to the efforts on the foreign scene, where interest-rate margins and time-rate (swap) changes were able to establish the desired balance-of-payments equilibrium, and it also is true with regard to the vanquished competitor fiscal policy, for fiscal policy changes domestic aggregate demand directly through cutbacks (budget surplus) or stockpiling (budget deficit), whereas monetary policy remains bound to the investable acceptance of its improved financing offers, a not inconsequential difference as regards the efficiency and inefficiency of anticyclical regulation of demand.

The political overdemand on fiscal policy by too high and too rigid welfare expenditures thus faces an "instrumental" overdemand of the politically less committed monetary policy because monetary policy does not possess the weapons to break through a profound investment lethargy or to eliminate overblown investment risks. It may be possible to do something about politically conditioned budget rigidities, but nothing can be done against instrumental rigidities. The only power monetary policy possesses is its braking effect. It can refract every upswing through monetary drying out—a skill which has been demonstrated repeatedly in modern times—while others (entrepreneurs or politicians but never the central bank responsible for the overkill) foot the bill.

Thus in the role distribution the domestic surplus monetary policy injects an antigrowth and antiemployment (deflationary) bias into the internal economic process whose intention may be altogether nonideological, yet it does not rule out ulterior political motives on the part of a central bank responsible neither to the government nor to the legislature.

Second, unavoidable frictions exist between external balance of payments and domestic demand. In the new policy mix, balance-of-payments equilibrium is the result of fluctuating exchange rates, not of capital movement. But what happens when the process does not function, for the reasons discussed in Chapters 7, 8, and 9, or rather, functions entirely differently than the model suggests?

We have already demonstrated that the policies of soft-currency countries that seek to equalize inflated domestic demand in relation to the balance of payments by permanent depreciation are based on exchange-rate illusions that have long since been discarded by almost everyone, certainly by all professional players on the international money and credit markets. Consequently, as in the case of fixed exchange rates, countries that in the course of time gamble away their foreign credit, which becomes dearer with each depreciation until it dries up altogether, have no choice after reaching the end of their road but to obey the "mandate of the balance of payments" (according to Von Böhm-Bawerk) and make the too-long-delayed painful adjustment: curb production, with all the attendant dangers to political stability.

What happens in the (surplus) hard-currency countries that manage their goal conflict between a still free margin of increasing domestic demand—measured against the balance-of-payments possibilities—by pegging their appreciation rate to that of world inflation so as not to forfeit their competitive position, and more important still, to avoid domestic export substitution? They destroy the symmetry of the adjustment process. Since the perpetuated appreciation expectations rule out the achievement of balance-of-payments equilibrium (via net capital exports) or reduction of balance on current accounts surpluses (via internal restructuring), the rest of the world is compelled to cope with declining domestic and foreign demand, with all the retortion measures brought on by this declaration of trade war.

Third, frictions exist between domestic goals and the goals of other partners—exported forced adjustments. Because surplus and hard-currency countries either cannot readily change traditional demand and production structures in the short run (for example, the OPEC countries), or do not wish to do so in the long run (for example, the German Federal Republic), they tell their trading partners what they must do at home. They misuse their balance-of-payments surplus in the sense of an *économie dominante* (according to François Perroux), or "in order to behave like a major power . . . an advantage one does not readily give up."[6]

Those who have the good fortune to live next door to these nonadjusting countries may join into a zone of regional monetary stability around the strong appreciation and reserve power, which guarantees to that power a domestic market free of destabilizing appreciating trends, i.e., transforming uncertain foreign demand into certain domestic demand while sparing its neighbors the necessity of importing inflation via the more expensive goods of the strong power. Those who have the bad luck to live too far away, in other parts of the world—which means most of the developing countries—have to make the best of their very restricted balance-of-payments scope. Since most of them no longer have any reserves to lose, the only losses they can still suffer are in growth, employment, and development.

Even though all this is known and demonstrably true, the policy makers of the surplus and hard-currency country exporters of forced adjustment maintain that the international economic crisis is imported, without however specifying from where. It is hard to say whether they really believe that they play no part in the deficits of others or whether they merely want to deflect attention from their responsibility.

The outcome of all this is that whatever regional block-building around determined surplus nations we look at—whether the OPEC block around the nucleus of oil-producing powers in the Arab Monetary Fund, or the IMF initiatives of the German Federal Republic and France—economically speaking they are simply a continuation of policies previously pursued by these central powers on the higher, more effective regional plane, not an attempt to conserve existing structures—a continuation of the tariff and agrarian protectionism via a domestic monetary policy of forced spatial adjustments.

If financing problems sooner or later force soft-currency countries into a self-blockade of autonomous or surplus economic policy, and if the domestic-deficit hard-currency policy practiced by West Germany leads to national or even regional trade wars, then the Austrian model, a combination of hard-currency and domestic surplus rather than deficit economic policy, avoids both the above results.

11

A WORLD MONETARY SYSTEM WITHIN ONE COUNTRY: THE AUSTRIAN MODEL

The outlines of Austrian economic policy of the seventies emerge more clearly against the (unfortunately real) background of conflicting economic policy principles and methods. Austria was one of the few Western industrial countries that did not experiment with these new international economic models. Despite the step-by-step dismantling of the old Bretton Woods system of stable but flexible exchange rates, Austria retained the old policy mix and merely changed the parity yardsticks and intervention basis of its exchange-rate commitments: the downward-floating U.S. dollar was replaced by an indicator of the trade and hard currencies most crucial to Austria. Since 1971 the schilling/DM relation of approximately 7:1 has remained comparatively stable, and, in tandem with the DM, the schilling's upward float has remained within a marginal range of less than 3 percent.

This gives rise to two questions: Why? And how has this affected Austria's economic development? Exchange-rate unions are usually formed to protect export markets. True, after the schilling changed from the U.S. dollar to the DM tie, Austrian export markets expanded, from a scant 5 percent of the U.S. and Canadian market to some 25 percent of the West German market. But this could hardly have been the overwhelming motive of Austrian policy, for had the schilling/dollar tie been preserved, given the continuing depreciation of the dollar, Austria would have been assured a far greater nominal market in all hard-currency countries, especially if one operates on the assumption of most soft-currency countries that in the

161

early float stages sellers (exporters) and buyers (importers) suffer from exchange-rate illusions. Austria could have improved its international trade position in U.S. dollar prices in the amount of the U.S. dollar depreciation rate at the same or slightly falling schilling prices of its exported goods and services and, like the German Federal Republic, have relied on export-led growth. Instead, Austria chose to strengthen its domestic (investment- and consumption-led) growth component. The reasons for that are quite obvious without a search for political motives.

First, like all industrial nations that depend on imported energy and raw materials, Austria after the oil shock had to be prepared for drastic shortfalls in domestic demand, both nominal and real. The higher oil bills, which led to less favorable terms of trade, had to be paid for with domestic real demand. The only question was whether they had to be paid now or later. "Now" would have meant rigorous internal savings programs (i.e., a cutback in investments as well as consumption), a savings policy geared to the preservation of what there was, not to the financing of future growth, investments, and jobs. "Later," on the other hand, would have meant raising the real transfer for the more expensive oil from a higher social or national product, hence less growth- and productivity-inhibiting.

Second, the oil shock hit Austria not, as it did most of the Western industrial nations, at the end of a catching-up and making-up process but midway; in 1973 Austria's real income was still substantially below that of the other industrial OECD and EEC countries. Paying cash for oil out of ad hoc forced export surpluses would have perpetuated this condition for some time to come.

Third, the question often asked by Austrian economists whether the policy tying the schilling to the DM was necessary to curb the wage demands of the unions can be dismissed as insignificant. It is not an established fact that a soft-currency policy (depreciation) results in higher wages, nor would that have been a determining factor. If, for example, the nominal competitive advantages of a permanent schilling depreciation had been absorbed permanently through "excessive" nominal wage demands, the unavoidable crisis would have forced a real adjustment of wage incomes. But there is no reason to believe that the Austrian trade union economists were unaware of this link between wages and jobs. Thus if the government started from the assumption that reason rather than unreason reigned among the architects of wage policy it did not have to base its hard-currency policy on that consideration.

The deeper reason for the continuation of the schilling/DM tie is connected with Austria's domestic development and situation. Being a young industrial country Austria had to give careful consideration to how and by what means it could sustain the tempo of domestic growth amidst the crisis, whether through full-employment–based export surpluses or through a policy of expanding productive capacity (capital stock) and domestic real income and savings potential. Whichever choice it made (export growth or expansion of domestic industry), Austria could never count on domestic financing. It always had to plan on long-range balance on current accounts deficits (import surplus) and commit itself to largely foreign refinancing (protecting the gross reserves) of this deficit (capital imports).

This forced equilibration of the unavoidable balance on current accounts deficit through foreign capital more than anything else determined the roles assigned to the various policy instruments. The decision to keep monetary and interest-rate policy tied to the goals of external equilibrium and stability was dictated by the need for preserving Austria's credit worthiness. Consequently, the only approach that was open was a fiscal policy that pegged domestic aggregate demand to the goal of full employment and growth.

Did the Austrian planners in 1971 and 1973 foresee the steady upward movement of a schilling tied to the DM? If they did, their basic commitment to a fixed rather than a variable rate of exchange, and their choice of a monetary and interest-rate policy tilted toward a balance of payments, or rather capital balance, would from the very outset have contained a margin for measured accelerated growth: the higher the schilling climbs, the greater the scope for a price-neutral expansion of domestic demand. If, as seems more likely, the upward trend of the DM and schilling was not fully anticipated, this latitude kept on being rediscovered and used, which also did no harm to the quality of the policy.

Whatever the case may be, the sustenance of domestic catching-up and growth required foreign capital to finance the import surplus without having to draw upon the reserves, and at the same time made possible a balance on current accounts and budget deficit; the causality of these two deficits was historically, not analytically, predetermined—initially the oil shock increased only the balance on current accounts and terms of trade deficits. But the inevitable transfer of real income and real demand to pay for the higher oil bills necessarily led to a decline in domestic demand. This in turn compelled the supporting expansive budget policy to sustain the catching-up momentum.

The causality grows out of the tangible objective connections. Because of its balance on current accounts deficit Austria was able to build up its domestic growth rate only to the extent that it fell back on additional foreign resources: tangible goods and services needed at home to continue its investments and to shore up consumption without inflationary foreign-exchange costs. Those who say that the domestic overconsumption of investment and consumer goods was solely responsible for Austria's balance on current accounts deficit ignore the fact that without the foreign loans Austria could not have afforded the import surplus that accelerated its growth. Austria's foreign credit framework determined the size of its balance on current accounts deficit and its domestic demand—not the reverse. And these foreign credits were generous enough to cover the foreign exchange requirements induced by the increased consumption of imports in step with the rising incomes. Had it been otherwise the "excessive" consumption would first have depleted all the country's reserves and then inflated prices, and the domestic boom would have dissipated because of balance-of-payments problems and inflation.

The foreign-financed import surplus thus had both a quantitative and competitive effect. The more plentiful and less expensive the unfinished and finished goods being offered on the domestic markets, thanks to the continuing DM/schilling appreciation, the more restrictive the effect on price, cost, and profit movements of domestic goods. The schilling prices, above all for finished goods in direct competition with imports, adjusted to the limits set by the DM prices: Austria imported DM stability. Thus in its domestic stability policy Austria—via the schilling tie to the DM—adjusted to the international low price and cost level of the German Federal Republic, yet it continued its autonomous fiscal policy to promote its domestic development goals: flexibility on internal matters limited only by the size of its foreign debt.

Despite (or perhaps because of) this linkage to its foreign credit the country achieved an almost ideal combination of Phillips curve values: high employment coupled with a very low rate of inflation and full financing of its balance on current accounts deficit, which protected the monetary reserves. This in turn created the tangible and financial basis for accelerating domestic growth, due above all to the use of a Bretton Woods type of policy mix—a policy that existed as though there still was an international monetary system with fixed exchange rates and an effective international price, cost, and financing network.

This gives rise to three important questions:

1. Is the policy of imported stability an "Austrian" or "German" achievement? Would it have been possible without the permanent DM appreciation?
2. How long can this policy of balance on current accounts and budget deficits continue—will it not sooner or later run up against the barrier of the ever-present foreign debt?
3. Can every international trading nation, regardless of size, in principle pursue a policy of this type of exchange-rate dependence?

The answer to the first question is relatively simple. The dependence on a "vital" currency, like the dollar in the past and the DM today, is basically symbolic, and at best a technical facilitation of the intervention mechanism, i.e., the Austrian National Bank. A hard-currency policy does not necessarily have to be tied to a neighboring vital currency. On the contrary, much is to be said for cutting the tie to the DM at some future time, not as much for reasons of prestige or fear that the schilling will be dismissed as a mere satellite currency of the DM, as for a desire to become free, or freer, of possible unexpected developments of the DM and the predictable and unpredictable

factors of its valuation. An exchange-rate union, particularly
one with a vital, and hence politically manipulated, index currency, calls for a close voting and coordinating relationship
between partners whose unity is always endangered by divergent
and, in the case of Austria, unnecessary national interests and
goals (see the complex problems of the former Euro-coil and of
the IMF).

By contrast, the tie to a "dead" (or abstract) index and reserve monetary unit (such as gold or special drawing rights)
would have the invaluable advantage of a politically independent
adjustment to a "reserve currency country." It was the fatal
miscalculation of the champions of floating to think that it
is possible to organize a market exchange (and equalization) in
an international market and price union without a common
denominator (or *numéraire*). Since the prices of currencies are
comparable among and with themselves only when one of them
becomes the official *numéraire*—or is promoted to that position
by the market—there always exists an $n - 1$ "reserve currency"
condemned to its own exchange-rate neutrality, regardless of
whether it sees itself in that role or not.

In the case of the gold standard this helpful role is played
by the pound sterling, because the gold price indispensible to
the parity determination of all other currencies was expressed
in pound sterling, and from 1815 to 1914 remained an almost
metric constant: £3/17s/9d per ounce. This allowed all currencies to fix "their" gold content in units of equal value (gram or
ounce). In the Bretton Woods system the U.S. dollar was the
only $n - 1$ currency (n = number of world currencies), at any
rate as long as it maintained its firm price in relation to gold.
Consequently, the breaking open of the gold market on March 19,
1969, not the subsequent official termination of the gold convertibility of the U.S. dollar on August 15, 1971, spelled the
beginning of floating and the attempt to manage without a
numéraire in our economic world community.

But as things turned out, for both logical and practical reasons such a system of competing monetary and price valuations
does not work. In the absence of a common denominator, given
today's n = 150 world currencies, there now exist 150(149)
$\div$ 2 = 11,175 exchange rates, which moreover fluctuate daily—

a telephone directory whose listings have to be revised daily. Concerned with keeping an overview of the valuations, the markets decided to let the U.S. dollar continue in its old function even after its official withdrawal as a gold-backed currency. For 149 dollar-denominated rates are still easier to handle than 11,175 separate rates. However, none of the 149 U.S. dollar users now has any assurance that the world banker supplying U.S. and Eurodollars (who as we have seen has become a dual entity) will not supply more than is demanded, maintaining his balance-of-payments disequilibrium as a minus balance today and perhaps a plus balance tomorrow.

The same redundancy problem, beyond all conflicts about a common agricultural policy, also blocks the (in this respect also unplanned) EMS. Unless the DM, as the strongest European currency, takes on the role of $n - 1$ (reserve) currency within the EMS and establishes a firm currency tie and conversion obligation, the monetary union will remain a private Eurodollar union with all the instabilities and inflationary pressures outlined in Chapter 9. A monetary union, regardless of whether worldwide or regional, must find a solution to the redundancy problem. Either a world banker or a group of superregional bankers relinquishes the "national right to inflation" (which, as we know, yields no "real" profit) and thus makes it possible for all members of the system to achieve an orderly balance of payments and financing of domestic development, or the market (in this case the Euromarket) will create a most unsatisfactory substitute. The liquidity and financing readiness of the world or superregional banker determines the scope for expansion of the remaining $n - 1$ partners, regardless of whether the supplier of final liquidity is a country, an exterritorial money or credit market, or a completely new supranational institute—a central world bank.[1]

Austria represents the only other alternative to the ultimately inevitable and necessary orderly and stable "monetarist" group solutions: If neither a world banker (simply another term for an international monetary system with its own *numéraire*) nor a functioning EMS (simply another term for an exchange-rate union embracing all sectors of a region, including agriculture) seems a likely possibility, there remains only the use of the available world liquidity reservoir and financing capability in a disciplined policy oriented toward the achievement of internal and external stability.

By taking up the many international loans in the essentially unstable Euromarkets that it needs for the price-neutral re-financing of its domestic programs, Austria provides the yard-stick for a rational and also "second-best" solution. Tying the exchange rate of the schilling to an already existing "neutral" (i.e., outside of official control) *numéraire* of the IMF—or, should the improbable become probable, the EMS—would undoubtedly be an improvement over this second-best solution. All these could serve the same function as the DM tie and would be better than the indicator of the Austrian National Bank known only to itself; the units known to and used by other monetary agencies would allow clear comparisons and constitute a true test of the schilling's hardness. At the same time, by breaking its DM tie and joining up with a group indicator, the schilling would gain a greater measure of international liquidity— not only because of its greater comparability but also because of its greater shiftability—without therefore having to give up the advantages of the DM-induced imported stability.

The second question can be answered affirmatively after a thorough analysis of the debt-liquidation processes built into the Austrian model (Chapter 6). The crucial point is this: the double-deficit policy of the public household and balance of payments cannot be continued forever, not because it cannot be financed but because it is not necessary. Once the built-up, rejuvenated capital stock has achieved the productivity and restructuring goals, it will automatically rectify the existing domestic and foreign debt. In addition, there is the flexibility offered by a priority-conscious fiscal policy whose planning objectives simultaneously determine its spending elasticity and rigidity, should that have crept in.

There is, however, one indispensible, essential condition: the synchronization of domestic tariffs and foreign transfers. The budget's financing of the debt service in schillings must be brought in balance with the effective repayment in foreign exchange. Why? Because domestic budget surpluses strengthen foreign transferability and thus stimulate the development of

balance on current accounts and capital balance surpluses—
a rule of fiscal policy strengthened further by the built-in
mechanism of the reversal of the debtor and creditor position.

The answer to question three, whether Austria's policy mix
combining hard currency and dual deficit can be generalized in
the sense of a Kantian imperative, i.e., be made applicable to
the conditions of other economies, has been given in the preceding two chapters as well as earlier in this chapter. If we get rid
of all "internal" money illusions, if income and profit are calculated and used only in real, not nominal, terms, the famous
Phillips curve (which measures the trade-off between the desired
rates of employment and unemployment and the consequent
rate of inflation) will become the Phillips line showing the hard
(and structural) core of unemployment that cannot be eliminated
either by a little more (or less) inflation or a little more (or
less) nominal aggregate demand, but only by an increase in real
demand or real growth—shorthand for an economic surplus
policy that guarantees full employment (see Figures 8 and 9).

The Phillips line (properly, not monetarily interpreted) therefore tells a government how much real growth it must create in
order to utilize the nation's labor potential. In this context
countries with too high a level of monopoly may have to change
from an income policy to a labor-market, or more properly a
job-market, policy—a problem that is not likely to arise in
Austria for some time, but that surfaced in West Germany a
long time ago.[2] Once "external" money or exchange-rate illusions have faded away, and depreciation and appreciation cease
to be substitutes for policy or cease to be used as weapons in
the war for better terms of trade, it will be possible to arrive at
a prompt agreement on realistic and stable exchange rates, for
in that event the renunciation of the "advantages" of floating
will be meaningless, except perhaps as a farewell gesture to the
discarding of an illusion.

If the members of the European or IMF monetary family
would conduct themselves in the "Austrian" manner and voluntarily adhere to their contractually and institutionally regulated
exchange-rate commitments, with possibly slight modification,
they not only would not be giving anything away but would all
gain something: a new voluntary international code of behavior

Figure 8. General Case of the Phillips Curve

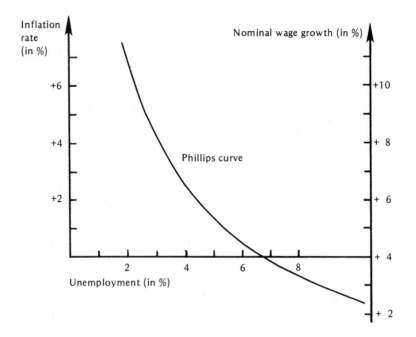

Figure 9. Phillips Line: Limiting Case of the Phillips Curve with Income and Profit in Real Terms Only

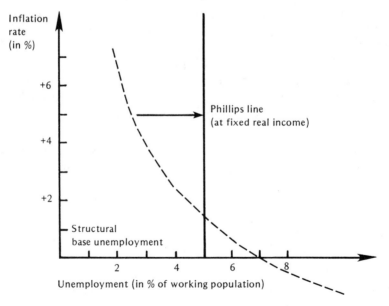

with minimal exchange-rate disturbances and far greater possibilities of solving problems of foreign balance of payments and
domestic development through long-term stable international
capital transactions. The world economy would once more
become what it was meant to be—a peaceful system of orderly
trade and monetary relations that eventually might even develop
its own international monetary system free from today's—and
tomorrow's—disruptive liquidity overproduction.

For the time being the difficult question of how much
supranational supervision and refinancing such a system of good
international economic behavior needs can be put aside. That
the giving up of needless national monetary sovereignty only
means giving up an illusion, not a real sacrifice, is obviously
something that experience still has to teach us. What the Austrian
model can teach the economic leaders of the world—and this
would not be the worst lesson—is that the renunciation of "free-
doms," "autonomies," and "jurisdictions" that in fact no longer
exist can be the beginning of an order that works all the better
the more the participants realize the advantages this brings
them. What the mininational economy of Austria—peripheral
in terms of international economic affairs—has gained by its
policy, maxinational economies can certainly gain for themselves if they re-establish their balance on current accounts
equilibrium through stable (or more stable) international exchange rates. This stability can exist regionally via interest-rate-
induced rather than expectation-induced capital transactions,
which would once more have predictable and balancing instead
of destructive effects. By this appropriation of monetary policy
for the creation of external equilibrium they can also "redis-
cover" their fiscal policy as a central factor of domestic demand
allocation and distribution.

PART 3

SUMMARY, RESULTS, AND CONCLUSIONS

One must choose between putting one's trust in the stability of gold or the decency and intelligence of governments. With all due respect to these gentlemen —I recommend gold.

—George Bernard Shaw

The following points summarize the results and conclusions arrived at in the preceding chapters.

1. To date, Austria has come through the world economic crisis of the seventies better than almost any other Western (or Eastern) industrial nation. Whatever yardstick is used—economic growth, employment, price stability, social peace, technological and industrial advance—the combination and sum total of the achievement are compelling. Both the overseers and critics of the free, social market economy must realize that this success was achieved without any concession to one of the evils of our time: the sacrifice of principles of a free-price—not intervention-guided—economy when internal problems of unemployment or external problems of balance-of-payments deficits arise.

Like all Western industrial countries since the escalation of the world economic crisis that began with the dismantling of the Bretton Woods monetary system and the OPEC price offensive of 1973, Austria had to contend with considerable balance-of-payments and employment problems. Because it is a small and landlocked country at the periphery of the international economic order, this crisis hit Austria harder than its neighbors and competitors with large domestic markets or trade hinterlands. Yet Austria has resisted both the temptation of the inflationary financing of full employment and the protectionist balance-of-payments equilibration.

2. Austria has refrained from availing itself of the so-called advantages of floating, nor has it joined the official regional

zones of protection (which in Europe serve as a protection against the outside rather than the cause of internal integration). Therefore Austria has resisted two widespread and dangerous nationalist illusions of the big industrial nations that have colored the world economic climate: the monetarist notion that disengagement from the international price and exchange-rate connection (floating) opens up new and greater possibilities for domestic employment and stability, and the protectionist idea that in our world economy it is possible to discriminate against others (and this includes the European refracted exchange rates— subsidized at home, floating outside the country) and still hold on to the advantages of a free world market (in which the others will tolerate anything).

On the international economic scene Austria acted like a soft-currency country by financing its balance on current accounts deficits (import surplus) out of foreign credits (capital imports), while at home it behaved like a hard-currency country by not letting the exchange rate of its currency depreciate; instead it stabilized it. That allowed Austria to import monetary stability as well as real development potential, and to finance the greater part of its domestic catching-up and modernization and the demand that guarantees full employment out of transferred foreign savings. This policy mix spared Austria and its trading partners painful and socially explosive shrinkages of domestic demand, employment, and prosperity.

3. Austria's prosperity amidst the energy crisis thus rests primarily on its economic policy adjustments. Like no other Western industrial country, Austria in the seventies, operating under changed international economic conditions, was able to achieve traditional policy goals (continued growth, job security, money value stability) through a new combination of policy instruments. Being free of the economic policy illusions described earlier, Austria's policy makers, in responding to the post-1973 decline in worldwide demand, decided on a course of domestic demand or budget adjustments rather than on one of foreign-exchange-rate adjustments.

The domestic demand lost to foreign countries as a result of the OPEC surpluses was compensated for at home, and consequently the demand deficit created by the real transfer of the dearer oil imports did not set off a production and job-destroying (deflationary) adjustment process. It thus seems fair to say that Austria's foreign balance deficit, together with its appreciating hard-currency surplus policy, explains and determines the nominal and real scope of its domestic surplus fiscal policy, not vice versa.

Through this policy mix Austria gave additional flexibility to its domestic-surplus policy. Also, because the continuing import glut (the prices of imports fell even more because of the higher rate of the Austrian schilling vis-à-vis the U.S. dollar) exerted permanent pressure on the domestic schilling prices, and because the income policy of the autonomous social partners was not seriously affected by inflation-caused and -exacerbated wage and income-distribution conflicts, fiscal policy was able to focus on growth and full employment instead of becoming bogged down by problems of inflation and conflicts about the distribution of wealth.

Austria developed a model of appropriate international economic behavior that should serve as a yardstick for industrial latecomers and developing countries alike. It not only refrained from any export offensives à la West Germany that were likely to stunt the growth opportunities of its trading partners, but in effect it used the crisis to close its investment and consumption gap. If Austria were a maxieconomy with its own big geographic area or hinterland and possessed more international economic clout, it might have been able to prove that individual engines with greater motive power are in an eminently better position to get the train of Western economic activity moving more rapidly.

4. After the dismantling of the Bretton Woods system Austria's economic policy continued to behave as though a functioning world order still existed. Its economic policy makers early on saw that the real threat posed by the oil offensive was not the higher cost of this most important of all energy sources but the changes in the international real income and real demand structure triggered by the improved terms of trade of the OPEC nations. Because they were much too "poor" to use

up their export surpluses over the short run, i.e., to transform
them into imports, they "lost" the real income flowing to them
from the industrial nations. The reinvestment of the unused
Petrodollars on the Euromarkets (recycling) was bound to raise
the nominal world financing and debt volume—not, however, the
real and effective world demand for goods and services. Consequently, the only choice left to the Western industrial countries
whose demand and terms of trade had been hurt after 1973
was either to compensate for these oil-price-induced losses on
the world market through still more exports and/or currency
appreciation, or to compensate for the losses on the domestic
market by accepting the (exogenous) deficit trend of the
balance on current accounts and the attendant decline in demand by stimulating domestic demand through budget deficits.

The German Federal Republic decided on the first alternative:
to force export surpluses and currency appreciation. The success
of this policy depended on keeping the appreciation rate of
the DM below the external (world) inflation rate, so that the
advantages of the better terms of trade could be reaped without
impairment of its foreign trade competitive edge. Austria
decided on the same course or, rather, on a combination of
the two. Letting the schilling appreciate together with the DM
and the other hard currencies gave Austria the same terms-of-
trade advantage as West Germany and safeguarded its foreign
trade position, but by encouraging domestic demand, something
West Germany failed to do, it gained the additional crucial
advantage of accelerated economic growth and continued full
employment. The German Federal Republic sought to maintain
full employment largely via a policy of export-related growth,
in which undesirable inflationary consequences of its foreign
surplus policy are counteracted by a hard policy of monetary
and fiscal stabilization.

Since the intensification of the world economic crisis, Austria,
on the other hand, has pursued a foreign-deficit, appreciation-
oriented, hard-currency policy, combined with a domestic-
surplus fiscal policy committed to internal growth and full
employment. The monetary policy (as in the old Bretton Woods
system) is oriented toward the external goal of balance-of-
payments equilibrium; it therefore cannot, as happens in almost

all other float countries, "interfere" in the domestic process with money-amount contingencies and the manipulation of interest rates in accord with the dictates of investment policy. This automatically compels fiscal policy to protect and finance domestic growth and full employment, with fiscal debt management regulating the domestic process not only in terms of demand but also of liquidity. The demand thrusts define the size of the effective domestic budget deficit and its allocation between domestic and foreign refinancing, as well as the most important signposts of domestic money supply—namely money supply deflected by the gross reserve position of the central bank (and in this respect contingent on the balance of payments and the budget, not on the central bank)—and the also largely budget-contingent domestic money demand. The two jointly determine the overall economic financing climate—credit conditions and interest-rate trends.

This role distribution rules out the sort of counterproductive goal conflicts typical of the German Federal Republic—conflicts between domestic employment and price equilibrium as well as the foreign balance-of-payments goals of the other world (economic) partners. For Austria's balance on current accounts equilibration by way of capital imports instead of intensified price and cost competition on the world markets does not threaten the domestic and external equilibrium and stability of any of its partners. In the Austrian policy mix, monetary policy (in line with the John Maynard Keynes of the thirties) remains the junior partner of a fiscal policy oriented toward growth and full employment, and is not, as in West Germany, downgraded to a junior partnership in a monetary policy oriented toward the stabilization of money value.

5. How "responsible" is this dual policy of balance of payments and budget deficits? Its critics (most of them are found in Austria, not in other countries) are more or less blind to two debt-liquidation regulators built into the development process itself: the real productivity effects and the occasionally no less significant financial savings and liquidity effects of the expansion and rejuvenation of the primarily industrial capital stock.

The growing cost-favorable production potential leads to

expectations of an already visible tendency toward the improvement of the (at least industrial) balance on current accounts:
to all effects and purposes the technological gap between Austria
and the EEC and European OECD industrial nations has been
closed. But more important still are the savings and liquidity
effects of the youthful capital stock. In the event of future presumably falling real reinvestment quotas, and conversely, rising
rather than falling financial write-off quotas of Austrian industry,
its cash flow is certain to improve (in the amount of the already
earned write-offs available as liquidity). This not immediately
investable real capital is available as potential savings capital.
Not only would a future higher savings cover of current investments ease the domestic price and cost climate, but it would
take the pressure off the hard-currency policy so that in future
it would not have to be ridden quite so hard. Most important,
the new and additional savings and liquidity potential could
become the basis for a more efficient Austrian capital market
available both for the domestic liquidation of the foreign debt
service and for the consolidation of domestic public debt, a
process that could be substantially accelerated by the fiscal
incentives discussed in Point 10.

The only threat to this successful dual-deficit financing policy
of foreign balance on current accounts and domestic budget
might come from a premature (exogenous) restriction of the
scope of foreign trade credits, that is to say, an international
balance-of-payments crisis. This will be pursued in Points 15
and 16.

6. It follows from this analysis that the frequently heard sus-
picion that the Austrian balance on current accounts deficit is
caused by an overall too high level of consumption confuses
cause and effect. Austria has been able to afford overinvestment
as well as overconsumption (both related to the sum of domestic
gross value creation, the so-called gross national product) precisely because so much foreign credit has been available to it.
Moreover, the observed overconsumption applies only to some
sectors, such as the strongly exchange-rate-elastic tourist market
and the strongly price-and-income-elastic durable consumer
goods market (particularly automobiles, household appliances,

and audio equipment), and it is debatable whether these private household investments involve national overconsumption rather than the national underproduction in these still too import-dependent markets.

7. The fixed schilling exchange rate vis-à-vis the other hard-currency countries reduces the uncertainty and unreliability experienced by other float countries in the calculation of planning data crucial to entrepreneurial decision making (according to Eucken). Exchange rates fixed by central bank intervention restrict the scope not only of imported but also of interventionist influence of the relative or intersectoral price and cost structure. The foreign prices of imported goods converted by the stable high schilling rate not only set ceilings to the upward movements of domestic costs, prices, and profits, but they also make possible the calculation of sales and purchases in the common schilling-neutral, hard-currency market of the German Federal Republic, Switzerland, and the Benelux countries, free from all incidental currency conversion profits—markets that account for approximately two-thirds of all Austrian imports, and almost two-fifths of all Austrian exports.

Since the effectiveness potential of monetary fiscal policy is limited to global demand- and liquidity-regulating incentives, and since the investment decisions of business (with regard to financing costs and profit value calculations) are unpredictable, and since selectively targeted interventions of a domestic-surplus credit and interest-rate policy are largely nonexistent, the developments of the price and cost structure taking place below the fixed intersectoral and relative price and cost levels are determined largely by the market, not by intervention.

If Austrian entrepreneurs and investors nonetheless complain about the excessive burden imposed by the intolerable frequent intervention of the government's tax, licensing fees, and redistribution policy, they do so out of the ingrained habit of private enterprise (a factor already commented upon by Adam Smith) to confuse the problems caused by competition with intervention.

8. Another reason for the blindness to Austria's almost classical comprehensiveness of expected and therefore also calculable

actual data changes is connected with the inevitable intrusion of the moods filtering in from the outside in an integrated market system: If the investors of the German Federal Republic feel insecure because of monetary risks—of problems relating to credit, interest-rate, and tax measures—their business associates are certain to adopt their pessimistic outlook (as they also adopt their more cheerful mood when their hopes, justified or unjustified, go up), an unavoidable psychological price for sharing the monetary and economic area of others.

If the investment risk in the seventies had been demonstrably higher in Austria than in most of the other OECD industrial countries, the Austrian investment quota would have had to be lower, not higher, than theirs; moreover, the countervailing trend could not have lasted more than ten years in comparison particularly with the German Federal Republic: a falling West German investment rate up to 1976 and a sustained high one in Austria (see Table 26).

9. The resort to foreign asset capital and financial resources not only expanded the global spending scope of fiscal policy, but also the possibility of selective fiscal steering in the direction of accelerated financing and development. The global income

Table 26. Investments and Social Product: Investment Quota[a] (in percent)

Year	Austria	German Federal Republic
1970	25.9	25.6
1971	27.9	26.4
1972	30.4	25.9
1973	27.4	24.5
1974	28.1	21.9
1975	26.7	20.7
1976	26.2	20.7
1977	27.2	20.9

Sources: For Austria, Öesterreichische Nationalbank, Vienna; for German Federal Republic, Deutsche Bundesbank, Frankfurt/Main.

[a]Gross capital investment measured against the gross national product of Austria and the gross social product of the German Federal Republic.

renunciation can be used to promote a policy of fiscal investment bonuses, which have channeled, and continue to channel, large portions of the tax revenue into an investment fund under entrepreneurial control that makes possible interest-free and indebtedness-neutral investment financing: "social" receipts (taxes) thus become private wealth, even if in the form of entrepreneurial asset investments. This long-standing linear and industry-oriented promotion of investment is complemented by a steadily rising trend of selective and project-connected promotion of investment based on overall economic priorities that make credits and publicly funded guarantees available at favorable interest rates.

By combining all publicly financed and supported private investment and all government investments in the public sector, the social quota of national economic gross capital investments is approximately two-fifths of the seventies' average, a magnitude that explains the size and stability of the investment process of that period yet also reveals the grave shortcomings of this business-oriented investment and development financing.

10. The generous support of investments by fiscal incentives has proved very successful with regard to growth, full employment, and domestic development. But as a future mainstay of restructuring and investment financing it poses a serious threat to productivity and savings potential. Even though the high and stable investment quota contributed significantly to the technological advance of an efficient, industrial export structure, it could have been still more effective had it discarded the linear, industry-oriented investment bonuses and concentrated the moneys thus saved on specific goals, or at least cut the industrial tie of the tax incentives that acted like an internal tariff on intersectoral tariff movements. The premium paid for reinvestment in one's own enterprise acts like a—even if unintended—tax on capital investments in other, and possibly more productive, enterprises, sectors, or capital markets.

Austria's underdeveloped private savings quota thus was the result not of overconsumption or lacking savings ability but of the misdirection of the most profitable savings source of industrial economies: the supply of goods resulting from the entrepreneurial cash flow. That flow to the money and capital markets is being blocked by a tax-rewarded capital endogamy, with the inevitable result that the linear and industry-oriented fiscal support of investment produces entrepreneurial self-financing, which, however, is in fact simply a forced savings of the non-entrepreneur and an undersupply of outside financing whose private and social costs will make themselves felt in the future. What is being promoted is not only the structural overconcentration of industrial sectors and wealth, but also today's profit position at the expense of the future, for the tax savings are biggest where profits are highest today, an almost foolproof recipe for refraining from innovative undertakings.

Austria's preferential tax system born during its industrial and technological infancy threatens to become counterproductive, and thus inimical to progress once the gap is closed. The underdeveloped Austrian capital market could become far stronger if the entrepreneurial investment activity were less energetically and less broadly promoted, for then a substantial portion of today's plant-targeted investment capital would be freed for savings.

11. On balance, despite this dissipation of productivity and structural and capital market potential, the development policy has had positive effects. As far as industrial modernization, diversification, and export ability are concerned, Austria made its greatest strides in the years of world crisis. The Austria of the seventies became an efficient industrial nation, a process that is sure to continue in the eighties, even if this successful growth and development could have been (still) greater given a different mix of fiscal policy incentives—one not tied to plants, and only selectively linear.

Austria's deficit fiscal policy, refinanced largely even if not exclusively through public capital imports, offers industrial as well as developing countries an example of highly successful growth policy that stabilizes employment and increases the real supply potential of the economy.

12. Both workers and employers, the social partners, benefited from this restructured policy of stable, high employment. Investment and growth created a demand for labor, and because

the demand for labor, particularly skilled labor, exceeded the supply, the favorable investment and profit situation worked to the advantage of both partners; the excessive wage demands that generally are part of labor conflicts never even surfaced. In view of the low unemployment rate the bargaining atmosphere between the social partners remained pleasant. But they also benefited from being spared inflation profits, which not only would have intensified the fight for income distribution but also would have led the entrepreneurs into error (into too high a degree of rationalization in the leading export sectors). However, neither labor nor distribution battles disturbed the balance between price and employment.

13. In the future, however, the income policy of the autonomous social partners is bound to play a more important role: the inevitable reduction in the balance on current accounts deficit vis-à-vis the so-called hard-currency countries (German Federal Republic, Switzerland, the Benelux countries) can be effected only if the social partners agree on a policy of real stable wage and labor costs in foreign prices vis-à-vis these countries so crucial to Austria's competitive capability. If Austria wants to utilize the real opportunities of debt liquidation inherent in its still increasing (industrial) export capacity, it must keep within the framework of a balance-of-payments–neutral income policy set by the internal (real) productivity and external inflation-caused increases of the hard-currency countries.

14. Austria's combination of domestic balance on current accounts surplus and foreign deficit cannot go on forever. The policy of dual (balance on current accounts and budget) deficits must, for reasons discussed in Point 5, be changed into one of dual surpluses, and it must be done before foreign and domestic debt and credit limits are reached, for an unplanned financial withdrawal of foreign creditors would lead to the unplanned (i.e., premature) end of the policy mix· planned overall economic growth rates and carefully thought out (and presumably financially feasible) projects would have to be shelved. The country would be faced with the sad alternative of having to

give up either full employment or the freedom of foreign trade and payment transactions, or possibly both.

Does that mean that the domestic critics of the dual-deficit-financing of balance of payments and budget are right in their contention that Austria's prosperity of the seventies is nothing but a flash in the pan, that it will come to an end when foreign countries become more reluctant to extend loans? How can it be proved that Austria's foreign exchange and budget debts (in domestic currency) merely anticipate certain balance-of-payments and budget surpluses?

The critics of the deficit fiscal policy fail to see the substantial real growth (capacity) as well as financial savings (liquidity) effects (inherent in the capital stock, shown in Point 5). More importantly, carrying forward income, spending, and debt rates of an antidepression budget to the next phase of a real as well as anticipated boom, they see the country as "poor"—a method almost guaranteed to bring about such a depression because of the effect of their calculations on future fiscal policy. The more certain the real as well as financial long-range growth trend of an economy, the less it is in need of the stimulant of higher government spending and of budget deficits out of proportion to tax receipts and the gross national product, not to mention disproportionate (linear and industry-oriented) investment incentives. Assuming that the near future will see a substantial decline in the financing of economic demand and in the "social" support of private investments as well as government subsidies coupled with greater efficiency of the private capital markets, it will also see an increase in the flexibility (refinancing scope) of fiscal policy. That which no longer can or has to be financed out of tax receipts can, thanks to the higher savings quota, be covered by new credits that replace the old credits and—over longer terms—can consolidate them.

The analysis and estimate of built-in regulators of both domestic and foreign debt liquidation, based on the development of real supply and real demand of the Austrian model, were the subject of the analysis of Part 1 of this study.

The problem of the synchronization of the foreign-exchange transfer and budget liquidation of foreign debt alluded to in Point 5 does not, as has been shown, pose an unsolvable dilemma either from the vantage point of the presumed foreign-exchange income or of the presumed budget income. Austria does not have to fear that because it lacks export surpluses it will have to pay for its foreign debts with domestic deflation (as in the crisis of the thirties) and a falling schilling rate; nor does Austria have the fear that because it lacks a budget surplus, it will have to pay its foreign debt in terms of growth and employment.

In the case of the domestic debt the inevitable increase in real savings, particularly from the reservoir of the entrepreneurial cash flow, insures its refinancing and consolidation at lower volume and interest-rate levels than in the past.

If these built-in debt liquidation processes should move too slowly or too feebly, they can be accelerated and strengthened via the more productive savings and foreign-exchange support of investment described in Point 10 and the income policy of the social partners, Austria's "iron income law" of the eighties as outlined in Point 13.

15. Two possible dangers may crop up along the way. One, exogenous in nature, is connected with the short-term unstable, if not explosive, situation of the free international financial markets not supported by any sort of central bank underpinnings. In principle they are as allergic to contraction as the free financial markets of 1929 and 1952. Large liquidity drains could easily set off a chain reaction of credit "destruction" and "cost increase" and thus force Austria (as well as other debtor countries) to give up its free schilling convertibility. It is beyond the ability of the government of a small country to banish the collaboration danger of the Euromarkets by its own policy; all it can do is to work toward the still possible—and increasingly more necessary—consolidation of these markets within the framework of international bodies such as the IMF and OECD.

The other danger point is of an endogenous nature. A policy that for the time being promotes only the international and national debt-liquidation process of dual surpluses (of balance of payments and budget) could easily turn into a permanent phenomenon, particularly since bad examples and theories (i.e., justifications) for budget-induced export growth do exist. The budget surplus would then be used as the stabilizing counterweight to the inflation imported through the balance on current accounts surplus. In this way Austria, after the liquidation of its foreign debt, would almost imperceptibly slide into a neomercantile policy of imported full employment, or export-led growth.

Can this danger—which is also inherent in the development process—be averted? Easily, if Austria after its foreign debt liquidation opens the way for the building up of private foreign capital. That is, Austria's future balance on current accounts surplus would, after reaching specific reserve limits (or goals) set by the central bank be financed out of private capital export, not out of public reserve accumulation (against the reserves of other partners). Austria's future goal, after the liquidation of its foreign-exchange credit, must be an equilibrated basic payments balance and a corresponding neutral reserve balance— a goal toward which budget policy also must work. In this, Austria's private foreign capital would help to (1) ease the balance of payments of the deficit partners and prevent imported depression problems from arising, (2) eliminate all domestic fiscal policy resistance growing out of stability policy considerations, and (3) secure Austria's position vis-à-vis less well capitalized trading partners (in Eastern Europe and the Third World) in whose markets it is yet to gain a firm foothold.

A capital market that performed turntable functions would facilitate not only the export of Austrian capital but also the transshipping of foreign capital. Austria could finance its bigger exports not only with its own saved capital but also with borrowed savings capital. The banking center Vienna would thus be able to link up with its pre–World War I tradition as an important site of international capital transfers; this, however, presupposes complete equality, in terms of both foreign exchange and policy guarantees of domestic and foreign financing.

16. Can Austria's tested economic alternative of fiscal rather than exchange-rate adjustment of the seventies be applied to other countries facing different problems? The German Advisory Commission recommended a policy along those lines in its 1968–1969 annual report. Austria tested this policy of domestic expansion through foreign trade. The heart of it is an expansive fiscal policy whose deficits are determined by the domestic

and foreign debt scope and limits of the national economy. Its pace in the debt-contracting phase is set by an appreciating hard-currency policy that eliminates the danger of any inflationary thrust, while in the debt-liquidation phase it is set by a policy of domestic production and savings surpluses that make possible not only real export surpluses but also their financing out of genuine domestic and foreign savings. Only in this way can inflationary tensions at home and a collision course with the other partners in an international economy be avoided.

Ignoring the possibility of critical developments on the Euro-markets (the only danger moment of this policy), this means that a country that, like Austria, adjusts its internal debt to its external credit possibilities not only helps itself but also spares its neighbors, whom it neither wages trade wars against nor deprives of export markets and jobs. Also, such a debt policy is not in the least irresponsible, for the debt limits expand with the real growth of capacities, while at the same time the proper use of foreign-exchange and capital markets can, as the example of Austria has demonstrated, even make the debt-liquidation potential grow by leaps and bounds.

Austria's economic policy of "as though there (still) existed a functioning world monetary system" thus fulfills an almost Kantian imperative of good domestic and foreign behavior. If all nations were to follow this guideline inherent in Von Böhm-Bawerk's "mandate of the balance of payments," an almost optimal world economic and monetary order for all nations, without supervision and policemen, could become a reality—a gold standard in which gold would be replaced by the observance of rules and a world order in which big and small nations could again live and work together in peace without encroaching on each other and of which the wise cynic George Bernard Shaw might say, to modify the introductory epigraph, "With all due respect for the earlier *stability* of gold, today I prefer to put my trust in the decency and intelligence of governments."

PART 4

THE MODEL

*Il semble bien que la compréhension des diverses inter-
connections d'une économie soit un facteur de réal-
isme aussi important . . . que l'énumération d'une
variété considérable de détails descriptifs non reliés
entre eux.*
                                        —Ragnar Frisch, 1949

*There is a limit to what we can do with numbers as
there is to what we can do without them.*
                              —Nicholas Georgescu-Roegen, 1966

How "theoretical" is the Austrian policy mix? Does it conform to any of the traditional econometric models?[1] This question is not prompted by the desire to make the heart of econometricians beat faster. We are concerned with finding out whether the economic policy pursued by Austria in the seventies, and our analysis of that policy, can pass the test of consistency. Are the measures that have been taken, in relation to their perceived goals and the perceived effectiveness of the instruments used to achieve them, in themselves free of contradiction?

In what follows we project the Austrian policy mix of a domestic-surplus policy dependent on other countries onto the model analysis developed by the International Monetary Fund in the seventies,[2] in its simple form for countries with an as yet underdeveloped domestic money and capital market.

Since the concern here is with the political logic of means and goals we will refrain from the sort of complicating dissection of the Ragnar Frisch kind of model. Also, because the central question relates to the "responsibility" of the domestic debt (finance) policy, we will begin the theoretical calculation in money amounts: in nominal national income or national product (wherein "gross" or "net" can be ignored), in nominal reserve or payments balances (wherein the sectoral origin of surplus and deficit are no longer of interest), and in only nominally representable foreign and domestic debts such as capital imports, domestic money holdings, and domestic credit volume (wherein "private" and "public" use of the overall observed financing potential can be combined).

By limiting ourselves to the problem, we consider the following eight macro factors:

National income expressed in monetary units Y
Private and public domestic consumer and
   investment spending A
Imports M
Exports X
Domestic money holdings Mo
Domestic credit or loan volume L
Reserve position of the central bank R
Volume of available foreign credits C

These factors are combined into the following four equations according to their internal relationships:

$$Y(A + X - M) = v \cdot Mo \qquad (1)$$
$$M = m \cdot Y \qquad (2)$$
$$dMo = R + dL \qquad (3)$$
$$R = X - M + C \qquad (4)$$

The structure of the model shows that the sum of the available foreign credits, C, at a "given" balance on current accounts, $X - M$, determines the size of R (wherein $R = 0$ stands for balance-of-payments equilibrium). $R + dL$, in turn, determines how much national money amount expansion, dMo, is "required" to finance the "desirable" national income, Y, at a given cash position (or liquidity preference), v.

The only "disturbing factor" is the rise of imports, M, paralleling the rise in Y, whose rate of increase is expressed through the marginal import quota, m. The greater the foreign credit or capital import volume, C, the more imports, M, our system can afford without incurring minus values in the balance of payments, R. As a result the scope for the increase of the national income, Y, expands both in "real" terms via m (rise in imports) as well as in "financial" terms via the expansion of the money amount, dMo.

The question, however, is, by how much? For that purpose

we must combine Equations 1 and 3 and differentiate them vis-à-vis dY. If we define the R of Equation 3 by the definitions of Equation 4, we get

$$R = \frac{1}{1 + mv} d(C + X) - \frac{mv}{1 + mv} + dL \frac{1}{1 + mv} R_{-1} \quad (5)$$

$$dY = \frac{v}{1 + mv} d(C + X) + \frac{v}{1 + mv} dL + \frac{v}{1 + mv} R_{-1} \quad (6)$$

Equation 5 shows that the balance-of-payments deficits $(R < R_{-1})$ are bigger the more domestic credit expansion, dL, takes place, wherein $mv/(1 + mv)$ functions as a negative reserve loss "multiplier": the bigger the marginal import trend, m, at a given domestic money circulation velocity (or cash-holding position), v, the more rapidly will balance of payments or external financing limits of domestic credit or debt programs be reached.

Equation 6 shows the "unified" effect of both "borrowed" and "earned" reserve flows, $d(C + X)$, domestic credits, dL, and the national income growth rate, dY, wherein a high cash-holding position ("savings tendency"), v, enhances the "technical" possibilities of internal credit expansion, dL, but conversely weakens a high marginal import tendency. The internal credit "multiplier" $v/(1 + mv)$ thus rises with $v > m$ and falls with $m > v$.

Both equations, however, describe only the short-term transition from one situation to another, from R_{-1} to R, the plus and minus trend of domestic debt activities from R and Y within one year, for example. However, we are not inquiring into the equilibrium conditions of one year but of an entire long-term period, in which $R_{-1} = R$, and consequently also $dY = dY_{-1}$.

This longer-term equilibrium at permanent (constant) growth rates of dY and $R = 0$ is achieved if[3]

$$R = \frac{1}{mv} d(C + X) - dL \quad (7)$$

$$dY = \frac{1}{m} d(C + X) \quad (8)$$

The "strategic coefficient" $1/mv$ of Equation 7 shows the economy's growth capacity for domestic debt or credit expansion, regardless of whether "private" or "public," for in the case of $R = 0$ (balance-of-payments equilibration via dX and dC) dL can increase only by the quotient $(dC + DX)/mv$.

But on what does this expansion-limiting factor of all dependent economies, mv, in fact depend? Since it is nothing else but

$$\frac{dM}{dY} \cdot \frac{dY}{dMo} = \frac{dM}{dMo}$$

and since we can assume equality between "marginal" and "average" growth of M and Mo, mv is always approximately equivalent to M/Mo.

In other words, the sum of the money amount, Mo, available for the financing of imports, M, determines how much real and how much debt increase an expanding economy can afford. M/Mo or mv thus quantifies E. Von Böhm-Bawerk's "dictate of the balance of payments," the "brake on the (internal) credit machinery," which in Schumpeter's days was still "golden" but has since become dependent on foreign credit.

The connection becomes still clearer if we write Equation 8 as

$$m\, dY = d(C + X). \tag{9}$$

We then find that the m financed out of earned reserves, dX, or borrowed reserves, dC, allows the real growth rate of the national income, dY, to climb beyond the capacity limits set by the country's own added value or domestic productivity. An increase in production later can be used to liquidate previous contracted foreign credits via $dX > dM = -C$ and without endangering the domestic absorption rate, A, of Equation 1. This too can be easily deduced from Equation 9. In the case of $dX > dC$, and consequently dX-dependent export-led growth, dY, m can be reduced to zero and minus. Of course, in that case a higher value for v must balance the minus value of m if one is to avoid "undesirable" reserve increases $(+R)$. A rising tendency of v however is only another term for a rising savings tendency, which would change an otherwise inevitable inflationary *Mo* expansion in line with Equation 3, particularly if intensified by the "technically" appreciated domestic credit multiplier $v/(1 + mv)$ of Equation 6 into a reserve-neutral equilibrium via $X > M = C$ in accordance with Equations 4 and 7.

Our model thus also demonstrates that the observed phase of the financing of growing balance on current accounts surpluses (= $X > M$) through capital exports ($-C$) instead of reserve imports ($+R$) following foreign debt liquidation conforms to the model conditions of balance-of-payments– and inflation-neutral expanding national economies, in which the public sector "hidden" in these aggregates has only one function: to set the direction in time and accuracy for the parallel processes of foreign and domestic indebtedness created by the need for reserve neutrality (i.e., balance-of-payments equilibrium). Now the new (strengthened) capital market "follows" the mandate of the new balance-of-payments surplus.

Quod erat demonstrandum.

NOTES

Preface

1. As a guide to the reader I would like to elaborate on three conceptual adjectives that recur throughout my analysis: *real, nominal*, and *optimal*. Conceptually, *real* stands for "physical," or statistically for "constant prices." But in a money economy there can exist justified doubt about whether we are dealing in constant prices with a "realistic" point of view. After all, the value of goods and services expressed in "current prices" determines the market process, size, and use of the social product, and until recently the distribution of income as well. Lately the distribution of income has also become known as "real," at any rate so far as this lies within the power and understanding of the participants in the bargaining process.

Conceptually, *nominal* stands for "financial," statistically for "current prices," ergo for "inflated." Of course, a price-inflated social product does not constitute "real" value creation or "productivity"; it merely gives this appearance ("illusion"). Nonetheless, these "fictive" nominal amounts and values trigger "real" distributive effects. If, for example, nominal selling prices of business increase more than the nominal, let alone real, wages of the nonentrepreneurs, the real income positions (shares in the social product) shift. "Real," however, does not necessarily mean "realistic," and nominal does not always mean "fictive" or "illusory." In their attempt to preserve the quantitative-theoretical (today we would say "monetarist") idea of money, which holds that it influences only the absolute prices of an economy and never its "relative" prices or price relations, which allegedly were based on real productivity, the post–Adam Smith generation of economists (above all David Ricardo) brought economic analysis to a conceptual dichotomy that could not be explained by the market behavior of the role players. According to this, political abstractions like the social product and the balance of payments ("macro aggregates") first had to be determined nominally (in nominal prices), but intersectoral production processes, in order to arrive at their productivity content, had to be determined in fixed (thus in fact fictive) prices. Thus, for the sake of comparison, macro-nominal magnitudes like the social product and foreign trade balance can be translated into "fixed" prices, and the production and value-creating processes into "current" prices.

The question of whether realistically one ought to think and calculate in real or nominal magnitudes is one that engages both Keynesians and monetarists, and the use of identical symbols for completely different concepts of money merely adds to the confusion. In his *General Theory of Employment, Interest and Money* (New York, 1935; London, 1936), p. 199, Keynes defines the money volume required for the financing of the real production processes (of the classical economists) as M_1, but differentiates between it and the purely expectation-related (precautionary as well as speculative) money as M_2 (which the classical economists did not know, even though Ricardo was an experienced stock-market speculator). If there existed only the M_1 money volume of the classical economists, and if M_2 were at best a marginal constant, then money volume could indeed give rise only to changes in price levels, never in price relationships. In that case "real" would almost always be equivalent to "realistic," and "nominal" almost invariably to "illusory."

Keynes in fact proved that a lively exchange takes place between M_1 and M_2: In times of crisis M_2 expands (his famous liquidity preference in a narrower sense) at the expense of M_1. In the absence of a counterbalancing M_1 expansion, interest rates rise and at first continue to strengthen M_2—with the result that the economy stagnates. So we see that under certain conditions money "illusion" does have "realistic" effects.

For the modern Friedmanians, M_1 and M_2 signify merely "technically" different types of money: M_1 refers to central bank money in circulation outside the banks, plus sight deposits in the banks, and M_2 refers to term and savings deposits, etc. The crucial point here is that their M_2 in the Keynesian sense, the so-called real cash position, represents an only marginally fluctuating constant. Consequently, the monetarists can make do with the quantitative-theoretical money of the classical economists. Disturbances on the monetary front are always caused by M_1, both in the Keynesian and Friedmanian sense. As far as monetarists are concerned, Keynes's M_2 is nothing but a chimera. Yet as we shall see in the discussion of the Eurodollar market in Chapter 9, it is indeed a reality.

In what follows, *real* is used in the physical sense and *nominal* in the financial sense—without any association to realistic or fictive—in the same way that the great Swedish political economist Knut Wicksell referred to his real interest rate as the interest rate that would obtain if all credits were granted "in natura" and all profits gained "in natura." (On this, see *Währungspolitik Geldwertstabilisierung, Währungsinflation und Sparerschutz* [Stuttgart, 1972], ch. 3, by the present author.)

Optimal, in a usage dating back to the classical economists, connotes a spatial dimension. Adam Smith considered large markets that allowed for a division of labor as "optimal." Ricardo narrowed this concept to domestic markets, since foreign markets according to his curious assumption knew only the movement of goods, not of factors. Robert Mundell ("A Theory of Optimum Currency Areas," *American Economic Journal* 51 [September 1961]: 657 ff.), defined optimal areas throughout all national economies as zones of maximum factor mobility, and hence also of rapid productivity equalization. According to Ronald McKinnon ("Optimum Currency Areas," *American Economic Journal* 53 [September 1963]: 717 ff.), neither China nor the United States constitutes an optimal area because of its balance-of-payments problems. Since that time a number of other definitions of optimal areas have been offered. On this, see the excellent survey by Yoshihide Ishiyama ("The Theory of Optimum Currency Areas: A Survey," *IMF Staff Papers* 22 [March 1975]: 344 ff.).

In this study the term *optimal* is for the first time used without any spatial attribution. Even a country like Austria, which by whatever definition one chooses is not an optimal area, can pursue an optimal policy, not through spatial adjustment like the member states of the European Monetary System (EMS), but through the adjustment of instruments, as the policy mix analyzed in this study demonstrates.

Three Austrian economists, F. Schebeck, H. Suppanz, and G. Tichy, in a research study (*The Effect of Exchange Rate Changes on Foreign Trade in Manufactured Goods in Small Open Economies: Preliminary Results for Austria* [Vienna, February 1978]), have pursued a similar course but limited it to foreign trade, terms of trade, and price competition. The present author differs with them on only one point, albeit a crucial one: It is not enough to examine only the exchange-rate adjustments and to omit the role distribution of the other instruments (particularly of monetary and fiscal policy) that grows out of this. The doubtful conclusion of Schebeck, Suppanz, and Tichy, that it is not easy to decide for which type of exchange-rate policy small and open economies should opt (p. 27) could have been avoided had they compared the eminently correct analysis of the costs of the exchange-rate adjustment with the benefits of the aggregate policy mix made possible by it, something we will attempt to do in this study.

Part 1
Chapter 1

1. J. K. Galbraith, *The Age of Uncertainty* (Boston, 1977).

2. F. Lutz, "The Interest Rate and Investment in a Dynamic Economy," *American Economic Review* 35 (1945).

3. See also my analysis of the middle-class sector in the German Federal Republic, in Wilfrid L. Kohl and Giorgio Basevi, eds., *West Germany: A European Global Power* (Lexington, Mass., 1980), ch. 2, "Economic Nationalism in the International Economy," pp. 36 ff.

4. See also K. G. Zinn, "Investitionsfinanzierung, Risikokapital und Lohnkosten," *Mitteilungen aus der Arbeitsmarkt- und Berufsforschung, Schwerpunktheft Löhne und Beschäftigung*, No. 3 (1978): pp. 358 ff., and the sources cited therein. Zinn demonstrated that in the German Federal Republic there exists

a countervailing trend of rising savings rate and declining capital in enterprises, including the giant corporation. He saw in the rising savings quota not only a change to a greater safety preference based on the psychology and mentality of "small savers," but a reciprocal effect inherent in the trend of development. Marx would most likely have called this one of the many contradictions of capitalist societies: as savings rates rise both the sales and investment risks of business increase. Because all business has to offer are risky projects for outside financing, more and more small savers are reluctant to invest in them (the so-called Kalecki-Keynes-Hansen stagnation hypothesis). Zinn's comments on this are as follows: "The increase in the savings quota of private households thus increases the investment risk in two ways: on the one hand from the demand side, and on the other from the financing side."

5. The present author and F. Lehner have jointly examined the economic and political costs of a rigid policy of domestic stability. See W. Hankel and F. Lehner, "Die gescheiterte Stabilitätspolitik und ihre politischen Folgen: Von der Unvereinbarket wirtschaftlicher Monopol- und demokratischer Konkurrenzsysteme," *Hamburger Jahrbuch für Wirtschafts- und Gesellschaftspolitik* 21 (1976).

6. See *Neue Zürcher Zeitung*, No. 32 (February 8, 1979): p. 16.

7. See W. Röpke, *Gegen die Brandung* (Erlenbach-Zürich, 1959): pp. 202 ff.

8. In contrast to the opinion of almost every professional analyst and politician, John Kenneth Galbraith and this author were among the first to prove almost simultaneously, and independently, that the effects of the oil shock were bound to be depressive or deflationary rather than inflationary. See Galbraith, *Money: Whence It Came, Where It Went* (Boston, 1975), pp. 299 ff., and this author's report for the German Marshall Fund of the United States, completed in the fall of 1975, *The Taming of the Petrodollar, or How Safe Is the Recycling*, portions of which were reprinted in *Der Ausweg aus der Krise* (Vienna, 1975), chs. 6 and 9. Galbraith shows the connection thus:

Everywhere the higher oilprice was considered highly inflationary, in the United States it served invaluably as an excuse for
official inadequacy in the control of inflation. In fact, it was defla-
tory. Especially in the Arab countries but also in Iran and elsewhere,
the revenues accruing from the higher prices were far greater than
could immediately be spent for either consumers' or investment
goods. So they accumulated in unspent balances. Thus they repre-
sented a withdrawal from current purchasing power not different
in immediate effect from that of levying large sales taxes on petroleum
or its products. . . . This effect of the oilprice increases was perceptively identified at one of President Ford's so called Summit Con-
ferences on Inflation in the autumn of 1974 by Professor Richard N.
Cooper. Few, not including the present author, saw the force of his
position. . . . The effect, increasingly evident as 1974 passed, was the
predictable effect of fiscal astringency. As demand faded, prices in
competitive markets—those for food, commodities, services—began
to weaken. Prices subject to corporate market power continued to
rise. So did unemployment. The oil-producing countries had provided the industrial countries with a surrogate tax increase. Its effect, like any general fiscal or monetary action against inflation, was
to increase unemployment well before acting to arrest inflation.
[pp. 299–300]

The present author in his Marshall Fund report said this:

Overnight the high price of oil has brought about what Western
economic and currency policy was unable to accomplish despite the
use of massive weapons such as cooling off the boom, which up to
that time had been uncontrollable. In the meantime a noticeable
change in atmosphere has occurred in all Western industrialised
countries—a general levelling off of demand, which in turn permitted
all the more painful emergence of a number of previously hidden
structural problems (in overcrowded sectors such as building, construction, automobile and textile production).
    What does all this have to do with petroleum and the increase
in its price? As long as the petroleum was still cheap, the situation
for decades was as follows:—a built-in countertrend to the constant
automatic cost increase of Western technology along with a growing
need for large capital funds and rising labor costs, in other words,
a factor of borrowed and imported productivity.—Petroleum played
the role of a built-in demand-support program, in which, due to the
relatively low cost of energy, demand retained an elbow room and

was available for buying a wide range of additional (demand-elastic) home products.—Especially because of its advances in productivity the competitive position of the industrialized countries, their balance of payments situation and terms of trade were bolstered.

The extent of this "petroleum subsidy" which was utilized for many years did not become apparent until it ceased to exist. The simultaneous and violent four-to-five-fold increase of crude oil prices brought to a head short term cost increases in all branches of energy-consuming domestic production. However, there was an element of danger, in that the uneven home and foreign market position in various branches of industry gave rise to major recessive and deflationary counterforces. Where the extra costs for energy could be passed on to the ultimate buyer in the prices he paid, they restricted demand which dropped off elsewhere. The business cycles in the industrialized countries began to separate in two: sectors with good outlets (small price and income elasticity in demand) kept on producing but at higher costs, sectors with weak outlets (high-price and income elasticity in demand) produced less, absolutely and relatively, and developed into centers of an emerging and intensifying recession.

In so far as the individual Western economies succeeded (by and large) in absorbing the higher petroleum prices in the total inflation rate, a third result supervened, burdening the entire gamut of economic activity across the board: to the extent of their ability to finance the higher petroleum prices, the national economies suffered a loss of domestic demand due to foreign effects. This freshly emerging short-fall in demand affecting the entire economy, which strained balances of payments besides the rate of business, brought about a greater recession trend, since most governments in the Western petroleum importing countries now were compelled to step up their generally already current anti-inflation policy "for balance-of-payments reasons." (In the process they were anxious to mitigate the recession effects by means of a more marked downward floating of their currencies.)

Thus, the oil shock presented or exacerbates in almost every country of the Western community a cyclical process, such as had last appeared on this scale and breadth during the 30's: the trends towards deficits in the balances of payments had to be combatted under a deepening recession inspite of inflation. To be sure, this action overburdened the mechanism of conventional economic and currency policy aimed at "global" cyclical effects. In other words, in order to overcome the balance of payment deficits, further restrictions became necessary, which in turn necessarily abated the already existing trends towards stagnation. And in order to cope effectively with the spreading recession, demand stimulating (reflating) measures were in turn necessary, which further widened the balance of payment deficits.

The question arises whether this development was unavoidable. Did Western economic and currency policy have to proceed, as it did, at least in 1974, according to the slogan: Petroleum which was lacking or could no longer be paid for could not be replaced with freshly printed money and demand financed thereby? This formula which was proclaimed in almost all Western industrialized countries until the 1974/75 turn of the year, and which was adopted in each case proved once again the error which unfortunately recurs in the history of economic policy, viz. what is correct for the individual enterprise and perhaps for a particular industry, too, cannot be unconditionally applied to the overall economy and especially not at all to the Western world economy.

Of course, instead of combatting inflation, one should have combatted deflation which had arisen as a result of the wiping out of real income and the transfer of domestic purchasing power to foreign countries (the OPEC countries) and do this promptly, i.e. immediately after the outbreak of the oil crisis. If additional demand had been created at that time, there would have still been lapses in demand in the weak sectors, but less severe ones, because they would have been smoothed out by counter-cyclical measures and not aggravated by cyclical factors. Consequently, the oil crisis would not have had a somewhat greater "inflationary" impact under such counter-cyclical policy. Since: demand was continuously draining off to the OPEC countries due to the exactions of extra expenditures for imported petroleum (imported deflation).

9. For a better understanding of this and the following paragraph the reader is advised to reread the preceding note and to read Jan Tinbergen, *"Beschäftigungsförderung ohne Preissteigerung,"* in B. B. Gemper, ed., *Bruno Gleitze zum 75. Geburtstag. Stabilität in Wandel* (Berlin, 1978), pp. 67 ff., especially pp. 70 ff. It is worthwhile.

10. See W. Eucken, *Grundsätze der Wirtschaftspolitik* (Tübingen and Erlenbach-Zurich, 1952), pp. 288 ff.

Chapter 2

1. The multiplier formula can be arrived at via a complex or

a simple method. The simple method is based on the formula of an infinite geometric progression: $1/(1 - r)$, in which r stands for the marginal spending or incremental factor, i.e., our a. If $r = a = \frac{1}{3}$, the arithmetic multiplier derives either from $1/(1 - \frac{1}{3}) = 1/\frac{2}{3} = 1.5$, or its corollary, since $1 - a = b + c$ is also equal to $1/\frac{2}{3} = 1.5$. See also P. A. Samuelson, *Economics*, 10 ed. (New York, 1976), pp. 228 ff. and 664 ff.

Of course these multipliers are highly dependent on expectations and reactions, i.e., they are unstable. The calculation with mixed magnitudes (constants) therefore yields approximations at best. Keynes himself therefore used the multiplier only to illustrate a trend, and he was appalled when Tinbergen, using the multiplier developed previously by Aftalion as well as Keynes's more recent one (which Keynes had developed for the 1929 election campaign of Lloyd George), later (1930) systematized by Kahn, based his model of an endogenous "calculable" business cycle and the anticyclical business policy on it. In this context Keynes, in a letter to R. Tyler, wrote: "We know that they [the coefficients] are not constant. There is no reason at all why they should not be different every year." (See Keynes, *Collected Writings*, 14, p. 287.) See also H. Theil, "A Reconsideration of the Keynes-Tinbergen Discussion on Econometric Techniques," *L'industria* (1963).

Keynes's attitude toward econometrics and its concepts of the quasiphysical predetermination of economic processes and the process changes emanating from the desired data changes of policy had been fixed in his earliest scientific youth. In his *Treatise on Probability* of 1921 (based on his dissertation), the book on which he worked from 1906 to 1920—longer than on any other—he defined social relations and reactions as subject only to the laws of mass-statistical probability and not to mathematical logic in individual instances. Consequently he saw no reason for assuming that in the economic calculation every reaction had to recur, not even ceteris paribus (see R. B. Braithwaite, "Keynes as a Philosopher," in Milo Keynes, ed., *Essays on J. M. Keynes* [Cambridge, 1975], pp. 227 ff.).

It can come as a surprise only to the epigones who misconstrue the "master" ("bastard Keynesians," in Joan Robinson's disdainful dismissal of them) that one or the other approach has changed since the thirties. Keynes would undoubtedly be pleased with our finding in Chapter 7 that the fading of the domestic and external money illusions is the result of a rational process of learning. He predicted the later behavior of the Euro-dollar marketeers in a letter to Joan Robinson in 1932 as logical: " . . . in truth all holders of securities are potential speculators." (See Keynes, *Collected Writings*, 13, p. 269.)

2. See A. Stanzel, "Kostenvorstellungen staatlicher Struk-turpolitik," in *Wirtschaftspolitische Blätter* 5 (Vienna, 1978): p. 68.

3. Keynes, *General Theory*, p. 378.

4. See N. Kaldor, "Conflicts in National Economic Objec-tives," *The Economic Journal* (March 1971): pp. 1 ff.

5. Named after the Prussian statistician Ernst Engel, who in his study *Die Lebenskosten belgischer Arbeiter-Familien* (Dres-den, 1895) found that as income rises, spending for basic needs such as food, clothing, etc., declines.

6. A. Kausel, "Der Schilling ist nicht überwertet," in *Wirt-schaftsbericht der Creditanstalt-Bankverein*, No. 5 (Vienna, 1977), pp. 5 ff.

Chapter 3

1. The supporters of the old banking principle were mistaken when they thought that the discounted letter of credit which the principle espoused would not create "additional" money because it was backed by accumulated produced goods. With-out the letter of credit, producers would have had to use their own or borrowed savings. In this respect the letter of credit was credit per se and therefore to be charged against the credit creation of the banks. On this, see also this author's *Währungs-politik*, p. 27: "Strictly speaking, the acquisition of commercial letters of credit by central banks are not credit creation, i.e., new credits. Rather, a supplier's credit previously created by commercial banks is transformed into a central bank credit. This however makes every previous creditor free to create new credits." The new (monetarist) school of banking is mistaken if it believes that the credit-creation multiplier between money supply and credit production based on this represents a "con-

stant," for only if that were so would it be sufficiently large to control M_1. Chapter 9 shows to what level of performance the credit-creation multiplier of the Euromarkets can be raised.

    2. See C. Köhler, *Geldwirtschaft* (Berlin, 1970), p. 185.

Chapter 4

    1. See T. Lachs, *Wirtschaftspartnerschaft in Oesterreich* (Vienna, 1976).

    2. Ibid., p. 90.

    3. Keynes, *General Theory*, pp. 257 ff.

    4. This "forgotten" factor of big-industry rationalization was studied for the first time by this author in *Währungspolitik*, pp. 61 ff., and recently more thoroughly in "Von der Einkommens- zur Arbeitsmarktpolitik, Vollbeschäftigung in weltoffenen Volkswirtschaften bei freischwankenden Wechselkursen und cash-flow-orientierter Finanzpolitik der (Gross) Unternehmen," *Mitteilungen aus der Arbeitsmarkt- und Berufsforschung, Schwerpunktheft Löhne und Beschäftigung*, No. 3 (1978).

    5. See Kausel, "Der Schilling," p. 6, and Kausel, *Beurteilung der nachhaltigen Wettbewerbsstärke der österreichischen Wirtschaft aufgrund makroökonomischer Tatbestände*, manuscript (Vienna, 1978), pp. 17 ff.

Chapter 5

    1. See A. Stanzel, "Kostenvorstellungen," p. 86.

    2. A very similar analysis with reference to the German capital market support during the fifties via fiscal incentives in the reinvestment of write-offs as well as the tax exclusion of interest income on securities of the building construction sector (mortgages and municipal bonds) has been made by Wolfgang Stützel, *Wirtschaftsberichte der Berliner Bank AG*, No. 2, 1957. In it Stützel asserted that "the taking out of profits from a corporation subject to corporate tax for purposes of investment in another with better long-term chances of success (because of tax incentives) impose a sort of 'internal tariff,' " and he recommended that these "tariff walls built around individual enterprises" be torn down.

Chapter 6

1. See Charles P. Kindleberger, *Die Weltwirtschaftskrise 1929–1939* (Munich, 1973), pp. 84 ff.

2. This is in addition to the repercussions of the infrastructure investments on our present-day prosperity. In his *General Theory* (p. 31) Keynes made some amusing observations on this point:

> Ancient Egypt was doubly fortunate, and doubtless owed to this its fabled wealth, in that it possessed two activities, namely, pyramid-building as well as the search for the precious metals, the fruits of which, since they could not serve the needs of man by being consumed, did not stale with abundance. The Middle Ages built cathedrals and sang dirges. Two pyramids, two masses for the dead, are twice as good as one; but not so two railways from London to York. Thus we are so sensible, have schooled ourselves to so close a semblance of prudent financiers, taking careful thought before we add to the "financial" burdens of posterity by building them houses to live in, that we have no such easy escape from the sufferings of unemployment. We have to accept them as an inevitable result of applying to the conduct of the State the maxims which are best calculate[d] to "enrich" an individual by enabling him to pile up claims to enjoyment which he does not intend to exercise at any definite time.

3. S. B. Linder, in his *Essay on Trade and Transformation* (Stockholm, 1961) called attention to this macroeconomic law of Engel, which is part of every development process. "Poor" countries use more investment and consumer goods than they themselves produce, and the difference between their domestic absorption quota and the simultaneously produced gross national product makes up their balance on current accounts deficit. See also the present author's *Weltwirtschaft, vom Wohlstand der Nationen heute* (Düsseldorf and Vienna, 1977), p. 224, on the consequences of development aid, export-led growth, and the treatment of the problem in the literature.

4. The stimulation of the balance on current accounts out of domestic surpluses can be the result of a "natural" productivity surplus, but it can also be the result of a politically

motivated manipulation of data. In Kaldor's export-led-growth model (see his essay "Conflicts in National Objectives," *Economic Journal* [March 1971]) the export surplus follows a budget-induced decline in demand. Also, the budget "leads" and the balance of payments "follows." In the event of an absorption of already earned foreign exchange by the budget, the balance of payments leads and the budget and its liquidation initiative follows the balance-of-payments opportunities that productivity had opened up. Kaldor's model is aimed at "fiscal dumping," while the one given here is aimed at utilizing otherwise less productively employed foreign-exchange means.

5. See Kausel, "Der Schilling."

6. See Kausel, *Beurteilung*.

7. Ibid., p. 21.

8. See E. J. Horn, "Technologische Neuerungen und internationale Arbeitsteilung," *Kieler Studien*, No. 139 (1976).

9. Kausel, *Beurteilung*, p. 18.

10. On the relationship of the multiplier (i.e., investment effects on income growth) and accelerator (i.e., reciprocal effect of income growth on investments), see Samuelson, *Economics*, pp. 220, 249 ff.

11. The different and, from the vantage point of goal-setting, contradictory concepts of budget neutrality are in fact concepts of "A" neutrality. That pertains to the full-employment budgets of Great Britain and the United States after World War II as well as their later refinement to a full-employment surplus budget with deferred fiscal adjustment. The following is a list of documents of full-employment fiscal policy:

White Paper on Employment Policy, CMND. 6527, HMSO, London, 1944.

White Paper on Public Investment in Great Britain, CMND. 1203, HMSO, London, 1960.

White Paper on Control of Public Expenditure, CMND. 1432, HMSO, London, 1961.

Samuel Brittan, *Steering the Economy, The Role of the Treasury*, 2nd ed. (London, 1969).

U.S. Employment Act of 1946 in G. Colm, *Das amerikanische Beschäftigungsgesetz, Vergangenheit und Zukunft* (Berlin, 1956), pp. 249 ff.

The Employment Bill of Sen. Murray in "The Employment Act in Economic Thinking of our Times: A Symposium," *AER Paper on Proceedings* (1957).

Alex Moeller, ed., *Kommentar zum Gesetz zur Forderung der Stabilität und des Wachstums der Wirtschaft* (Hannover, 1968).

Council of Economic Advisers, Annual Report 1962 in *Economic Report of the President* (Washington, D.C., 1962).

M. Lecy, *The Full Employment Budget Surplus in Public Finance and Fiscal Policy, Selected Readings* (Boston, 1966), p. 319.

W. Heller, *Das Zeitalter des Ökonomen, Neue Dimension der Wirtschaftspolitik* (Tübingen, 1968) (ed. and trans. by W. Noelling).

12. Smith's famous four tax maxims in the *Wealth of Nations* give no indication that taxes are anything more than compensation for the costs of running the state enterprise—a balancing of the administrative budget. See the present author's *Heldensagen der Wirtschaft* (Düsseldorf and Vienna, 1975), pp. 237 ff.

13. H. Seidel, *Bericht über die Lage der Finanzen in der Republik Oesterreich*, manuscript (Vienna, June 1978).

14. Ibid., p. 125.

15. Ibid., p. 129.

16. Ibid., p. 160.

17. See Beirat für Wirtschafts- und Sozialfragen, *Budgetvorschau 1978 bis 1982* (Vienna, 1978).

18. Ibid., p. 11.

19. Ibid., p. 7.

20. Ibid., p. 27.

21. On the problem of tax-receipt elasticities, see K. Häuser, "Wirtschaftliches Wachstum, wirtschaftliche Stabilität und die Rolle der öffentlichen Finanzwirtschaft," in *Public Finance Policy and Techniques for Economic Stability and Balanced Economic Growth* (Congrès de Budapest, 1964; Institut International des Finances Publiques, La Haye, Paris, Saarbrücken, 1966), pp. 153 ff. See also G. Hagemann, *Aufkommenselastizitäten ausgewählter Steuern in der Bundesrepublik Deutschland 1950–1963* (Tübingen, 1968), pp. 141 ff.; and W. Albers and A. Oberhauser, *"Die Entwicklung des Sozialprodukts und der öffentlichen Einnahmen in der Budesrepublik Deutschland 1970–1975,"* in Deutscher Bildungsrat, *Gutachten und Studien der Bildungskommission*, Band 5 (Stuttgart, 1975), pp. 36 ff.

Part 2
Chapter 7

1. See Hankel and Lehner, *Die gescheiterte Stabilitätspolitik.*

Chapter 8

1. See the various studies by this author on the background of the German economic miracle and its export-led growth, especially, "Germany—Economic Nationalism in the International Economy" in Kohl and Basevi, eds., *West Germany: A European and Global Power,* p. 28:

> Until recently the appreciation rate of the DM vis-à-vis the U.S. dollar was equal only to a fraction of the world inflation rate expressed in U.S. dollars. While the world market prices (in U.S. dollars) rose 165.3 percent since 1972, German export prices (in DM) and cost of living (in DM) rose at only 37.7 and 35.5 percent, respectively. A "mathematical balancing" of this thus mediated average price and cost advantage of German export products would have required a DM upward float in this period of 165.3/37.7 = 127.6 percent vis-à-vis the DM–U.S. dollar parity of 1972, but in fact only 34.6 percent eventuated, which shows more clearly than any theory how little the exchange-rate movements depend on and are determined by developments in real purchasing power. At the same time the mathematical difference of 127.6 – 34.6 = 93 percent shows how little "over" and how greatly "under" valued the DM still is, at any rate measured by yardsticks of the not necessarily correct purchasing power parity theory of exchange rates, or to put it differently, how "successfully" German monetary policy has "defended" the DM exchange rate in the sense of safeguarding the German export position.

On the background of a policy of perpetuated surplus policy, see T. Balogh, *Internationale Wirtschaftsbeziehungen—Doktrin und Wirklichkeit* (Frankfurt/Main, 1975), pp. 100 ff.

2. Keynes, "A Tract on Monetary Reform," in *The Collected Writings of J. M. Keynes* (Cambridge, 1971), Vol. 4, p. 742.

3. B. Hansen, "Zinspolitik und Devisenpolitik," in *Skandinaviska Banken,* No. 4 (1959), p. 164.

4. See this author's *Weltwirtschaft—Vom Wohlstand der Nationen heute* (Düsseldorf and Vienna, 1977), p. 185, and the literature cited therein.

5. See O. Veit, *Grundriss der Währungspolitik* (Frankfurt/ Main, 1961); *Reale Theorie des Geldes* (Tübingen, 1965); and *Währungspolitik als Kunst des Unmöglichen* (Frankfurt/Main, 1968). Unfortunately, Veit consistently and unprofessionally avoided any dispute with his friends in the monetarist floating as well as central bank sectors.

6. See Eucken, *Grundsätze*, p. 169.

Chapter 9

1. Opinions differ about the assumptions about the credit multiplier of these Euromarkets. It is a mystery how early analysts (e.g., Einzig, Klopstock, Machlup, and Bell), at a time when Eurocredit expansion was comparatively modest, could arrive at extremely high credit-creating capacities, while later analysts (e.g., Mayer, Carli, and Niehans), who had already witnessed the explosive credit-granting phase of the early seventies, managed to prove extremely low credit-creating capacities. H. Mayer ("Moltiplicatione e creatione di credito sul mercato dell Eurodollaro," *Moneta e Credito*, No. 95 [1971], p. 231) grants the Eurobanks a multiplier of no more than between 0.50 and 0.90, which, by adding the refinancing lines guaranteed by the home-office banks, can be raised to a maximum of 1.05–1.09. J. Niehans cannot find any credit-creating multiplier at all ("Geldschaffung und Kreditvermittlung im Euro-Dollar Markt," in *Verstehen und Gestalten der Wirtschaft*, Festschrift für F. A. Lutz, W. Bickel, ed. [Tübingen, 1971] pp. 279 ff.). P. Einzig (*The Eurodollar System*, [London, 1964]), F. Klopstock ("The Euro-Dollar Market: Some Unresolved Issues," in *International Finance* [Princeton, March 1978]), F. Machlup ("Eurodollar Creation, A Mystery Story," *Banca Nationale di Lavoro Quarterly Review* [September, 1970]) hint at far higher levels. G. Bell (*The Eurodollar Market and the International Financial System* [New York, 1973]) considers Einzig's maximal multiplier of 18–20 as completely realistic. W. Frattiani and P. Savone, on the basis of the monetarist international monetary

base concepts of Friedman, Schwarz, Brunner, Meltzer, and Carli, arrive at a medium value of between 3 and 7, which, if it were applicable, would still be a good 100–350 percent higher than all similarly calculable national credit-creation coefficients. On this, see M. Frattiani and P. Savona, "La creazione dei Eurodollari: Soluzione di un enigma," *Moneta e Credito*, No. 3 (1971), and this author's calculation of a credit multiplier for the German Federal Republic of the sixties ("Mittelfristige Finanzplanung ohne Kapitalmarktrechnung," in *Zeitschrift für das gesame Kreditwesen* [Frankfurt/Main, 1967], pp. 761 ff., with G. Zweig).

In fact, all Eurodollar multiplier calculations contain two statistical unknowns—the individual (voluntary) bank liquidity reserve r (which is kept in other banks or for which the guarantees of the home-office bank can serve as substitutes), and the aggregate liquidity base available to the system, which is composed of U.S. dollar inflows (based on the running balance of payment deficits of the United States), and outflows to national money and credit markets (drain effects).

In the well-known credit-creation formula

$$\frac{1}{r + c(1 - r)}$$

"everything" thus depends on the assumptions for r as well as for c. The estimates of Klopstock, Machlup, and others for c vary from 5 to 20 percent. Friedman gives no rate whatever for the cash position of the Eurobanks. The estimates for c are even more diverse. Mayer believes the deposit losses to the national U.S.-, DM-, and other money and capital markets to be enormous. In his opinion all Eurobanks are in the same situation as individual commercial banks within the national system. The Eurobanks create "only" credit, but the deposits that are theirs disappear more or less completely within the national systems in which the Eurobank customers keep their accounts (H. Mayer, "Multiplier Effects and Credit Creation in the Euro-Dollar Market," *Banca Nationale di Lavoro Quarterly Review* [September, 1971], pp. 240 ff.)

The only correct point of the outflow thesis is that in the

course of participation the individual bank cash position r is distributed among more than one central liquidity holder. Whether it therefore becomes bigger is another question. But even if it were to become bigger, the additional interbank credit facilities resulting from this business connection would have to be taken into account. Even if these internal refinancing lines do not enter into the Eurodollar credit volume granted to non-banks, they still give rise to a higher c (aggregate liquidity), and thus a higher aggregate multiplier. Thus dividing the multiplier formula by the number of players does not yield any additional information:

$$\frac{1}{r + c(1 - r)^m}$$

where only the quantity of m is known, but not its effect on r and c.

The Mayer thesis can at best be partially valid for a small group of genuine U.S. firms that render their foreign payments in Eurodollars but keep their cash in U.S. dollars. The multinationals, European, and other non-U.S. firms that constitute the bulk of the Euromarket users have no reason to do so. On the contrary, they can maximize their monetary profits if they take up as many Eurodollar credits as possible and invest the equivalent amount in strong currencies.

2. Quoted by J. R. Micks (*Essays in World Economics* [Oxford, 1959], p. 157).

3. J. M. Keynes, "Proposals for an International Clearing-Union," *The International Monetary Fund 1945–1964, Vol. III: Documents* (Washington, D.C., 1965), pp. 19 ff.

Chapter 10

1. See J. Tinbergen, *On the Theory of Economic Policy* (Amsterdam, 1952), chs. 4 and 5. Kaldor elevated this Tinbergen principle to the rank of a "law"; Balogh asserts that "like other explanations and models of Professor Tinbergen it does not pass serious muster." In my opinion it does very well, but it leaves open the problem of the instrument's coordination.

2. R. A. Mundell, "The Appropriate Use of Monetary and Fiscal Policy for International and External Stability," *IMF Staffpapers* 9, No. 1 (March 1962): 70 ff. The present author, without being acquainted with Mundell's work, developed the same idea of a division of labor between externally oriented monetary and domestically oriented fiscal policy at the meeting of the Verein für Sozialpolitik held at Innsbruck in 1970. See "Probleme der Finanzierung von langfristigen staatlichen Infrastruktur-Investionsprogrammen," in H. Arndt and D. Swatek (eds.), *Grundfragen der Infrastruktur-Planung für wachsende Wirtschaften* (Berlin, 1971).

3. Keynes, *A Treatise on Money*, Vol. II (London, 1971), p. 276.

4. The development of this two-dimensional economic policy aimed at the achievement of external and internal equilibrium was the lifework of John Maynard Keynes. It was not an easy birth. Keynes first revolted against the one-dimensional subordination of internal goals to the external objectives of the old gold standard in his *Tract on Monetary Reform* (1923), when, citing the swap rate practices of the Austro-Hungarian national bank before 1914, he somewhat casually recommended floating in larger volumes between cash and term rates. In his *Economic Consequences of Mr. Churchill* (1925) he developed the first model of an "imported depression," based on Churchill's untimely appreciation of the pound sterling, and correctly predicted the mining crisis. In his *Treatise on Money* (1932), he presented a two-dimensional model embedded in a great deal of monetary history: flexible exchange rates are to ease internal policy and create balance-of-payments equilibrium, while interest-rate policy, because of the greater reactability of short-term foreign credits, should continue to balance the capital account (see vol. 2, ch. 36)—a peculiar mixture of new, more or less "monetaristic" and classical ideas. In the *General Theory* (1935-1936) he completes the breakthrough to the primacy of domestic over external goals. The former internationalist has turned into an economic nationalist, as Hayek in 1937 prophetically dubbed the new direction. In *How to Pay for the War* (1939), the domestic fiscal surplus policy is expanded into the price stabilization policy; the budget "can" form surplus if full

employment is assured. In 1941 Keynes broke with the primacy
of domestic over external goals in his plans for a world currency
system. In his famous *Proposals for an International Clearing
Union* (1943) he called for "equal weight" and "symmetry" of
the balance-of-payments adjustment of deficit and surplus countries, with worldwide control of international liquidity creation
through a world central bank. Mundell's appropriate-use-of-
instruments model is thus complete, yet it is ignored by most
students to this day. See the nationalist fiscalists who are still
mired in *How to Pay for the War* and the *General Theory*.
Among the "great" Keynesians, only J. R. Hicks, L. Robbins,
R. Triffin, C. Kindleberger, A. Shonfield, and a few others
unreservedly support Keynes's rediscovered internationalism,
and "optimal currency area" theoreticians like Mundell,
McKinnon, and Tinbergen do so with some reservations.

5. See also G. Magnifico, *Eine Währung für Europa, ein Weg
zur europäischen Währungsvereinigung* (Baden-Baden, 1977), to
whom I owe the discovery of this source.

6. Balogh, *Internationale Wirtschaftsbeziehungen*, p. 100.

Chapter 11

1. The redundancy problem for monetary analysis rediscovered by Robert Mundell (*Monetary Problems of the International Economy* [Chicago, 1969], p. 21, with A. K. Svoboda)
has long been known to economic theory. Cournot and Walras
had already formulated it with mathematical precision, even
though they did not "solve" it. See the present author's *Weltwirtschaft*, pp. 322 ff. and the literature cited therein. The consequences connected with this for the EMS have been treated
by Giogio Basevi, "Sistema monetario europeo," ch. 1, in
L'economia italiana 1978-79, Quinto rapporto CEEP—a must
reading for all EMS negotiators. The still valid consequences
for the Atlantic defense treaty have been treated by this author
in E. O. Czempiell and Dankwort A. Rustow, eds., *The Euro-
American System* (Frankfurt/Main and Boulder, Colo., 1976),
under the title "A New Order for American-European Monetary
Policy" (pp. 51 ff.), as well as more recently, "Der Euroscheck
ist besser als das ganze EWS," *Frankfurter Rundschau* (March
10-11, 1979).

2. The present author has analyzed this major structural problem of the German Federal Republic in great detail. See "Von der Einkommens- zur Arbeitsmarktpolitik," pp. 289 ff., which is also the source of Figures 8 and 9.

Part 4

1. Heinz Handler of the Austrian Institute for Economic Research, for example, in an internal paper (*The Exchange Rate as an Intermediate Target of Stabilization Policy*) sought to explain the hard-currency policy by the Scandinavian model developed by Frisch, Aukrust, Edgren-Faxén-Odhuer, and other Scandinavian authors. However, his understandable confusion that the Scandinavian model and the Austrian policy mix of the seventies do not really fit together is due more to his preconceived notion that the two did have something in common than to reality. As Handler rightly points out, the Scandinavians are primarily concerned with intersectoral adjustment processes, moreover under the disquieting conditions of both wage- and exchange-rate–induced inflation. In the Austrian model the financial macroequilibrium conditions of the balance of payments and budget are in the forefront: it sets forth the financial overall framework of a market-economic (entrepreneurial) planned and determined sectoral structural policy in which the state participates only insofar as it itself (through its public and licensed enterprises) acts as the entrepreneur.

In addition, Handler burdens himself unnecessarily with false notions and prejudgments. The DM, which determines the exchange rate of the schilling, is not "overvalued," as the present author proved (it is hoped convincingly) in his analysis of German economic policy of the eighties ("Aus Politik und Zeitgeschehen," supplement to the *wochenzeitung das parlament*, p. 30), and more recently in Kohl and Basevi, *West Germany: A European and Global Power,* pp. 28 ff. Nor would Austria therefore be compelled to import a depressive structural impairment of its neighbor: It has a far too strongly divergent production, capital, and cost structure. (On this, see Kausel's analyses referred to in chapters 4 and 6.)

Handler's advice to his government to depreciate the schilling for reasons of employment and to protect Austria's international

competitive position through greater pressure on income and
real wages would seem to be the surest way to put an end to the
era of social symmetry and harmony—and Handler knows it,
for he is firmly convinced of the rigidities and ratchet effects
of a downward wage movement. (See p. 33 of his paper.)

2. See J. J. Polak and V. Argy, "Credit Policy and the Balance of Payments," *IMF Staff Papers,* 17, March, 1971, pp. 1 ff.
The present author has incorporated the IMF Model into his
Weltwirtschaft, pp. 243 ff. The presentation in Part 4 of the
present work substantially follows both these sources.

3. The derivation of these equations can be proved as follows:

$$R = \frac{mv}{1 + mv} dL + \frac{mv}{1 + mv} 2dL + \frac{mv}{1 + mv} 3dL + \ldots = dL$$

$$dY = \frac{v}{1 + mv} dL - \frac{mv}{1 + mv} 2dL + \frac{mv}{1 + mv} 3dL + \ldots = 0$$

Thus $R = 0$ as well as $dY_{-1} - dY = 0$. The long-term internal
credit expansion takes place within the framework of the
external (R) as well as internal (dY) growth equilibrium; the
long-term equilibrium is adduced through the cumulative sum
of all individual period effects.

INDEX

Adenauer, Konrad, 11
Advisory Commission. *See* German
  Federal Republic, Economic
  Advisory Council
Advisory Committee for
  Economic and Social
  Questions. *See* Commission
  for Economic and Social
  Questions
Agricultural policy, 167
Amortization, 15, 82
Anticyclical fiscal policy, 29–31,
  36, 119, 156
Appreciation nations, 16, 128,
  133, 157
Arab Monetary Fund, 159
Austria
  added value ratio of, 11
  balance on current accounts of,
    164, 165, 176, 179, 180,
    185–186, 188
  balance of payments of, 46,
    60–61, 85, 89, 95, 113, 169,
    175, 178
  banking system of, 48–49, 112
  bankruptcy rates of, 13(table)
  and budget, 104, 105(table),
    108, 109(table), 185–186
  and budget balance, 83, 96,
    99(table), 103, 106–107, 168
  budget deficit of, 36(table), 79,
    98, 101, 106, 179

  and capital-import-financed
    business policy, 50, 149, 163,
    176
  and Commission for Economic
    Partnership, 55, 56
  consumer quota of, 38, 40
  and debt liquidation, 84, 86,
    87, 88, 89, 95–96, 106, 107,
    108, 109, 110–111, 179, 187,
    188
  as debtor nation, 117
  and domestic trade surplus, 97,
    104, 163, 177
  and economic growth compared,
    39(table)
  economic policy of, 17–18, 21,
    48, 60, 102–104, 161–165,
    167–168, 171, 176, 177–178
  and economists of Austrian
    school, 15
  employment in, 11, 12, 23,
    41, 55, 175, 178, 184–185
  and expenditures, 80(table),
    101–102, 106–109
  and exports, 40, 42(table), 60,
    64, 84, 85, 86, 88, 89–90,
    92–93, 109, 111, 161, 163,
    181
  federal guarantees of, 75(table)
  federal tax collection share in,
    35(chart), 49, 50, 87, 106,
    186

fiscal policy of, 24, 27–31, 33,
38, 50, 51, 52, 54, 89, 96,
108, 110, 169, 177, 179, 186
and fixed exchange rates, 62–63,
64, 181
foreign indebtedness of, 36,
37(table), 43, 48, 51, 52–54,
82, 84, 86, 88, 104, 106,
107, 149, 186, 187
and gross domestic product, 12,
83
and gross national product (GNP),
29, 56, 65, 66(table), 67(chart),
83, 84, 89, 98, 101, 102,
103(chart), 104, 106, 107, 180
hard currency policy of, 13, 52,
63, 84–85, 86, 88, 91, 93, 95,
110, 113, 148, 178
and imports, 51, 71, 164, 176,
181
income policy of, 55–64, 185,
187
investment rate of, 4(chart),
33, 40, 49, 65, 71
investment ratios of, 3
investments of, 31, 32(table),
33(table), 34(table), 41,
66(table), 74, 162
investments and social product
of, 182(table)
liquidity of, 46, 47(table), 48,
50, 52, 54, 71, 90, 91, 180
marginal investments and savings
rates of, 7, 8(table), 9, 43
and medium-sized entrepreneurial
structures, 11
as net-capital import country, 61
policy mix of, 23–24, 46, 50,
113, 161, 169, 176–177, 179,
185, 193
price increases and interest rates
in, 68(table)
and productivity, 40, 60, 63, 90,
91, 93, 94, 95, 179, 184
progressive income tax of, 30

public guarantees for, 78(table)
public indebtedness of, 81, 82,
86
and real-capital formation, 49
and savings, 74, 91, 94, 162,
180, 183, 186, 187
and structural policy, 76
subsidies in, 77(table), 108–109
tax policy of, 181, 184
technological progress of, 40,
41(table)
war debt of, 88
See also Central bank;
Econometric model; "Iron
income law"; National Bank;
Real income, and Austria;
Schilling

Balance of payments, 13–14, 16,
18, 25, 26, 29, 51, 127, 128,
130, 147, 151, 152, 153,
155, 156, 157, 158, 168,
171, 178, 180, 189, 194,
195, 196, 197. See also
Austria, balance of payments of
Balance on current accounts, 51,
52, 54, 70, 71, 82, 89, 91–92,
95, 102, 108, 111, 113, 124,
125, 128, 153, 163, 171,
197. See also Austria, balance
on current accounts of; Benelux
countries, and balance on
current accounts; German
Federal Republic, and balance
on current accounts; Switzerland,
and balance on current accounts
Banking. See Austria, banking
system of; Central bank;
Eurobanks; Euromarkets;
Export-Import Bank; Federal
Bank; International monetary
system; National Bank
Banking theory, 45
Bank restrictions, 21
Bankruptcy rates, 13